THE
cajuns

THE
cajuns

AMERICANIZATION
OF A PEOPLE

Shane K. Bernard

University Press of Mississippi / *Jackson*

www.upress.state.ms.us

Library of Congress Cataloging-in-Publication Data

Bernard, Shane K.
The Cajuns : Americanization of a people /
Shane K. Bernard.
p. cm.
Enlargement of author's thesis (Ph.D.)—University of
Louisiana at Lafayette. Includes bibliographical
references (p.) and index.
ISBN 1-57806-522-4 (cloth : alk. paper)—
ISBN 1-57806-523-2 (pbk. : alk. paper)
1. Cajuns—History. 2. Cajuns—Cultural assimilation.
3. Cajuns—Ethnic identity. 4. Americanization.
5. United States—Ethnic relations.
6. Louisiana—Ethnic relations. I. Title.
E184.A2 B47 2003
305.84'10763—dc21   2002005652

British Library Cataloging-in-Publication Data available

To Kara and Colette,
qui me sont plus chères que tout le reste

**The trouble wit' most Anglo-Saxon
people in America is that they
want aver'body to t'ink lak' they do.**

—Anonymous Cajun,
quoted in *Southern Voices,* 1974

CONTENTS

PREFACE

This study resulted from personal exploration: I am a descendant of Acadian exiles who settled in Louisiana in the eighteenth century, who intermarried with other ethnic groups on the semitropical frontier, and who in the process became a new ethic group—the Cajuns.

I am, however, an Americanized Cajun. Although I was born and reared in the heart of Cajun country, my mother is not Cajun but Anglo-American. By a twist of fate I was baptized Protestant, not Catholic, the traditional Cajun religion. And what little French I speak ("un 'tit peu") is standard French, not Cajun French, which I learned in college or taught myself. Even the pronunciation of my Acadian surname has been Americanized (BER-NARD, not BEAR-NAH).

I grew up in suburbia, read comic books, built model airplanes, played Little League ball, and watched many of the same TV shows and movies that other budding Generation Xers watched throughout America. Most of my childhood friends were Cajuns, but like me none spoke French. Rarely did we join activities that might be considered traditional or ethnic: perhaps a fishing trip to the Atchafalaya Basin or Bayou Courtableau, an Easter game of *pâcque-pâcque*, or a family crawfish boil or gumbo.

Regardless, when I visited my Cajun grandparents on Crochet Street in Opelousas, I heard Cajun French. They used it as a secret code, so that my cousins and I could not understand what they were saying. They spoke English, too, of course. They had to speak it to survive in the modern world. Maw Maw worked for South Central Bell, Paw Paw, for the U.S. Postal Service.

As I grew older, I became increasingly aware of the cultural rift between our generations. How was it, I wondered, that after more than three hundred years in the New World, our family had suddenly lost the ability to speak French? What had occurred between my generation and that of my grand-parents to bring about this significant change?

Americanization is what occurred—rapid, widespread Americanization, sparked by the onset of World War II and fueled by the convergence of several ensuing trends and events during the postwar period: the advent of mass communications, rampant consumerism, interstate highways, the jet age, educational improvements, even the rise of rock 'n' roll, to name only a few major factors. The twentieth-century notion of progress had come to south Louisiana.

I first explored the theme of south Louisiana's postwar Americanization in my book *Swamp Pop: Cajun and Creole Rhythm and Blues* (Jackson: University Press of Mississippi, 1996). A musical genre invented by teenaged Cajuns and black Creoles during the 1950s and early 1960s, swamp pop combined rhythm and blues, country and western, and most importantly Cajun and black Creole music. The sound resulted from a collision of cultural elements: folk and mainstream, rural and urban, traditional and modern, French and English. Americanization made swamp pop music.

In many ways this work extends from that book. My goal this time, however, is more ambitious: to examine the sweep of Cajun history during the last six decades of the twentieth century—for beginning in 1941 the Cajuns underwent a transformation so dramatic as to fundamentally alter their ethnic identity. In doing so, they redefined the meaning of the word *Cajun*. They were still Cajuns, but not the same kind: they were Americanized Cajuns.

ACKNOWLEDGMENTS

I wish to thank Professors Terry H. Anderson, John H. Lenihan, Albert S. Broussard, Rogelio Saenz, and Richard Furuta of Texas A&M University and Professor Carl A. Brasseaux of the University of Louisiana at Lafayette, who helped to prepare the dissertation on which this study is based.

I also extend my gratitude to Professors Barry Jean Ancelet and James H. Dormon of the University of Louisiana at Lafayette, who offered advice informally during the course of my work. Professor Ancelet's personal archives served as an important resource in reconstructing the last three decades of Cajun history.

Dozens of interviewees and other individuals also volunteered information, and several of them deserve special mention: Colonel Wallace J. Moulis, U.S.A. (Ret.), Brigadier General Curney Dronet, A.U.S. (Ret.), and Brigadier General Robert J. LeBlanc, A.U.S. (Ret.) for assisting with military and civil defense research; Professor Matthew J. Schott of the University of Louisiana at Lafayette for permitting me access to his unpublished manuscript about Axis POWs in south Louisiana; Floyd Soileau of Flat Town Music and Kim McIlvain of Crazy Cajun Music, as well as songwriter-poet Zachary Richard, for permitting me to quote copyrighted lyrics; and Judge Allen M. Babineaux, Warren A. Perrin, David J. Cheramie, Edgar G. Mouton

Jr., Philippe Gustin, Richard Guidry, and Raymond Spencer Rodgers for assisting my research concerning French preservation.

In addition, I wish to thank the curators, archivists, and librarians who offered help, especially Professor I. Bruce Turner, Jean Schmidt Kiesel, and Al Bethard of Dupré Library, University of Louisiana at Lafayette; and Debra DeRuyver of the National Archives and Records Administration.

Professor Elemore Morgan Jr. of the University of Louisiana at Lafayette practically donated historically important photographic images, for which I am appreciative.

The Louisiana Endowment for the Humanities kindly awarded my project a research and writing grant. I am most grateful to my LEH contact, Celeste Uzee, for guiding me through the grant process.

I owe a considerable debt to my employers, McIlhenny Company and Avery Island, Inc., and particularly to Paul C. P. McIlhenny, Tony Simmons, Edward McIlhenny Simmons, and Gray Osborn, who supported me during this endeavor.

I commend the thoroughness of my editors, Seetha Srinivasan and Anne Stascavage of the University Press of Mississippi; my copyeditor, Ellen D. Goldlust-Gingrich; and my anonymous critical reader.

Most importantly, I wish to thank my family, especially my wife, Kara Tobin Bernard, and my daughter, Colette Amie Bernard, for their patience and inspiration.

"A Tear in a Lady's Eye" (R. Bernard-B. Mehaffey) Crazy Cajun Music BMI © 1968.

"La vérité va peut-être te faire du mal," poem by Zachary Richard, from *Faire récolte,* Moncton, N.B.: Les Éditions Perce-Neige, © 1997.

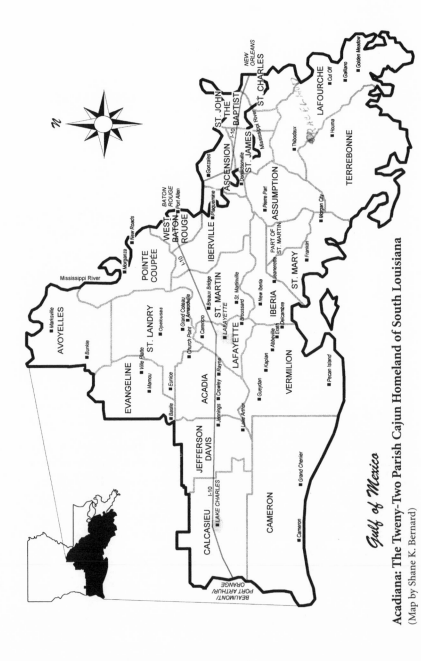

Gulf of Mexico

Acadiana: The Twenty-Two Parish Cajun Homeland of South Louisiana

(Map by Shane K. Bernard)

INTRODUCTION

The Americanization of the Cajuns took place after decades of intense, scornful Anglo-Saxonism, the belief that Anglo-Saxon culture is superior and therefore should be imposed on other ethnic groups. Both the Cajuns and the Acadian exiles from whom they descended had been slandered as backward, ignorant, and un-American. In 1856, for instance, a journalist described the Acadians as "lazy vagabonds, doing but little work." A New Yorker referred to them during the Civil War as a "most ignorant and wretched" people, who to his disgust were "unable to speak the English language, or convey an intelligent idea in the national tongue." A Protestant minister noted during the same period, "These people seem to be living in the year 1500, such are their limited ideas, singular habits, and unparalleled ignorance." These negative stereotypes persisted as the Acadians intermarried with other ethnic groups after the Civil War and evolved into Cajuns. In 1873, for example, a journalist described the Cajuns as "the least intelligent" of south Louisiana natives, while the author of an 1887 Harper's article quoted a local as calling them a "no good" lot who "don't know more'n a dead alligator." One postbellum journalist referred to them as "good representatives of the white trash," reviled even by local blacks as "Acadian niggers."[1]

It was in this Anglo-Saxonist context that the rapid, widespread Americanization of the Cajun people began with U.S. involvement in World

War II. Indeed, this book maintains that the unifying thread of recent Cajun history is Americanization—the process of becoming like the Anglo-American establishment that has traditionally dominated the nation's mainstream culture. It meant, for example, embracing the work ethic, materialism, and patriotism of Anglo America, all of which were foreign to the majority of Cajuns. It also meant speaking English, despite the fact that the Cajuns and their forebears had spoken French as their primary (and usually only) language since coming to the New World three centuries earlier. Americanization thus ranks as one of the most important events in the entire Cajun experience, along with the expulsion of their ancestors from Nova Scotia and south Louisiana's devastation during the Civil War. These events resulted in sea changes that forever altered the nature of the ethnic group. While Acadian and Cajun history during the colonial era and nineteenth century have been examined in detail, the mid- to late twentieth century has been almost wholly ignored by historians. As such, this book constitutes the first detailed examination of recent Cajun history.

Significantly, the concept of Americanization has traditionally borne an undertone of Anglo-Saxonism. This ethnic bias has existed in America since colonial times and persisted into the twentieth century. It expressed itself in numerous ways, but it commonly centered on the issue of language. During and after World War I, for example, Anglo-Americans focused their xenophobia on German-Americans by outlawing the use of German in public places, including churches and schools. Some school libraries removed German-language books from shelves, burning them or selling them as wastepaper. In the Midwest between 1917 and 1921 at least eighteen thousand German-Americans were fined for speaking German in public. Similarly, Anglo-Americans in the Southwest banned the use of Spanish, punishing Hispanic students "like little outlaws" for speaking their native tongue on school grounds. Hispanic educators were also criminalized for using the language in classrooms. As late as 1970 a high school teacher in Texas was indicted for using Spanish during a history course. American Indians also suffered from punitive practices. Government agents removed thousands of Indian children from their families—sometimes by force—and educated them in distant English-only boarding schools. As late as the 1960s Indian students who were caught speaking their ancestral tongues at school were locked in closets, had their mouths washed out with soap, or had their heads shaved. Despite the coming of multiculturalism during the 1960s, when the struggle for civil rights and various liberation movements sparked feelings of ethnic pride and empowerment, this Anglo-Saxonist bias continued to exert itself sporadically. In the mid-1990s, for example, many Americans embraced a neo-nativist English-only movement aimed at stamping out "foreign" languages, particularly Spanish. The Cajun people, as will be shown, have also endured linguistic discrimination and were treated harshly in the past for expressing their ethnicity through French.[2]

A distinct ethnic group, the Cajuns can be viewed, ironically, as the product of Anglo-Saxonism, for their eighteenth-century Acadian ancestors were brutally exiled from Nova Scotia by the British government, which viewed the French-Catholic minority as a threat to its North American empire. Of the roughly fifteen thousand Acadians displaced from Nova Scotia, about three thousand sought refuge in south Louisiana, settling in a region eventually called Acadiana. There they intermarried with other ethnic groups on the semitropical frontier, including French, Spanish, and German settlers and even a small number of Anglo-Americans and Native Americans. They were also influenced by Afro-Caribbean slaves and their descendants, who, like the Cajuns, shared a French-Catholic heritage. This cross-cultural pollination transformed the region's white ethnic groups into a single new ethnic group, the Cajuns, whose population now numbers over a half million. It included not only persons with Acadian surnames, like Breaux, Guidry, Hebert, and Theriot, but also those with French surnames, like Begnaud, Fontenot, and Soileau; Spanish surnames, like Castille, Miguez, and Romero; German surnames, like Hymel, Schexnider, and Stelly; and Scotch-Irish and Anglo-American surnames, like McGee, Miller, and Walker. Elements from all these groups contributed to the new ethnic landscape, but Acadian culture remained the predominant influence. This is demonstrated by the persistence of French as south Louisiana's primary language until the mid-twentieth century. Cajun musician Dennis McGee thus rightly claimed, "McGee, that's a French name. I don't know anyone named McGee who doesn't speak French."[3]

Although the developing Cajun people and their ancestors remained largely untouched by Americanization prior to World War II, they were not totally removed from the currents of national history. Major events like the

American Revolution, the Civil War, Reconstruction, and World War I influenced the ethnic group. Of these, the Civil War had the greatest impact, for by destroying south Louisiana's economy it lowered rival ethnic groups, such as the French, Spanish, and Germans, to the same impoverished social stratum inhabited by most Acadians. As a result, these ethnic groups began to intermarry with the Acadians in sizable numbers. More than any other factor it was this postbellum blending process that created the people called Cajuns. However, the Civil War had only a minor Americanizing influence on the forming ethnic group, which tended to regard the conflict as someone else's fight. *La guerre des Confédérés,* many south Louisianians called it, the Confederates' War. A magazine illustration from the period showed a typical Acadian conscript on picket duty, chained to a tree to prevent him from deserting.[4]

Similarly, the superpatriotism of the World War I era failed to exert a strong Americanizing effect on most Cajuns. Few actually fought in the conflict, for most were discharged from the service because they had contracted influenza, a national epidemic, or because the war ended prior to their deployment. Even the practice of punishing Cajun children for speaking French on the school playground or in the classroom, a byproduct of the era's intense Anglo-Saxonist nationalism, did not result in immediate Americanization. Many south Louisiana children did not attend school and so were spared the humiliation of writing lines or being paddled. Those who did experience punishment still tended to use French at home, but when they became parents around World War II, many declined to teach the dialect to their children, viewing it as a shameful impediment to social and economic advancement.

Thus, most Cajuns remained culturally isolated from the rest of America for nearly the entire first half of the twentieth century, even as radio made its way into south Louisiana during the 1920s and 1930s. Although a folklorist noted in the 1930s that "Radio stations for many years have been broadcasting Acadian music. . . . Not only Acadian music and singing, but also newscasts in Acadian-French, commercials and all," evidence suggests that less than half of Acadiana dwellings possessed radios. This reflected not only the Cajuns' isolation but also the poverty in which they had been mired since the collapse of the local economy after the Civil War. By 1940 only about 17 percent of rural farm dwellings in Acadiana had electric lighting, about half the average for the entire country. Similarly, only 22 percent, less than half the national average, had adequate plumbing, defined as an indoor bathtub or shower, an indoor toilet, and running water. Cajuns in more urbanized areas, such as Lafayette, Lake Charles, New Iberia, and Opelousas, also suffered such deprivations. Like other minority groups, including whites in Appalachia, blacks in the South's cotton belt, Hispanics in the Southwest, and Indians on reservations across America, the Cajuns were so isolated from mainstream culture and so immersed in poverty that, according to some historians, most did not notice the Great Depression.[5]

On the eve of the Cajuns' rapid, widespread Americanization that began with U.S. entry into World War II, outsiders still viewed the ethnic group through the lens of Anglo-Saxonism. As late as 1929 a historian dismissed the Cajuns as unworthy of study. Overlooking their contributions to important rural industries, such as hunting, fishing, trapping, logging, and farming, the historian observed, "Such a people were not to be of great influence in hastening the development of Louisiana." A decade later a WPA writer portrayed the Cajuns as "uncultured . . . impetuous, highly inflammable, ultra-sensitive [and] unrelenting in hatreds." The same writer noted that Cajun males possessed "dull, rather unimaginative eyes," while the ethnic group in general led "a life without stability, responsibility or conventionality . . . one in which the sole purpose and solitary desire is the satisfaction of fundamental necessities and emotions."[6]

This image of the Cajuns as hedonistic bumpkins would continue to haunt them for decades. Beneath it always lay the specter of Anglo-Saxonism. One journalist betrayed this persistent bias when he derisively penned, "He of Anglo-Saxon stock regards American civilization as the highest in the world, and insists that this [Cajun] native shall square himself to it, but he persistently refuses . . . and to the urgent demands of the Anglo-Saxon neighbor his 'Non, monsieur,' comes back as unerringly as the refrain of Poe's raven."[7]

It took a historical event of unprecedented scale to trigger the rapid, widespread Americanization of the Cajun people, and that event was World War II. Unlike previous historical events, this global conflict and its aftermath served as major Americanizing agents in south Louisiana, resulting, for instance, in the near demise of Cajun French by the end of the century: in 1990 only about 30 percent of Cajuns spoke the dialect as their first language, and most of these were middle aged or elderly. Practically no Cajun youths spoke the dialect, even as a second language. This reality suggests the dramatic changes the Cajuns had undergone during the previous sixty years, a period that remained unexplored in detail despite the rise of new social history, or "history from the bottom up," as some have described it.[8]

Appearing in the 1960s, this field made a decisive break with the past by dismissing wars, revolutions, diplomacy, politics, and "great men" as subjects of study. A new generation of historians, influenced by ongoing protest and liberation movements, instead placed stronger emphasis on the roles of immigrants, women, workers, races, and ethnic groups and published a deluge of significant books and articles on these subjects. Historians examined black history from colonial times through the civil rights movement. Women historians studied not only feminism but the role of women and gender throughout American history. Hispanic historians focused on Mexican-Americans from the Spanish colonial period to the advent of the "Brown Power" movement. Historians of the Jewish and American Indian experiences also appeared, as eventually did Cajun historians, but they tended to focus on south Louisiana during the colonial era and nineteenth century.

This book seeks to fill a major gap in Cajun history by using a variety of previously untapped sources, including personal interviews, courthouse records, manuscript collections, newspaper articles, and even poems and songs. One particularly useful source was a database of written responses to questionnaires submitted by the author to newspapers throughout south Louisiana and east Texas. These questionnaires, which so many editors kindly published, asked average, ordinary Cajuns to comment on a variety of subjects from the effects of military service during World War II, to their feelings about the ethnic label *coonass,* to how they perceived their own ethnicity. The response was tremendous, resulting in more than a hundred often extremely detailed and surprisingly candid letters.

The questionnaire subject that generated the largest number of responses concerned the punishment of Cajun children for speaking French at school. Many victims and eyewitnesses described with evident sorrow the harsh treatment meted out by some educators until well after World War II. Significantly, a few respondents expressed concern that younger Cajuns, and non-Cajuns in general, have increasingly tended to discount these stories as mere fables, a trend also discerned by the author. Yet such punishments did occur throughout south Louisiana for roughly two generations, instilling many Cajuns with lifelong feelings of shame and humiliation. "Please let it be known how we were treated for speaking French," implored one respondent. "This is the first time I have had to write a letter to express my bitterness on this subject. . . . I guess after writing this letter I realized that I'm still not completely over my pain and anguish."

Another invaluable source was the U.S. Census, particularly the 1990 census, which the author accessed in two formats: the standard, multivolume print version, available to the general public through numerous libraries; and a digital version, known as Public Use Microdata Samples (PUMS), available mainly to scholars through academic institutions. PUMS offer raw census data extrapolated from 5 percent of households in specific geographic regions and allow researchers to generate customized statistical analyses and tabulations. For example, it can determine for 1990 the number of primarily French-speaking Cajuns in south Louisiana who identified themselves as World War II veterans. The print version of the census does not possess such capabilities.

It is important to note, however, that researchers have discovered a major discrepancy between the 1990 census and preliminary results from the 2000 census. The 1990 census counted more than four hundred thousand Cajuns in Louisiana, while the 2000 census counted only about forty thousand, roughly a 90 percent decline in only ten years. The U.S. Census Bureau clearly miscounted, either in 1990 or 2000 (or both), for the disappearance of almost the entire Cajun population in only a decade is highly improbable.

General opinion in south Louisiana holds that the 1990 census remains the most accurate measure of the Cajun population, while the 2000 preliminary results are considered, to cite one editorial, "a colossal miscalculation." Louisiana historian Carl A. Brasseaux has estimated the state's Cajun population at between five and seven hundred thousand, figures that approximate the findings of the 1990 census. Brasseaux thus has discounted the 2000 statistics, noting wryly that there are probably forty thousand Cajuns on the north side of Lafayette Parish alone. Nonacademics also have scoffed at the 2000 statistics. Lafayette's *Daily Advertiser* ridiculed the figures as "cockeyed" and observed, "Our government advises [us] that there aren't as many Cajuns . . . as we saw dancing in the streets during festival time." "If You're One of 365,000 Missing Cajuns," ran one of its headlines, "Please Send up a Flare." Asked another newspaper, "Where Did All the Cajuns Go?"

The 2000 census results are obviously incorrect to anyone familiar with south Louisiana's cultural landscape. And because no reason exists to doubt the accuracy of the 1990 results, this study relies on those earlier figures.[9]

A few other matters of interpretation demand attention. For example, the terms *south Louisiana* and *Acadiana* are used interchangeably when referring to Cajun Louisiana, and sometimes they implicitly include a small part of southeast Texas that boasts a large Cajun population. Furthermore, the labels *Cajun* and *Acadian* are used synonymously in quoted material, although the author's own term of preference is *Cajun*. In addition, the phrase *south Louisianian* is often used as a convenient synonym for *Cajun*, although other ethnic groups also regard south Louisiana as their homeland. For example, a sizable Creole population inhabits the region and has exerted a major influence on the local cultural landscape. The word *Creole*, however, is a slippery one, meaning in a broad sense "native to Louisiana." As a result, persons of black, white, and mixed-race heritage have all referred to themselves as Creoles, both in the past and present. Unless otherwise stated, the word *Creole* is used in this book solely in reference to south Louisianians of Afro-Caribbean heritage, including those of mixed-race ethnicity.

Finally, it should be understood that criticism of "Anglo-Saxonism," defined in this work as the imposition of Anglo-Saxon ways on other ethnic groups, does not impugn Anglo-Saxon culture and values in general. Similarly, criticism of "Americanism" during World War II and the early Cold War periods, when Anglo-Saxonist biases permeated the concept, should not be misconstrued as disparaging American culture and values.

THE
cajuns

ONE

CAJUNS DURING WARTIME

Quand j'ai parti pour aller dans l'armée.
J'ai quitté tout ça moi, j'aimais.
Moi, j'ai pris le grand chemin de fer
Avec le coeur aussi cassé.

When I left to go in the army,
I left all that I loved.
I took the train
With such a broken heart.

—Cajun musician Nathan Abshire, "Les blues du service militaire [Service Blues]," date unknown

It's my job to convince them that it's more fun to use a bayonet on a Jap than a knife on a muskrat.

—Captain Robert L. Mouton, on recruiting Cajuns for the U.S. Marines, 1942

Four thousand miles from his hometown of Breaux Bridge, Ralph LeBlanc, or "Frenchie," as Navy pals called the twenty-year-old sailor, sat reading comics in Kingfish Hangar's ready room. Usually occupied by pilots receiving orders and briefings, the room this morning, as every Sunday morning, served as a hangout where off-duty sailors drank coffee while glancing through stateside newspapers.

For the past three days LeBlanc and his crew of mechanics had been awaiting aircraft from the carriers *Enterprise* and *Lexington,* so the roar of diving planes came as no surprise. Just a few aviators showing off, LeBlanc figured, before swooping down to land. LeBlanc went outside with some of the other sailors to watch the display. "We thought they were going to give us a little show," he recalled a half century later, "and then one of them drops a bomb right on the PBY hangar."

The bomb's spinning nose propeller landed at LeBlanc's feet. He stooped down and picked up the fragment. "It was so hot," he recounted, "I burned my fingerprints into it." LeBlanc could only surmise that a "crazy" American pilot had bombed the hangar—then it dawned on him what really was occurring.

A short distance from LeBlanc's post, another Cajun, twenty-one-year-old Louis Provost of Lafayette, watched from the heavy cruiser *San Francisco* as planes swarmed around his vessel, firing machine guns and dropping bombs and torpedoes. "People were being blown up and thrown in the water," he recalled. "I was like a scared rabbit." As Provost watched, an explosion ripped through the nearby battleship *Arizona,* killing a thousand sailors, including three Cajuns—Charles Donald Frederick of Abbeville, Russell Durio of Sunset, and Felix Ducrest of Broussard.[1]

The day was December 7, 1941, and the place was Pearl Harbor. Cajun GIs had just witnessed the opening salvo of Japan's sneak attack on American soil, the event that marked the U.S. entry into World War II and the beginning of a chain of events that over coming decades would immerse most Cajuns in mainstream culture.

Cajuns participated in the war effort by the thousands, compelling many to leave their south Louisiana enclave for the first time. In training camps, fox-holes, and trenches, Cajun GIs encountered solely English-speaking Americans, and some, like Lovelace Viator of Vermilion Parish—"one of more than a dozen in his original company from the bayou country," reported his local newspaper in 1945, "who could neither speak nor understand English"—learned the new language in order to serve and survive in the military. They saw new peoples, visited strange places, and were exposed to influences that changed their traditional values. Some Cajun GIs found wartime service an ordeal, experiencing culture shock and suffering ethnic slurs. Others excelled as soldiers, exhibiting heroism on the battlefield and winning the admiration of their comrades.[2]

Back on the home front, Cajun civilians united with other Americans to support the war effort. They volunteered as air raid wardens, plane spotters, firefighters, auxiliary policemen, and nursing aides, and they participated in bond, stamp, and scrap drives. Like combat experience, these activities promoted feelings of national unity, drawing Cajuns closer to mainstream America. Emphasis on "the American way of life" strongly affected Cajun children: census data shows that the use of Cajun French as a first language dropped 17 percent for Cajuns born during U.S. involvement in World War II, the single largest decrease since the beginning of the century. This trend resulted not only from intense Americanism but also from the practice of punishing Cajun students for speaking French at school.[3]

The war also brought south Louisiana civilians into contact and sometimes conflict with different peoples and cultures. Anglo-American GIs, oil field workers, their families, and Axis prisoners of war all moved into the formerly insular region. Other Cajuns left Acadiana to take jobs in New Orleans and east Texas, where despite their frequent trouble with English they worked in shipyards, refineries, and defense factories. Wartime movies, newsreels, newspapers, books, magazines, and radio programs introduced home front Cajuns to the outside world, influencing both positively and negatively their feelings about themselves and other Americans.

World War II unified Americans more than any other event of the twentieth century, and no other event spawned so many profound and lingering aftereffects. Between 1941 and 1945 more than fifteen million men and women entered the U.S. military, and millions more left home to work in defense-related industries. Never had so many Americans picked up roots and moved so far, so frequently, so quickly. Soldiers who as civilians had strayed no more than a few miles from their birthplaces were whisked halfway around the globe, where alongside Americans from other sections of the country they fought common enemies and encountered "foreign" peoples and locales previously unknown. One ethnic historian has aptly asserted that "it would be difficult to exaggerate the importance of the war as the central event in shaping Americans' understanding of their national identity." World War II shaped this identity primarily by hastening the Americanization of minorities, including blacks, Germans, Italians, Hispanics, Jews, and Native Americans.[4]

Like these and other ethnic groups, Cajuns were caught up in the turmoil of wartime. Census data indicates that about 24,500 Cajuns served in the military during World War II. As might be expected, they made up the majority of inductees in the heart of Acadiana. Of 69 white St. Martin Parish men inducted between January and April 1942, for example, 68 percent had Cajun surnames, nearly the same percentage as for the 95 Lafayette Parish whites inducted in November 1942. For 26 Vermilion Parish whites inducted in November 1943, the figure was 77 percent, about the same as for the 41 whites inducted in Iberia Parish in February 1942. The percentage was smaller but still significant outside central Acadiana. In Terrebonne Parish, 42 percent of the 160 men inducted in May 1942 were Cajuns.[5]

Cajuns not only were drafted into the military but, shocked into newfound patriotism by the attack on Pearl Harbor, volunteered with enthusiasm. On the morning after the disaster, a recruiting officer arrived at work in Opelousas to find three teenagers waiting to enlist. "We three had been thinking for some time of enlisting," explained one, "and this Jap bombing decided us." A few weeks later Captain Robert L. Mouton of the U.S. Marine Corps traveled across southeast and central Acadiana, sometimes using motorboats or pirogues (shallow-draft boats), to recruit fellow Cajuns for the "Bayou Battalion," sometimes called the Bayou Brigade. His rationale was simple: "They can shoot straight, they can handle a knife, they're good physical specimens and they love a scrape. . . . If that doesn't make good Marine material then *moi, je suis fou* [I'm crazy]." According to Allen J. Lasseigne, a Bayou Battalion veteran, the force eventually consisted of about 150 to 200 men who trained together in San Diego, California. In spring 1942 the group went to Hawaii, where its members were split up and scattered throughout the Pacific, serving alongside other Americans in the fight against Japan.[6]

Mouton frequently relied on his French-speaking skills when recruiting in the bayou country, for in 1942 it was the primary language of almost 75 percent of prospective Cajun GIs. Most were bilingual, speaking English and French, but some knew little or no English, an unsurprising trait, since older inductees had been born shortly after the turn of the century, when French

was still the region's unrivaled tongue. Of those older GIs, more than 80 percent used French as their first language.[7]

Because of their ethnic peculiarities, Cajun GIs attracted attention when
they settled into training camps across the country. The arrival of a group of
Cajun inductees in South Carolina, for example, stirred the interest of the
local *News and Courier*: "A 'Foreign Legion' has come to Charleston in the
French-speaking soldiers from the Louisiana bayous," the paper observed. An
officer explained that most of his inductees grew up on rice, sugarcane, and
cotton plantations and had spent most of their days outdoors, farming, fishing, or hunting. As a result, they made excellent soldiers and marksmen.
Another officer, himself a Cajun, boasted, "The men in this outfit are noted
as the best fighters, the best cooks, and the best lovers in the army!"

The *News and Courier* praised the Cajun GIs as "absolutely American" but
hinted at the Americanization they were experiencing. Officers first instructed
the soldiers in French, but English soon dominated training exercises. "Now,
several speak English only," the paper reported, "and sometimes find it necessary to find a bilingual fellow officer to help translate the gesticulations and
machine-gun rattle of the patois when some emergency arrives."

These soldiers adapted to their new environment, but they also made
their surroundings more familiar. They spoke French among themselves and
prepared traditional dishes, including crawfish bisque and chicken-oyster
gumbo, which made their mess hall the most popular in camp. They also
sang folk songs, as demonstrated when a cook broke into a mournful ballad
in front of the *News and Courier*'s reporter:

Je passai devant la porte.	*[I passed before the door.*
Je criai bye-bye la belle.	*I cried bye-bye, sweetheart.*
Il n'y a personne que me reponde.	*There is no one that answers me.*
Oh, yé yaille! Mon coeur fait mal.	*Oh it hurts! My heart hurts.]*

In these ways, Cajun GIs battled homesickness and eased the strain of
Americanization, for many found their sudden immersion in Anglo-American
society a bewildering experience.[8]

Despite the message of national unity proclaimed during World War II,
Anglo-Saxonist bigotry led to discrimination and outbreaks of ethnic violence. For example, blacks were initially denied entry into some branches of

the military, such as the Marines, and those who did join other branches were usually given menial positions, such as laborers in the army or stewards in the navy. As more blacks attempted to get jobs in the military and in defense industries, tensions flared over inequalities, leading to riots in New York City, Detroit, Mobile, and other places, including Beaumont-Port Arthur, Texas, and Alexandria, Louisiana, both just outside Acadiana. Similarly, wartime discrimination against Hispanics caused a race riot in Los Angeles, whose Mexican-American residents had been denied the right to work in defense industries. At the same time, the U.S. government regarded Japanese-Americans on the West Coast as potential traitors, even though they had committed no acts of sabotage, and relocated them to inland concentration camps. German-and Italian-Americans were encouraged to mimic Anglo-Americans. As one historian has observed, "'Blend in,' was the wartime imperative: 'Hush, speak English.' We are not German, or Italian, or Japanese, or Jewish: 'We are AMERICAN.'"[9]

It was amid this oppressive Anglo-Saxonist environment that Cajuns joined the military during World War II. Although treated better than non-white ethnic groups, they nonetheless were perceived as different because of their ancestry. As a result, they often became victims of ethnic discrimination. Comrades nicknamed Cajuns "Frenchie" or "Frog" or subjected them to slurs like "coonie" or "coonass," both denoting ignorance. Delton Joseph Menard, who trained at Little Rock, Arkansas, recalled, "There was one soldier in particular that laughed and made fun of me because I was Cajun. One day we were practicing throwing hand grenades and he kept calling me a coonass and making fun of my English. I finally got fed up and took a dummy hand grenade and hit him on the back of the head with it." In some cases, more worldly GIs preyed on unwary Cajuns. L. Harvey Adams, who grew up in the countryside between Crowley and Kaplan, recalled being "*very naive*. I trusted everyone. Everyone knew better than I. I had never been allowed to express myself, or make decisions. That's the Cajun upbringing. I was duped many times by the city-wise kids. Guys would borrow money from me and never repay me, yet I said nothing. It seemed to be my duty." Some lone Cajun GIs felt alienated amid so many English-speaking comrades. "I couldn't express my thoughts and feelings well in English," noted Réaux Meaux, "so I couldn't really talk to anyone. No one else in my outfit spoke French." Culture shock overwhelmed a few inductees. "I felt I had come from a foreign country," recounted Gerald B. Champagne of Breaux Bridge, "and everybody else seemed to think I did."

Although the U.S. military needed French-speaking GIs to act as interpreters in France, Belgium, North Africa, and Southeast Asia, officials often disregarded the linguistic skills of Cajun servicemen. Some recruiters, often Gulf Coast Anglo-Americans with preconceived notions about their French-Catholic countrymen, saw Cajun French as a bastardized dialect, understood only by south Louisiana hayseeds. Thus, when a Cajun informed an induction officer at Fort Shelby, Mississippi, that he spoke two languages, the officer brushed off the information, stating that Cajun French "would be of no benefit to the U.S. Army."

Yet the military sometimes used the linguistic abilities of Cajun GIs. Elvin Thibodeaux translated while serving in France and was once called on to question captured Nazi soldiers. Speaking no German, he was perplexed until he found that the soldiers were French-speaking Alsatians and Lorrainers who claimed they had been threatened with death if they did not fight for Hitler. Dudley J. Theriot also served as a translator in Europe: "I would ask the French people where some of the Germans were dug in the ground, or the building they were hiding in. . . . They spoke very fast, but after asking them to speak slower I could understand them easily." An infantryman from Vermilion Parish used his linguistic skills in North Africa, where Free French troops were stationed. On one occasion, he was introduced to a French officer, recalling, "I spoke to him in his native tongue. . . . He said for an American I had an unusual accent. I told him we all spoke French at home, and he then told me that the French I spoke was seventeenth-century French that had been forgotten in France."[10]

The Office of Strategic Services (OSS) recruited a few Cajuns to act as secret agents, sending Robert J. LeBlanc of Abbeville deep into Nazi territory to liaison with the French resistance, known as the Maquis. According to LeBlanc, he made these forays across enemy lines only after months of linguistic training in which he learned to suppress his Cajun colloquialisms. "Many times my radio operators and driver would wonder if I was coming back," he noted. "My ability to speak French was crucial." The OSS also recruited Sam Broussard of New Iberia. Serving as an intelligence officer,

Broussard sat in on D-Day planning sessions with Eisenhower and participated in the Omaha Beach landing. Once in France, he slipped through German lines to aid the resistance. "I was assigned to infiltrate Brittany to contact the Maquis," he recalled. "We had ammunition, guns, etc., dropped and prepared for an attack on the Germans. We put that enemy company out of action." When the German army retreated, Broussard moved on to Belgium and assisted its resistance movement.[11]

Like most American soldiers, the majority of Cajun GIs took enormous pride in their wartime service. As one wrote from an army camp in Texas, "It's an honor to be an American and able to help his country. I left home nothing but a poor working boy, now here I am an American soldier serving my good Uncle Sam." Another enjoyed his life in the navy, where, "No man is better than you, and you're better than no one." Cajun women also served their nation, among them four Castille sisters from Sunset, who signed up in the Women's Army Corps (WACs). One sister, Mercedes, worked near the front lines in western Europe, setting up hospital units and evacuating wounded soldiers during the Battle of the Bulge.[12]

Indeed, some Cajuns, such as Wallace J. Moulis of St. Martinville, excelled as soldiers. He attended the U.S. Military Academy at West Point and served with distinction in western Europe, seeking out German troops as an intelligence and reconnaissance platoon leader and as a battle patrol commander. "A lot of us owe our lives to the risks you took," wrote one of his privates. "You didn't have to go out on those patrols—nor did you have to brief us as thoroughly as you did before each mission—nor did you have to sleep in a pup tent back in the Ardennes—or eat last, or see that we were well-bedded down—but you did—without exception." Similarly, Joe Thibodeaux of Lafayette displayed heroism as a member of Darby's Rangers, a special forces unit that participated in the invasions of Sicily, Italy, and North Africa. "We got annihilated at Anzio," he recounted. "About 700 went in and about six of us came out." Among aviators who performed remarkably was Wiltz P. Segura of New Iberia. Piloting a P-40 fighter in China with the squadron known popularly as the Flying Tigers (officially the Twenty-third Fighter Group), Segura fought about twenty-five dogfights and shot down six Japanese aircraft, qualifying him as an ace pilot. He also was shot down, bailing out of his flaming aircraft after being struck by ground fire. Jefferson J. DeBlanc of St. Martinville flew F4U Corsairs in the

Pacific and was shot down while defending U.S. dive bombers and torpedo planes. Parachuting out of his aircraft, he swam for hours to reach a tropical island, where headhunters captured him and then traded him to allied coastal watchers for a bag of rice. "Being in the war made a man out of you in a short time," he recalled. "It was kill or be killed. That will certainly make one grow up fast." For his heroism, DeBlanc received the Congressional Medal of Honor.[13]

The war exerted a profound influence on Cajun GIs, giving them a new sense of national identity and beginning the process of rapid, widespread Americanization. Proud of their wartime contributions, they came home staunch patriots, defenders of the American way of life. They had at long last become part of the national melting pot. "I wanted to be an American," asserted Robert J. LeBlanc, explaining why even Cajun GIs who had served as translators did not teach their children French after the conflict. Many south Louisiana servicemen returned home mispronouncing their own surnames in the Anglo-American manner. "I was always called HE-BERT," complained former B-24 crew member Isidor L. Hebert, because other GIs "could not understand A-BEAR." Prejean became PREE-GENE, LeBlanc became LEE-BLANK, DeRouen became DEE-RUIN. This trend was so common that it prompted one south Louisiana civic leader to plead, "Those of you with pretty French names like Roger, Mouton, Broussard, and the like should be the last ones to allow your names to be changed to the more prosaic English or hill-billy ones."[14]

Just as ethnic GIs experienced Americanization during World War II, millions of ethnic civilians also underwent changes on the home front, pushing them toward a common national identity. "Americans All!" ran a popular slogan, as wartime anxieties and heightened patriotism created an atmosphere that demanded consensus and conformity for victory's sake. Influenced by this trend, Cajun civilians reacted to the coming of war much like Americans anywhere in the country. "The dastardly attack by Japan," reported the *St. Martinville Weekly Messenger*, "was taken calmly, but with suppressed anger, by citizens of St. Martinville and St. Martin Parish. The subsequent declaration of war . . . received patriotic approval." The *Abbeville Meridional* noted that citizens of Vermilion Parish responded to the declaration of war by making "plans to cooperate with the national defense organizations to meet the crisis well prepared."[15]

Yet the idea of a "world war" at first perplexed some on the home front, who knew little about events beyond their parish borders. According to storyteller Allen Simon, when an elderly Kaplan resident heard that the Germans had bombed Abbeville, France, he thought the target was actually Abbeville, Louisiana, less than ten miles away. "They're already here?" he asked. When informed that the attack had occurred in Europe, he replied, "I'm sorry for these French people way over there, but that'll teach them a lesson. If they'd stayed here where they belong and not gone over there, we could have helped them." Simon's account may be of the "urban myth" variety, for a Louisiana State University educator recorded in his memoirs the story of Cajun named Alcide who responded in a similar manner to the German invasion of France. "'Well,' said Alcide, 'What all those Frenchmen doing in France? Me, I don't have any sympacy for dem. Dey never should have left Louisiana in the first place.'" Regardless of authenticity, both stories reflect much of south Louisiana's isolation at the dawn of World War II.[16]

Most south Louisiana civilians, however, grasped the nature of the conflict and organized to defend the home front. Immediately after Pearl Harbor, local sheriffs followed directives from the FBI to collect the names of all Japanese residents, the beginning of the nation's internment of about 120,000 U.S. citizens and resident aliens of Japanese ancestry for the duration of the conflict. The sheriff of St. Landry Parish duly turned over the name of his only Japanese constituent, a Mr. Nagada who for years had operated a fruit stand and market in Eunice. In Jefferson Davis Parish the sheriff reassured citizens by informing them, "there are no Japs in this parish."

Local police also went on the lookout for spies and saboteurs, sometimes with a vengeance. Only one day before Germany declared war on the U.S., the *Daily World* announced that alert Opelousas city police had arrested two men "suspected of being a different nationality than American." One of the men spoke German, the paper observed with suspicion, while the other was of German descent. Eventually, it was determined that they were not Nazi saboteurs but hoboes from Pennsylvania. Around the same time, Opelousas police arrested another foreigner suspected of being a Nazi spy, but he turned out to be Canadian.

Acadiana officials heeded the FBI's advice to protect local industrial, utility, transportation, and communication facilities. Announcing that the coastal industries under his jurisdiction were "fair game for saboteurs," the sheriff of Iberia Parish vowed that his department would deputize locals "to combat menace," including "activities of fifth columnists." He placed public buildings under twenty-four-hour watch, erected fences and floodlights, put guards at the massive saltworks on Avery, Weeks, and Jefferson Islands, and assigned patrols to the parish's oil fields.[17]

Across the nation, wartime anxiety infected the civilian population, giving rise to fears of enemy attack, infiltration, and subversion. Acadiana was caught up in this national trend, aided in part by Louisiana Governor Sam Jones, who toured the region in 1942 to stir interest in civil defense. Noting that the Japanese had swiftly carved out an empire by "marching through Malayan jungles as impenetrable as the Atchafalaya swamps," he warned that the region's oil fields could become targets for aerial attacks. "An airplane can fly from the Pacific Coast to Abbeville in four hours," the governor warned a Vermilion Parish audience. "You had better give up the idea that it can't happen in Louisiana."[18]

Spurred by such warnings, Acadiana citizens mobilized for home front defense. In Iberia Parish more than 5,500 residents signed up as volunteers; in St. Martin Parish the number reached 6,500, a quarter of its population. Towns as small as Parks (population 460) conducted blackouts, which were also observed in the countryside miles from the nearest town. "You'd hear the siren in Kaplan," recalled farm dweller Allen Simon, "and they'd blow this thing long, so many blasts, and you had to either turn your lights off, or it was kerosene lamps, or put a black paper around it and close your shades."[19]

As occurred elsewhere in the nation, wartime anxiety sometimes escalated into wartime hysteria. When a highly contagious disease wiped out hundreds of muskrats in the coastal marshlands and spread to nineteen south Louisianians, killing eight, rumor circulated that the outbreak had been caused by Japanese germ warfare. Fearing widespread panic, the federal government moved in, quarantined all possible disease carriers, and asked the media to refrain from reporting the incident. The disease was eventually identified as psittacosis, or "parrot fever," a viral infection transmitted by birds.[20]

More than Japanese germ warfare, coastal residents of south Louisiana feared German U-boats in the Gulf of Mexico. From December 1941 to August 1942 the Germans conducted a vigorous U-boat campaign in U.S. waters, sinking 609 ships weighing 3.1 million tons—an average of about 70 ships per month. Some of these attacks occurred in the Gulf of Mexico, resulting in the destruction of several tankers and freighters off the mouth of the Mississippi River, along the Acadiana coastline, and near Sabine Pass at the Louisiana-Texas border. "Trawlers Bring up Wreckage in Gulf," reported the *Houma Daily Courier* after an attack off the Terrebonne coast, where fishermen discovered adrift three empty life rafts and a lifeboat, all apparently machine-gunned and one stained with blood. When survivors of a U-boat attack arrived in Houma for treatment, their presence, according to the local paper, "shocked residents . . . into the full realization of the grim reality of Axis submarine warfare." One coastal resident mirrored the concerns of her community when she wrote, "Goodness! How we hope those subs will get caught." The lurking U-boats "brought the war closer to Louisiana," observed the *Abbeville Meridional,* "and made Vermilion Parish residents aware of the impending shore attacks."

Indeed, when a Vermilion Parish man found mysterious footprints on an isolated beach, the U.S. Coast Guard suggested that they may have been left by Nazi submariners looking for sources of fresh water. As a result of this report and others, the War Department authorized the formation of the Swamp Angels, also known as the Cajun Coast Guard. Ranging in age from seventeen to sixty-five, the unit's roughly one hundred volunteers searched south Louisiana's marshes and *chênières* (coastal sand ridges) for signs of U-boat activity and saboteur infiltration. Patrolling on horseback or in pirogues, they guarded a thirty-mile stretch of coastline from Southwest Pass in Vermilion Parish to Grand Chenier in neighboring Cameron Parish. The Swamp Angels never encountered any German submariners, but the unit played an important role by rescuing pilots-in-training who crashed in the region's salt marshes, whose voracious mosquitoes, razor-sharp reeds, and impenetrable muck could make survival for the uninitiated nearly impossible.[21]

While most south Louisianians prepared to defend their homeland, thousands moved away to work in defense-related industries. A large south Louisiana landowner fretted over the resulting lack of field hands, most of whom, he wrote, had "gone into higher paying jobs—especially the shipyards in New Orleans, Orange, and Beaumont." In New Orleans these transplants worked for such firms as the Delta Shipyards and the Higgins Boat Company, the latter of which made landing craft for amphibious assaults, most notably the D-Day invasion of Europe. Cajuns employed by Higgins were described as "hard workers" and "proficient," and the company eventually opened a facility in southeastern Acadiana to produce rocket-launching support boats and more landing craft. Meanwhile, transplants in the Beaumont–Port Arthur–Orange area of east Texas worked for firms such as the Pennsylvania Shipyards or the Consolidated Steel Corporation. So many Vermilion Parish residents moved to Port Neches, Texas, located between Beaumont and Port Arthur, that they called their neighborhood "Little Abbeville." Others referred to east Texas as "Cajun Lapland," because south Louisiana seemed to lap over into the Lone Star State.

The move to Texas was so common that the experience became the subject of several Cajun songs, including "Les blues de Texas," "Valse de Port Arthur," "Port Arthur Blues," "Austin Special," and "Grand Texas." Most of these compositions portrayed the migration negatively, for many transplants suffered abuse from the local Anglo majority and for the first time felt like members of an ethnic minority. "Kids used to laugh at our Cajun brogue," noted Rita Dartez Reed, one of those transplants, while another, Eola Miller Wright, recalled, "Sometime they would call me 'cooney.'" Transplants had to contend with frequent coonass jokes but retaliated by making Texans the butt of jokes, as demonstrated by this perennial favorite:

Q: What's the difference between a coonass and a horse's ass?
A: The Sabine River.[22]

Meanwhile, the war shattered Acadiana's isolation, exposing Cajuns who had remained at home to Anglo-American culture. Outsiders poured into local military bases; others, mainly from Texas and Oklahoma, found work in the region's oil fields. As these newcomers took up residence in the bayou country, tensions flared between them and the native population. In 1942, for example, state social workers observed "friction between culture groups" and identified Ascension, Avoyelles, Jefferson Davis, Lafourche, and St. Landry Parishes as those having the largest newcomer populations. Relations were most strained in Lafourche, where a sizable group of Anglo-Americans worked in oil fields around Golden Meadow. This prompted social workers to observe a cultural rift between upper and lower Lafourche, "caused by the influx of . . . a population different in its mode of living." As a result, Cajuns became targets of ridicule in their own homeland when they strayed into areas dominated by newcomers. In turn, the Cajuns called the newcomers "les maudits texiens" (damned Texans) regardless of their place of origin and derided them for bringing honky-tonks, bad credit, drunkenness, fighting, prostitution, and polygamy to the parishes.[23]

Anglo-Americans were not the only outsiders encountered by home front Cajuns during World War II. Between 1943 and 1946 some 450,000 German and Italian prisoners of war were detained in the United States, and more than 50,000 of them passed through Louisiana. Many ended up in Acadiana's rice-and-sugar-growing coastal parishes, where they partially replaced native field hands who were serving in the military or working in factories. At one time at least 8,500 German and Italian POWs were imprisoned in twenty-six Acadiana towns spread throughout seventeen of the region's twenty-two parishes. These POWs made a lasting impression on the residents of Cajun Louisiana: even today the town of Broussard boasts in tourism literature that its dismantled Billeaud Sugar Factory was the "largest employer of German POWs in World War II."

South Louisianians often came into direct contact with these POWs. Rumors even circulated about fraternization between locals and captured enemy soldiers, rumors that have been attributed to the persistent negative stereotype of the hedonistic Cajun. "In context with *Cajun,*" one historian has observed, "the word *fraternization* . . . conveyed pictures of unpatriotic debauchery associated peculiarly with the mythical degeneracy of the Deep South, moss shrouded bayous, and the Gothic of Latin Francophones, a spicy brew long favored by romantically inclined novelists and playwrights." The most common rumor concerned POWs dallying with south Louisiana females. Stories circulated that POWs at Port Allen flirted openly with high school girls on the sidelines of the prison's soccer field, engaged in "midnight sex" with local women through the barbed-wire fences at Franklin, and had wild sex parties with Cajun females in St. Martinville and Lake Arthur.

News commentator Walter Winchell twice "exposed" these scandals on his national radio program, alleging that "Nazi orgies" had taken place in Cajun barrooms, where German POWs cavorted with local prostitutes and indulged in banquets of spicy seafood and free-flowing beer. In response to these reports, American Legion Post 29 in Vermilion Parish petitioned President Franklin D. Roosevelt and Congress to halt these embarrassing incidents. Louisiana State Police rushed to the scene to investigate the Lake Arthur incident, only to determine that no orgy had occurred. Citing the police report, the *New Orleans Times-Picayune* reported that a Jefferson Davis rice farmer had merely treated his POW field hands to a seafood dinner at a local restaurant. Ridiculing Winchell's accusation and the hysteria it generated, the paper summed up the episode in a December 1943 headline: "'Great Nazi Orgy' Was Only Dinner." These rumors obscured an important fact: home front Cajuns encountered POWs and in doing so felt closer to the war raging overseas, and these encounters, to a degree, helped to erode Acadiana's former insularity.[24]

Across the nation, children were influenced by the war through popular culture, through their participation in activities such as scrap drives, and especially through the classroom, which more than ever became a medium for disseminating Americanism, the idea that the American way of life was superior to others and should be emulated by everyone. Louisiana followed this national trend: alarmed by growing Axis belligerency, the state's superintendent of education declared more than a year before the bombing of Pearl Harbor, "Ordinarily, we are urged to teach children how to think and not what to think. Thus we avoid indoctrination; however, it seems to me that in America we have about reached the point at which we should do some definite indoctrination in favor of democracy."

To facilitate this indoctrination, the Louisiana Department of Education issued dozens of circulars about the role of schools in civil defense. One, for example, appealed to social studies teachers to organize classroom programs for instilling Americanism. Another urged teachers to have their students celebrate "I Am an American Day." The department also recommended that students read books that promoted American values, such as James Frances Dwyer's *The Citizen,* Edward A. Steiner's *From Alien to Citizen,* and Edward Bok's *The Americanization of Edward Bok.* The Department of Education urged that a variety of instructional and propagandistic wartime literature, some published by the military, be made available to students, such as *He's in Submarines Now, Your Job and American Victory, What the Citizen Should Know about Our Arms and Weapons,* and *Jump into the Fight with Parachute Troops!* Students were encouraged to join the Victory Corps, a coed paramilitary organization that existed to provide students with a curriculum "basic to citizenship training for American life."[25]

A major consequence of this indoctrination was a sharp decline in the number of Cajun children who spoke French as their first language: the figure nose-dived from 63 percent for those born during the five-year period before America's entry into World War II to 38 percent for those born during the five-year period after the conflict. As one observer noted during wartime, "The children are, these days, more and more inclined to lay aside the French of their forefathers for the English that is taught them in the schools. All their enthusiasm is for modern things and manners."[26]

Some educators helped to bring about this change by punishing Cajun children who were caught speaking French at school, a practice that began prior to the 1940s. Caught up in the Americanism of World War I and the following Red Scare sparked by the Russian Revolution, numerous states had designated English as the sole language of classroom instruction. Louisiana was among those states: in 1916 the state's Board of Education banned French from classrooms, a move sanctioned by lawmakers in the state constitution of 1921. The policy of punishing students for speaking French, however, does not appear to have been condoned by the state, even after the outbreak of World War II. Literature issued by Louisiana's Department of Education made no mention of punishment, and some former students and teachers recalled that punishment was rare or nonexistent in their schools, even as the practice occurred commonly in other schools during the same period. This lack of uniformity implies that individual teachers, principals, and school boards seized on punishment as a means of dealing with French-speaking students, acting locally without the endorsement of high-ranking state administrators.[27]

Nevertheless, by using the classroom as a pulpit for teaching Americanism tainted by Anglo-Saxonism, the Department of Education created an environment that encouraged punishment. It also did little to discourage the practice. As a result, some educators subjected French-speaking students to harsh, humiliating penalties. They called them names like "swamp rat" and "bougalie" (a Louisiana term meaning "lower-class Cajun"), forced them to write lines ("I must not speak French at school"), made them kneel in corners on kernels of corn, or slapped them with rulers. "I started school at the time of World War II," recalled Arlyn Berthier of Avoyelles Parish. Although knowing little or no English, "We were not allowed to speak or ask the teacher in French to let us go to the rest room or be excused for personal reasons. . . . If French words were spoken, we were turned over to the principal's office, where this big old man had a set of rubber tubes tied together and we were whipped. The girls caught were punished different, as they were forced to walk around the flagpole with bricks in their hands."

Forced by Anglo-American teachers—or by misguided Cajun teachers trained by Anglo-Americans—to act like mainstream children, south Louisiana youths put aside their ethnicity, learned to speak English, and joined in the war effort like good Americans. Prompted by schools, churches, and scouting groups, they bought and sold war bonds and stamps, grew victory gardens, canned fruits and vegetables, rolled bandages, made hospital beds, and collected scrap items. In Lafayette, Girl Scouts adopted the slogan "All Out for Defense." A boy in Eunice saved pennies to buy a one-dollar membership in the American Red Cross. "The spirit of America will never be downed as long as its citizenship is composed of youths like Frank Frugé," observed his local newspaper, "AMERICA MARCHES ON." In Port Barre students in the Future Farmers of America and 4-H encouraged residents to grow more vegetables, raise more hogs and cattle, and buy more war bonds and stamps. Students in New Iberia won first prize in a statewide salvaging contest, collecting more than forty-eight thousand pounds of waste paper. In Broussard students grew vegetables for their cafeteria, raised fifteen hundred dollars at a war bond rally, and pledged fifty thousand dollars toward the purchase of a warplane. A seventh grader from Arnaudville promoted salvage drives by writing a short story for his local newspaper. It told of an automobile dredged from Bayou Teche to make "beautiful bullets . . . for the heads of Hitler, Mussolini, and Hirohito."[28]

For Americans of all ages, newspapers and other media played an important wartime role, informing them about the conflict, stirring patriotic feelings, and furthering the Americanization of minorities. Despite a high illiteracy rate, increasing numbers of Cajuns were learning to read by the 1940s, albeit in English. Literacy was encouraged by the Louisiana Library Commission, which sent out bookmobiles to service rural Cajuns. Books and magazines opened south Louisiana to outside influences and helped to ingrain the belief that to succeed, one had to read, write, and speak English. This perception was reinforced by Acadiana's several English-language daily and weekly newspapers, which the U.S. Treasury Department used to reach Cajun readers by tailoring advertisements to them. "American boys fight, suffer, and die today to perpetuate freedom," a war bond advertisement read below a drawing of Evangeline, an ethnic icon to more educated Cajuns, who viewed the fictional milkmaid as the personification of their culture. If the poet Longfellow "had not enjoyed liberty," the advertisement continued, "he could not have written 'Evangeline.'"[29]

Like millions of Americans each week, Cajuns flocked to theaters during wartime to see motion pictures and newsreels. These were powerful Americanizing agents, especially since many contained patriotic themes, some imposed by the U.S. Office of War Information. In addition, movies did not require literacy, only a grasp of spoken English. By the 1940s many Acadiana towns had at least one theater, such as the Evangeline in New Iberia, the Jefferson in Lafayette, the Rose in Opelousas, and the Liberty in Eunice. In their wartime compendium, *Gumbo Ya-Ya,* a team of folklorists noted,

> Movies are popular all over the Cajun country, cowboy and other types of action pictures being first choice. "Quiet, please!" signs are wasted in Cajun cinemas, for no Cajun ever stops talking except when he's asleep, much less when Gene Autry is chasing rustlers across the screen. At such tense moments, leaning forward in their seats, Cajuns will yell: "Come on, Gene! Get him, you! I would not let him get away with that, no. Not me!" And with anxious sighs, "*Sacré bleu!* That Gene Autry is sure dead now. There ain't never gon' be no more pictures from him. That's for true!"[30]

Of all wartime media, however, radio exerted the strongest impact on Cajun culture, for, like television in coming decades, its broadcasts reached isolated residents who might not subscribe to newspapers or view motion pictures. In 1942, researchers found that 41 percent of rural Lafayette Parish homes possessed a radio, concluding, "It is probable that it is through this medium that most of the rural people of this parish obtain their entertainment, news, and such agricultural information as is available." Like Americans elsewhere, Cajuns tuned in to hear news programs, jazz and big band music, and popular serials like *The Shadow, Tom Mix,* and *Jack Armstrong—The All American Boy.*

A few Cajuns, however, partly co-opted wartime radio by featuring their own dialect and music through local programming. State senator Dudley J. LeBlanc of Vermilion Parish used radio to reach out to his French-speaking constituency. The response was phenomenal: so many south Louisianans skipped Mass to hear his weekly Sunday program, according to one source, that priests begged LeBlanc to reschedule it. "That was a ritual, man, that was like the way of the cross," recalled Allen Simon. But even LeBlanc sensed a change in south Louisiana's cultural landscape, for although he delivered the first half-hour of his program in French, he aired its second half-hour in English.

Similarly, the Hackberry Ramblers, a popular Cajun string band from Cameron Parish, hosted their own live music program on KPLC radio in Lake Charles. The Ramblers received letters and postcards from fans throughout south Louisiana and east Texas requesting traditional Cajun songs like "Jolie blonde" and "Dans le grans bois." Ultimately, however, the Ramblers mirrored the ongoing Americanization process, for despite their Cajun roots, the band had embraced Anglo-American western swing music, a genre popular in neighboring Texas. Furthermore, a survey of the Ramblers' fan mail shows that requests for Anglo-American tunes like "The Soldier's Last Letter," "There's a Star-Spangled Banner Waving Somewhere," and "I'll Be True While You're Gone" greatly outnumbered requests for French songs, even though Cajuns composed most of the Ramblers' audience.[31]

When the war ended, Cajuns celebrated victory like other Americans across the United States. In Opelousas the usually tranquil streets "broke out in bedlam," observed a journalist, "as horns squeaked and people shouted." Some townsfolk flocked to churches to offer thanks for victory and to pray for the safe return of loved ones. Others ran to liquor stores, "coming out with little round packages under their arms, bent on a little more 'out of this world' celebration to last far into the night." The scene was much the same elsewhere in Acadiana. "An automobile horn sounded somewhere up the street," noted a reporter in Houma. "There was another and another until it seemed that every automobile in town had suddenly awakened in a spontaneous burst of enthusiasm. Boat whistles and horns joined in—bells began to ring—sirens and whistles." St. Martinville went "completely wild with joy," and Kaplan citizens held a parade, which in addition to furloughed servicemen, boy scouts, and the local fire brigade included a horseman pulling two lassoed revelers dressed like Hitler and Tojo.[32]

As the home front celebrated, Cajuns GIs around the world eagerly awaited orders sending them back to south Louisiana. Never in their ethnic group's history had so many Cajuns been so far from home. Even the dispersal of their Acadian ancestors from Nova Scotia paled in comparison, as thousands of Cajun GIs found themselves scattered across Europe, Asia, Africa, the Pacific, and North America. Cajuns were there in 1945, from Germany to Japan. "Berlin used to be a big city," wrote L. J. Broussard of Vermilion Parish from the former capital of the Third Reich. "Now it is nothing but a big pile of bricks and sand." A kinsman, Ray Broussard of Iberia Parish, witnessed Japan's formal surrender in Tokyo Bay aboard the battleship *Missouri*. "I almost broke my neck," he informed his parents, "but I saw most of the ceremony from a gun mount." He added, "Now that I've seen it and it's all over, I want to go home."[33]

Some never came home. Census data suggests that more than six hundred Cajun GIs died during the war, many falling in the conflict's major battles: Anzio, Iwo Jima, Leyte, Luzon, Okinawa, Saipan, and the D-Day invasion of Normandy, where twenty-one-year-old Private Houston D. Duhon of New Iberia met his death. The thousands who did come home, however, were not the same Cajuns who had left Acadiana; those who stayed on the home front also had changed. Separated by thousands of miles, all underwent similarly profound transformations during the four years of wartime. United with others against common foes, Cajuns in foxholes and at home emerged from the conflict a more Americanized people. The process was far from complete, for World War II had set into motion a series of trends and events that in the postwar era would hasten the ethnic group's assimilation into mainstream society. It was the end of World War II, yet the Americanization of the Cajuns had only started.

TWO

ATOMIC-AGE CAJUNS

Moi, J'aime Ike [I Like Ike]

—Presidential campaign button issued in Acadiana, 1956

"Allons Rock and Roll [Let's Rock and Roll]"

—Song title, Cajun musician Lawrence Walker, 1959

Around 10 P.M. on March 15, 1957, a fiery meteor emitting a shower of red sparks hurtled over south Louisiana, turning darkness to broad daylight before slamming into West Côte Blanche Bay. Windows rattled, some shattered, and police throughout central Acadiana fielded calls from hundreds of frantic citizens. No, they replied, it wasn't a midair collision, an oil-rig blowout, a "space ship from Mars," or "la fin du monde," the end of the world. It was only a chunk of rock from outer space.

Significantly, some Acadiana residents assumed that what they had witnessed was an incoming missile and the flash of an atomic blast. They believed that the Soviets had launched a nuclear attack on Baton Rouge or New Orleans. According to the *Abbeville Meridional,* for example, a local resident "who prefers not being identified said he thought the meteor was a guided missile . . . sent to this area by the Russians for some destructive purposes." The same article cited Vermilion Parish resident Preston Broussard as describing the meteor's impact as "like the explosion of weapons used in warfare." Lafayette's *Daily Advertiser* stated, "Some thought it was . . . 'an atomic bomb dropped over New Orleans.'" In the rural community of Kaplan, schoolteacher Earl Comeaux was putting his daughter to sleep when he observed "the yard light up as in daytime." At first the event puzzled him, but as he recalled, "It dawned on me that that was the flash of an A-bomb exploding. Since it was in the east, I immediately thought of Baton Rouge, a prime target of the Russians. They would be after the petroleum plants there."

Comeaux knew more than most locals about atomic warfare: a few years earlier, he had served with the Strategic Air Command (SAC), flying on B-50 bombers that carried nuclear warheads targeted for Moscow rail yards. Waking his wife anxiously, Comeaux told her about the mysterious flash and explained that if the capital had indeed been bombed, the resulting shock wave ought to reach Kaplan at any moment. "Well, no sooner was that said than a great boom shook the house," he recalled. "I was convinced that we had been attacked by the Russians." Gathering their children, the Comeauxs huddled around their television, awaiting official word of doomsday. After a long night, they learned about the meteor that had crashed nearby. "How terrified I had been for my family and myself!" he recalled. "How ridiculous my reaction to a natural occurrence."[1]

Obviously, Cajuns were as susceptible to Cold War anxieties as other segments of American society. But the Atomic Age brought more than the threat of nuclear annihilation to south Louisiana. It heralded a number of trends and events that moved Cajuns toward mainstream America. For example, Cajuns sought protection from communism in their newfound role as staunch patriots, and they assisted in the vigorous national effort to weed out subversives through McCarthyism. Compulsory military service accelerated the ethnic group's Americanization, while World War II and Korean War veterans used the G.I. Bill of Rights to complete their schooling, buy homes, and start businesses. This led to improved economic conditions, as did the booming oil industry, which gave many Cajuns their first good jobs. No longer burdened by rural poverty, Cajuns cast aside the antimaterialism of their ancestors and embraced the age's rampant consumerism. The most popular luxury item they purchased was a television, which further introduced the ethnic group to an English-speaking world beyond the Cajun homeland.

Because of the Cold War, the 1950s represented an era of patriotism and Americanism, and in south Louisiana this meant that many Cajun children continued to be punished for using French at school. As a result, the number who spoke it as a primary language continued to decline. At the same time, older siblings grew discontent with the trappings of their heritage and sought to emulate "typical" teenagers elsewhere. They even created their own distinct genre of rock 'n roll, which in itself served as a powerful Americanizing agent. Moreover, the rise of tourism during the era brought thousands of visitors to Acadiana, eroding its cultural insularity and boosting the commercialization of its culture. Although depicted by the tourism trade as a serene fairyland, the region was increasingly caught up in the struggle for black civil rights. The combined effect of these factors was that by the early 1960s, Cajun Louisiana was engulfed in the currents of mainstream American history.

As for all Americans and the world, the Atomic Age began for Cajuns in August 1945 with the dropping of A-bombs on Hiroshima and Nagasaki. Many rural Cajuns had difficulty grasping the nature of this frightening weapon. "We couldn't understand what an atomic bomb was," explained Allen Simon. "I mean, all of a sudden, ka-boom." Toby Hebert recounted elder family members calling it the "*Thomas* bomb," because there was no Cajun French equivalent for *atomic.* Those who were more Americanized, however, better understood the new weapon's significance. Congressman James "Jimmy" Domengeaux of Lafayette, for instance, informed his constituents only days after the bombing of Japan, "Use of the atomic bomb means that two roads are open to the world's future. One leads toward destruction of civilization, . . . the other leads toward a new and brighter era for all mankind."[2]

Nuclear anxieties increased throughout America after 1949, the year the Soviets acquired the bomb. By the end of the 1950s about two-thirds of Americans listed the threat of nuclear war as the nation's most serious problem. This looming fear reached deep into Acadiana. "I well recall the nuclear attack drills at school," reminisced Michael W. Talbot, a Cajun from the Teche country. "You sat on the floor, preferably concrete, next to a sturdy wall, placed your head between your legs, covered and pressed the back of your head with the intertwined fingers of both hands, and kissed your ass goodbye." W. J. Ducote recalled "nightmares of mushroom clouds," and Zilda M. Hebert wondered "if we would actually be bombed. . . . We greatly feared nuclear war and the devastation it would bring." Their fears were not unfounded: a federal study found that most of Cajun Louisiana stood at least a 30 percent chance of contamination by radioactive fallout should a nuclear bomb hit Lake Charles, a likely scenario in the event of war because of the city's vital industrial complex and major SAC air base housing two bomber wings. (Perhaps the closest south Louisiana actually came to being nuked occurred when fire destroyed an atomic warhead aboard a U.S. bomber parked at Lake Charles; fortunately, radiation contaminated only the aircraft wreckage.)[3]

By spring 1962 Acadiana had 360 public fallout shelters, some of which were located in communities as small as Gueydan, Kaplan, Bayou Boeuf, Cut Off, Basile, and Mamou. A few Acadiana residents even built their own backyard shelters, but these did not always relieve nuclear anxieties. Zilda Hebert's father built a shelter, sprang surprise midnight drills on his family, and harshly penalized stragglers. "My brother was punished by having to stand at attention for hours," recalled one family member. "He was just a little boy being lectured that he was going to be the cause of our entire family failing to survive the bomb by having to wait on him."[4]

"Don't believe it can't happen here," civil defense officials warned residents of St. Martin Parish, "it can." The message was the same in Lafayette, whose leaders regarded their community as a secondary target for Soviet bombers overshooting Baton Rouge. "We are only 6 minutes flying time away and could be the substitute spot." Lafayette's daily newspaper sought to allay fears by informing readers that "in small amounts, radioactivity seldom is harmful" and advising them to "wait a few minutes" after an atomic explosion, "then go and help fight fires." Even the sleepy Cajun town of Opelousas observed a mock nuclear attack. The local paper averted panic by informing townsfolk that "The bombing will not be real. There will be no bombing planes overhead and no bombs dropped."[5]

Mock nuclear attacks continued throughout the 1950s and into the 1960s, becoming more elaborate and realistic with each exercise. During the 1961 statewide Operation Alert, participants acted out a detailed scenario that included pretend broadcasts from President John F. Kennedy and simulated nuclear attacks on ten Louisiana targets. Three bombs fell on Cajun parishes. Two blasts equaling twelve megatons wiped out Lake Charles and, inexplicably, a single ten-megaton blast obliterated Lac des Allemands, a rural fishing and boating area in southeast Acadiana. "The attack on the state of Louisiana commenced with a strike on Chennault Air Force Base at 4:14 P.M.," read the scenario. "At 7:53 P.M., a very heavy nuclear bomb was reported to have struck in the Lake DesAllemands area. . . . A huge ball of fire followed by a pink mushrooming cloud was observed. . . . At 7:57 P.M., the center of Lake Charles was hit." The exercise called for 16,500 dead, injured, or wounded in Lake Charles. Nevertheless, civil defense leaders promised residents three hours and twenty-two minutes of warning prior to nuclear attack, sufficient time, they stated, to evacuate a forty-square-mile radius around the city. They cautioned citizens about Soviet fifth columnists, however, who might infiltrate the parish "to sabotage and spread panic at just the right moments."[6]

In 1947 President Harry S. Truman announced a global plan to contain communism, pledging "to support free peoples who are resisting attempted subjugation by armed minorities or by outside pressures." In 1950 the United States put the Truman Doctrine into action in northeast Asia, using American troops to repel a communist invasion of South Korea: "Korea, Here We Come," sang Cajun musician Harry Choates. Approximately 13,200 Cajun GIs served during the three-year conflict; perhaps as many as eighty-five never returned home alive. Of all these Cajun servicemen, about 67 percent used French as their first language. Like those who served in World War II, however, they were rapidly Americanized through immersion in English-speaking society. The difference in cultures was apparent: shortly after Marvin Ducote arrived at boot camp in Fort Smith, Arkansas, he overheard a number of elderly locals speaking among themselves. "You know what's wrong with that group?" he asked a fellow south Louisiana soldier. "They should all be speaking French." As in World War II, some Cajun GIs who served during the Korean conflict faced ethnic discrimination. As a soldier in the early 1950s, for example, Earl Comeaux encountered "prejudice against me personally for the first time. I never thought of myself as a Cajun until then."[7]

On the other hand, south Louisianians who comprised Marine reserve squadron VMF-143 expressed ethnic pride by nicknaming themselves the Ragin' Cajuns, the earliest known use of this now familiar phrase. The squadron's emblem was a charging cartoon pelican (the Louisiana state bird) bedecked in boxing gloves and carrying a lighted bomb in its mouth. According to former squadron commander Carol Bernard, the Marine Corps activated several Ragin' Cajun pilots during wartime, transferred them to other squadrons, and sent them on combat missions over Korea in new jet fighters.

Despite their intense patriotism, Cajuns could become irate or apathetic when Cold War necessities conflicted with their way of life. During the war, residents of coastal Acadiana protested the creation of a twelve-hundred-square-mile air force gunnery range off Vermilion and Cameron Parishes. The proposed range, they observed, would destroy "the best fishing area in the section" and ruin the shrimping industry that operated out of nearby ports like Delcambre and Morgan City. While assuring Washington that they had no wish to impede plans for defense, the protesters suggested that the range be established farther into the Gulf. A decade later regional civil defense authorities had to cancel a mock nuclear attack on eight central Acadiana parishes because of cultural conflicts. According to a civil defense memo, those conflicts included the annual sugarcane harvest and its accompanying festival in New Iberia.[8]

During the late 1940s and early 1950s, many Americans believed that communist agents had infiltrated their government, educational institutions, and even Hollywood. President Truman responded by issuing Executive Order 9835, which called for the investigation and dismissal of federal employees suspected of disloyalty. The nation's most powerful antisubversion group, the House Un-American Activities Committee (HUAC), carried out Truman's mandate using the powerful Smith and McCarran Acts, which criminalized the teaching or advocacy of subversive ideas and required communists to register with the federal government. Two Cajun congressmen served on HUAC. One of them, F. Edward Hébert of New Orleans, whose family hailed from Terrebonne Parish, joined the committee in 1948 and played an active role in the noted Hiss espionage case. Former communist turned informant Whittaker Chambers called Hébert "the most unsparing of interrogators." The other Cajun member, E. E. Willis of St. Martin Parish, joined HUAC in 1955, and from 1963 to 1969 he chaired the committee. Meanwhile, states formed their own antisubversion groups. At one time, Louisiana's ten-member Joint Legislative Committee on Un-American Activities included three Cajuns, one of whom, Senator Sam Broussard, served as its vice chairman and operated a branch office of the committee out of his suburban New Iberia home.[9]

The zealous national campaign to ferret out communists eventually became known as McCarthyism, after Senator Joe McCarthy of Wisconsin, whose practice of haphazardly accusing alleged subversives lasted from 1950 until his censure by the U.S. Senate in 1954. In the South, including Louisiana, racist authorities used McCarthyism to intimidate civil rights proponents, particularly the National Association for the Advancement of Colored People (NAACP). Yet during its national peak, McCarthyism was almost nonexistent in Acadiana. As Leroy J. Curole of lower Lafourche Parish recalled, "Communism was talked about, watched on the news and talked about some more. A few people were even pointed out as being communists in disguise, but this was all people's vivid imagination." "Subversives Not High Here," observed a south Louisiana newspaper. This perceived lack of subversion owed much to the Cajuns' traditional dislike for political extremism and their exemplary service during World War II. Joel Fletcher, president of Southwestern Louisiana Institute (SLI), Acadiana's chief school of higher education, informed a northern audience, "While the Acadian still speaks the French language, there is in his heart no divided allegiance. He is a citizen of the United States, and, as I told countless F.B.I. investigators during the last war, who were looking into the loyalty of men being considered for strategic positions, 'When a man has an Acadian name, there is no need of further investigation. Without exception, an Acadian loves this country devotedly and will give of his all to preserve it.'"[10]

Yet McCarthyism was itself subversive, and by the early 1960s it had infected south Louisiana. Its presence was demonstrated by the case of Dr. Alexander Sas-Jaworsky, a Ukrainian refugee who became a U.S. citizen and settled in rural Vermilion Parish to practice veterinary medicine. Sas-Jaworsky embraced his new south Louisiana home and endeared himself to locals by picking up some of their traditional dialect. "Comment ça va? [How goes it?]" he greeted them. In his spare time, he crusaded tirelessly against the evils of communism, telling more than two thousand schools, churches, and civic groups how communists had seized his homeland, confiscated his family's property, and imprisoned his father, a Russian Orthodox priest and prodemocratic politician. Sas-Jaworsky praised the virtues of Americanism in his book *The Best Answer Is America* and received dozens of awards and citations in recognition of his ardent patriotism, from an "honorary Acadian" certificate to a U.S. Immigration Service award for "Outstanding Immigrant of the Decade, 1948–58" to the Daughters of the American Revolution's "Gold Medal of Americanism."

Nevertheless, Sas-Jaworsky lost a bid for the Louisiana senate in 1963 amid rumors that he was a communist. He responded by filing a fifty-thousand-dollar lawsuit against his accuser, an Abbeville grocer who had announced to several customers, "I hope that damn communist Dr. Sas-Jaworsky loses the election because they said he was a communist. That is the way the communists operate. They send over here people like him." Although both the plaintiff and defendant were transplants to the region, the judge, attorneys, and almost all the witnesses were Cajuns. Their conduct revealed the extent to which south Louisianians had been indoctrinated about the Red Menace. When attorneys quizzed a young witness about the meaning of the word *communist,* he replied that it meant "Something like a thief, a traitor to his country. Somebody that don't believe in God." Another witness replied, "I think it's one of the lowest things that a person could possibly be. As a matter of fact, I think [it's] even lower than a thief or a murderer, because—well, he supports communism and communism doesn't believe in God, and they want to control the whole country like we were taught in books."

Taking the stand, the grocer not only declared himself innocent but claimed that he had spoken up for Sas-Jaworsky when one of his teenaged clerks had called the immigrant a communist. Judge Jerome Domengeaux (brother of Congressman Domengeaux) was unconvinced. Calling the defendant's story "poppycock," he accused the grocer of perjury and witness tampering and awarded Sas-Jaworsky forty-five hundred dollars in damages. Domengeaux concluded the trial by commenting, "In Vermilion Parish, Louisiana, as in every other section of these United States, the appellation 'communist' carries with it contempt, vileness, Godlessness and disregard for Constitutional free government. To call one a communist, except in jest, is as bad, if not worse, as calling one a member of the Mafia." Furthermore, said Domengeaux, the word was "akin to thief or, to use the vernacular, an S.O.B., or bastard or something like that . . . excuse the language." Ultimately, the Sas-Jaworsky incident demonstrated not only that the Red Scare had penetrated Acadiana but also that south Louisianians were willing to revive the specter of McCarthyism nearly a decade after it had lost its intensity elsewhere. The unfounded suspicion among some Cajuns that Sas-Jaworsky was indeed a communist perhaps revealed an overzealousness to prove themselves "good Americans."[11]

The fight against communism strongly influenced American classrooms, which were viewed as particularly vulnerable to subversion. Fearful of McCarthyism, teachers on the elementary, high school, and college levels often avoided controversial topics. Students of the era likewise shunned intellectual discourse, prompting critics to label them "the silent generation." These trends made their way into the heart of Cajun country, prompting SLI professor Bernard Bienvenu to complain, "It is difficult to introduce a controversy in the classroom. The person is subjected to accusations of 'communist.'" He lamented that "America is in the midst of intellectual intolerance," condemning the era as one of "complete conformity." SLI nonetheless escaped much of the red-baiting found at other universities. In 1956 Amos Simpson arrived from Berkeley as a new professor and found SLI relatively open-minded, a trait he attributed to the laissez-faire Cajun values that permeated the campus. When the recently appointed professor refused to sign a loyalty oath as required by law, nothing happened: no hearing, no charges of "communist," no dismissal.[12]

By the early 1960s the intellectual climate in south Louisiana had changed. The state required SLI and other universities, as well as high schools, to teach a course titled "Democracy versus Communism." L. D. Dupuis Jr., an educator who taught the course at Cecilia High School, recalled, "It was an ultimatum: You stop teaching American history, wherever you are. That's it. Then you start tomorrow . . . teaching Democracy versus Communism, and buddy, you get the information where you can. The state provided us with absolutely nothing. . . . It was handled very poorly, from the very, very top, but it looked good."[13]

The fear of communism had accelerated in 1957 when the Soviets launched the first artificial satellite, Sputnik. Americans learned about the spacecraft through sensational media reports, heard its ominous bleep on radio, and saw the glowing sphere sail defiantly across the night sky. The result was near hysteria: Americans immediately called into question their military preparedness, their educational system, and most of all their deep-rooted sense of national purpose and superiority. Washington responded to public fears not only by increasing defense spending and founding NASA but by passing the National Defense Education Act, which allocated federal funds for the study of science, mathematics, and foreign languages. These skills were viewed as indispensable for waging a successful global struggle against communism, which now seemed to have jumped ahead of democracy in technological prowess.

Despite the nation's new emphasis on foreign-language skills, Louisiana educators did not view the French-speaking abilities of Cajun students as potentially helpful in winning the Cold War, with at least one notable exception. SLI President Joel Fletcher argued, "It is the patriotic duty of young men and women who come from Louisiana French families to study French. . . . The position our nation now occupies as a world power makes it mandatory that more of our citizens understand the languages of the people of other lands."[14]

Most educators disagreed, however, and continued to use the classroom for promoting a strongly Anglo–Saxonist form of Americanism. For example, the state's geography textbook, *The People of Louisiana*, published in 1951, described Cajuns as "an unsophisticated agrarian people . . . slow in adopting 'American' ways," which it defined as "the values and standards of their English-speaking neighbors." Furthermore, the textbook linked poor educational results not to rural poverty or to isolation but directly to Cajun culture itself: "The educational standing of the population is lowest in those particular parts of the French section in which the Acadian influence has been the greatest." Indeed, the textbook blamed the entire state's educational ills on its French-speaking Cajun minority. "More than any other factor," it explained, "this contributes to Louisiana's poor national standing, just as the Spanish-speaking population of New Mexico is responsible for that state's low ranking educationally."[15]

This denigration of Cajun culture in a state textbook no doubt stung many south Louisiana students, particularly as more children than ever were enrolled in school. This larger student population resulted not only from the period's baby boom but from a tougher state compulsory attendance law, known as Act 239. Passed by the state legislature in 1944, it required all children between ages seven and fifteen to attend school regularly; it also provided for the punishment of parents who failed to comply. In addition, Louisiana created "visiting teachers," whose jobs combined the roles of truant officers and social workers. Educators greeted the subsequent flood of new students by discouraging their use of French, even as a second language because it allegedly corrupted their mastery of English. A teacher in rural St. Martin Parish thus blamed Cajun French for common abuses of English like "I stuck me a nail" (I hammered a nail), "The dog barked after the lady" (The dog barked at the lady), and "He gave me some shit rock" (He gave me some sheetrock).[16]

As a result, some educators continued to punish Cajun children for speaking French at school. Virginia Verret Landry, a former Lafayette Parish student, first attended school in 1946 and recalled, "My first-grade teacher knocked me on my knuckles with a wooden ruler for speaking half English and half French. I stood in the back corner of the classroom for what seemed like all day at the time. I had no recess ever. I had to read English books while other children played outside. I remember my first-grade teacher discussing with the second-grade teacher what a waste of her time I was." Paul L. Landry remembered one of his Calcasieu Parish teachers resorting to barbaric punishments to break students of speaking French, locking violators in a closet or forcing them to wear nooses around their necks—a symbolic death for anyone who dared to speak their native tongue in the classroom.

Punitive practices continued into the 1950s. Kenneth L. LaBorde of Marksville recalled, "I will never forget my first-grade teacher for making me kneel on two pieces of chalk and putting another chalk between my nose and the blackboard for speaking French. . . . It was humiliating and embarrassing." In remote areas, teachers punished children late into the decade. Morgan J. Landry, who began school in rural Assumption Parish in 1958, recounted, "There was one teacher that would make us place our fingertips together meeting at a point and then we were made to place these fingers facing upwards; she would then take a yard stick and take careful aim and give these fingers one very good whack. This was very painful. . . . The odd thing about the situation was that she herself was Cajun and spoke French."

The consequences were disastrous for Cajun French, pushing the dialect to the brink of extinction. For the first time, a minority of the ethnic group's children spoke French as their primary language. The percentage would plummet to 21 percent for those born between 1956 and 1960, a woeful decline from the 83 percent for Cajuns born at the dawn of the century. French became a mystery to most postwar Cajun children, a peculiar code their parents slipped into when they wanted to speak in confidence.[17]

While educators across the country molded baby boomer children into good Americans, the national economy skyrocketed: during the 1950s the gross domestic product doubled, inflation remained low, and consumerism surged. As a result, many American families cashed in on a variety of novel luxury items, including suburban homes located far from polluted, congested cities. Suburbia in turn gave rise to the modern drive-in culture, symbolized by chrome-laden automobiles, serpentine freeways, and sprawling shopping centers that appeared on what had been farmland only a few years earlier. Critics called the period the Age of Affluence and decried its emphasis on conformity and materialism.

These Americanizing trends quickly made their way into the heart of Acadiana. The same SLI professor who warned about the intrusion of McCarthyism into south Louisiana classrooms likewise complained, "Today, we teach our children to respect wealth. This is the age of Lincoln and the Cadillac." Although a traditionally antimaterialistic people whose Acadian ancestors hailed from precapitalist France and whose recent forebears had been subsistence laborers, the Cajuns now found it increasingly difficult to resist tantalizing goods offered by mainstream America. Many embraced its consumer ethos: they wanted good jobs so they could acquire luxury items and participate in the American Dream.[18]

Dudley LeBlanc of Vermilion Parish demonstrated that Cajuns could compete in the modern capitalistic world. Growing up amid rural poverty, young LeBlanc knew only a few words of English. Regardless, he convinced SLI to admit him and on graduation he worked selling shoes, newspapers, and cigarettes. But LeBlanc stumbled on his key to riches during the early 1940s, when a vitamin shot cured him of a persistent ailment. Analyzing the ingredients of various patent medicines, he brewed up a concoction dubbed Hadacol, a term derived from the name of his new business, the HAppy DAy COmpany, plus L, his surname's initial. He introduced the tonic in 1945 as a curative for a variety of ailments, publishing testimonials that claimed Hadacol relieved blindness, cancer, diabetes, epilepsy, paralysis, and tuberculosis.

Public response was phenomenal: sales for 1949 totaled two and a half million dollars, and by early the next year LeBlanc was spending a million dollars per month on advertising in thirty-one states. He commissioned numerous Hadacol promotional items, such as comic books, T-shirts, lipstick, thimbles, water pistols, cowboy holsters, and even a hit song, "Hadacol Boogie." In 1950 LeBlanc launched an ambitious scheme for making Hadacol a household word, the Hadacol caravan, a traveling variety program offering "free admission" in exchange for two Hadacol box tops. Covering more than thirty-eight hundred miles its first year, the caravan consisted of more than a hundred vehicles and featured such stars as George Burns, Mickey Rooney, Milton Berle, Bob Hope, Minnie Pearl, Roy Acuff, and the favorite among southern audiences, Hank Williams Sr. Each show started with LeBlanc greeting the audience from his chauffeured Cadillac and ended with the lighting of a pyrotechnic sign reading "Hadacol for a Better Tomorrow."

By 1951 the Hadacol fad was fizzling out, while the Federal Trade Commission and the American Medical Association investigated the tonic's dubious curative powers. Just before the bottom fell out, LeBlanc unloaded Hadacol on a group of Wall Street tycoons. When the investors accused LeBlanc of fraud, he supposedly replied, "If you sell a cow and the cow dies, you can't do anything to a man for that." Critics labeled LeBlanc a con man and shameless self-promoter, but most rural south Louisianians regarded him as a folk hero who showed that Cajuns could beat *les américains* at their own game. In addition, LeBlanc used his charisma and influence (he held office several times) to campaign tirelessly for the preservation of Cajun culture, organizing goodwill tours of Canada and France, forging alliances with Francophones worldwide, and publishing three books that espoused Cajun pride.[19]

Other formerly impoverished Cajuns also pursued the American Dream, albeit on a smaller scale. A catalyst for elevating the economic status of many south Louisianians was the Servicemen's Readjustment Act of 1944, better known as the G.I. Bill of Rights. Passed for World War II and later Korean War veterans, this federal legislation provided tuition for schooling and loans for purchasing homes, farms, and businesses, among other benefits. Like millions of other American veterans, former Cajun servicemen left rural folk occupations to take advantage of the G.I. Bill, finishing high school, acquiring vocational training, or enrolling in college.

As a result, enrollment at SLI more than doubled between 1945 and 1946, reaching a record high to date when in 1947 its student body numbered about thirty-five hundred students, roughly half of whom were war veterans. While SLI officials scrambled to provide temporary classrooms and new housing, the state expanded John McNeese Junior College at Lake Charles (now McNeese State University) into a four-year institution and established Francis T. Nicholls Junior College (now Nicholls State University) at Thibodaux. Cajuns who attended these and other schools on the G.I. Bill of Rights became accountants, architects, lawyers, physicians, and engineers, among other white-collar occupations.[20]

Even those Cajuns who were not college bound left folk occupations in large numbers after World War II, moving from outlying rural areas to more urban settings in search of better paying blue-collar jobs. Many were former sharecroppers displaced by the mechanization of agriculture, a trend that occurred throughout the rural South because of field hand shortages during wartime. Cajuns who had previously subsisted as farmers, trappers, fishermen, moss pickers, loggers, and boat builders now became carpenters, mechanics, butchers, grocers, electricians, and oil-field workers.[21]

Indeed, the oil industry played a major role in changing south Louisiana's cultural landscape. Soon after oil was discovered in Acadiana in 1901, hundreds of oil companies, from small, independent wildcatters to major corporations, were extracting oil and natural gas from fields bearing names like Anse La Butte, Coteau Frêne, Evangeline, and Hell Hole Bayou. In following decades Anglo-Americans, mainly from Texas, poured into the region, lured by jobs and dreams of striking it rich.

Cajun country would never be the same. As one observer noted of rural Lafourche Parish at midcentury, "Golden Meadow presents the greatest scene of activity and bustle in the marsh area. This settlement is strung out along Bayou Lafourche with only one road, which runs along the bayou. Because of the oil fields in the vicinity, huge trucks are constantly rumbling up and down this road, while automobiles weave in and out among them. Tugs chuff up and down the bayou towing oil barges. And seldom does a day pass when an amphibious plane of one of the oil companies does not land in the bayou carrying important people on important business. The whole tempo of life has been speeded up."[22]

Cajuns at first lamented the influx of outsiders who came in search of oil, but as one Texan wildcatter recalled, "When they found out what we were paying, the Cajuns stopped complaining." Indeed, they soon became the backbone of the Gulf Coast oil industry. By the mid-1950s so ubiquitous were Cajuns in the "oil patch" that they merited their own entry in *Jerry Robertson's Oil Slang,* a book of industry jargon. *Robertson's* defined *Cajuns* as oil-field workers "of mixed Spanish-French ancestry most likely to be a native of Louisiana . . . quaint, brave and skillful . . . who laugh as they risk their lives on deep wells in high pressure offshore areas in the Gulf Coast."[23]

Lafayette illustrates how the oil industry rapidly changed Acadiana. What in 1940 had been an agricultural town of about 19,200 was transformed in only a decade to a thriving petroleum city of about 33,500. "Oilmen have flocked to the city, swelling its population threefold and more," noted a local newspaper in 1949. With this surge in population came new stores, restaurants, theaters, hotels, bakeries, and automobile dealerships, converting Lafayette into "a modern city, sprawling beyond its original boundaries into subdivision after subdivision, building after building. . . . The buggies and leisurely pace of an earlier Cajun day have given way to all the furor and speed of modern wealth and initiative." In response, SLI's departments of math, science, and engineering taught Cajun students the skills they needed to prosper in the oil business, helping them to break through the "glass ceiling" that previously kept many from occupying white-collar jobs. The creation of the Oil Center office and shopping complex in 1952 hastened Lafayette's transition from a sleepy Cajun town into a modern American city. What began as a few office buildings on a former turnip patch grew by the mid-1960s to more than sixty buildings employing four thousand workers and included a municipal auditorium, hospital, two-screen movie theater, planetarium, and art museum. Lafayette also became headquarters to Petroleum Helicopters, a commercial helicopter fleet that serviced oil platforms in the swamps, marshes, and Gulf of Mexico; by the late 1950s it was the nation's largest independent helicopter operator.[24]

Other Acadiana communities were also strongly affected by the burgeoning oil economy. In Lake Charles, corporations built sprawling petrochemical facilities employing local and transplanted workers. Refineries sprang up in Acadiana parishes lining the Mississippi River, primarily from West Baton Rouge Parish south to St. Charles Parish. Coastal communities such as Abbeville, New Iberia, Morgan City, Houma, and Thibodeaux supplied the industry with thousands of oil-field workers and prospered from the abundance of petroleum businesses in their vicinities. As one south Louisiana editorialist noted during Oil Progress Week, "Yes, the oil industry has found solid root on our soil. We are happy to salute all of its components, from the policy makers behind mahogany desks to the sweating roughnecks in the fields. . . . They truly make every week another period of economic progress."[25]

In reality, the changes that attended the coming of Big Oil were not always positive. Marsh dredging and waste dumping polluted the Cajuns' traditional fishing, trapping, and hunting grounds. The industry also contributed to the decline of traditional Cajun culture by introducing mainstream American values, from consumerism to country-and-western music to various strains of Protestantism. The 1948 docudrama film *Louisiana Story*, directed by renowned pioneer filmmaker Robert Flaherty, overlooked these negative consequences by depicting only the benefits showered on a backwoods Cajun family by oil exploration. Helped by a Cajun boy's gris-gris amulet, congenial oil men find what they are looking for and depart, leaving the bayou virtually untouched, except, as *Life* magazine noted, "now the Cajun family has more groceries to eat and the boy has a new hunting gun." Most viewers were unaware that the film's $258,000 budget was entirely underwritten by Standard Oil Company of New Jersey. *Time* magazine thus called the critically acclaimed film "a subtle piece of public relations."[26]

The case of Lennis Hebert demonstrates how the oil industry served as an Americanizing influence. In the late 1950s Hebert quit a job digging potatoes for five dollars a day to assemble and repair wellheads. He eventually rose to division manager of an oil-field supply company, acquiring all the trappings of success offered by mainstream society: cars, television, a new home. But success came at a price not only for himself but also for other upwardly mobile oil-field Cajuns. "They've got big campers, bass boats and swimming pools," he explained, "but they had to spend half their lifetime offshore to pay for them. When I was growing up on the farm, money didn't mean much to us, but oil's changed us. Now, everyone's trying to keep up with the Joneses." Not only were Cajuns trying to keep up with the Joneses, they were marrying them, a natural result of the influx of transplants to the region. "Proud French names are now joining with the Smiths, Joneses, Schmidts, Garcias, Gallaghers et al.," observed a journalist writing in the late 1940s about oil's impact. "Yvette is marrying Tony; Pierre is engaged to Sally; Etienne and Greta are showing off the twins."[27]

Bolstered by soaring oil industry revenues, many Cajuns enjoyed the same modern conveniences found across the United States. Of roughly three hundred mostly French-speaking white households queried throughout small-town Lafayette Parish between 1951 and 1953, 97 percent had natural gas, 96 percent had electricity, 91 percent had running water, 87 percent had indoor bathrooms, and 61 percent had telephones. In addition, 77 percent of these families owned their homes. Modernization also came to the parish's rural citizens. For example, 94 percent of farm households had electricity, compared to only 15 percent a decade earlier; 58 percent had running water, an increase of 43 percentage points since 1942; 54 percent had indoor bathrooms, compared to 20 percent previously; and 18 percent had telephones, more than four times higher than ten years earlier. In addition, 85 percent possessed an automobile or truck, almost all manufactured within the past decade. Yet motor vehicles had been uncommon in the parish's outlying areas during the early 1940s—only one to every three horse-drawn vehicles. And despite the 1942 survey's claim that "tractors are not thought to be necessary or even desirable" by Lafayette Parish farmers, they had almost universally adopted mechanization within a decade. "The old days of the plow and the horse are gone," observed a 1951 survey.

These changes mirrored national trends and could be found throughout the twenty-two-parish Acadiana region. By the end of the 1950s about

85 percent of Acadiana residents had radios, 80 percent had clothes wash-ers, 64 percent had telephones, and 77 percent had access to one or more automobiles—figures only slightly trailing or roughly equaling those for the South and nation. Acadiana residents were actually more likely than other Americans to own goods that fended off heat and humidity, perhaps no surprise considering the region's semitropical climate. For example, 29 percent of dwellings had home food freezers, at least 10 points higher than the nation, the South, and the rest of Louisiana, and 22 percent had air-conditioning, higher than the rest of the state and the South and 10 points higher than the nation. Most south Louisianians rejoiced at the coming of these modern conveniences. As Cajun homemaker Beverly M. Bernard of Avoyelles Parish noted about her home appliances, "You don't know how good it is to have, until you have it."[28]

The Cajuns eagerly accepted postwar consumerism, and that eagerness was aptly illustrated by the community of Pecan Island. A *chênière* located on the coastal marshes of Vermilion Parish, the island remained inaccessible to automobiles until October 1951, when a shell road connected it to the "mainland"; the state finished improvements to this road in June 1953. Electricity did not arrive until May 1954, however, spurring Pecan Island's four hundred residents to embrace consumerism with a vengeance. "Age of Electricity Comes to State's 'Last Frontier,'" a newspaper reported only days after electrification. "TV sets, deep freezes, electric ranges, automatic wash-ers, and electric irons came in almost as quickly as did the last of the electric poles and lines," it observed, moving the island "from the primitiveness of yesterday to the luxury of today as quickly as it took to flip a switch." One res-ident declared, "I've used the scrub board to wash my clothes too long. The first appliance we're buying is an automatic clothes washing machine." When a journalist visited the community three years later, one of her first impres-sions was "TV antennas . . . silhouetted against an overcast sky at sun-down."[29]

Television exerted the most Americanizing effect of all consumer goods. Because of it, everything seemed to happen to everyone at once, whether the event was the birth of Little Ricky in a 1953 episode of *I Love Lucy* (described as "a national event"), the 1954 humiliation of Joe McCarthy ("Have you no sense of decency, sir, at long last?"), or the 1963 assassination of President

John F. Kennedy. Television offered Cajuns a seemingly magical world populated with fascinating people from distant places like New York and Hollywood. It also tantalized them with flashy commercials for products that promised to improve their workaday lives. Because all national programming was in English, television further diminished the perceived value of speaking French. It also induced Cajuns to remain at home instead of joining in more traditional folk activities, like the Saturday night *fais do-do* (communal dance) or the evening *viellée* (gathering of neighbors for food, conversation, and sometimes live musical performances). Growing up in the 1950s, Sylvia David Morel recalled, "Television, unfortunately, replaced the quality time I remember spending with cousins and extended family. Instead of listening to the 'old folks' and their stories about *les vieux temps* [the old times], we watched make-believe on TV. What a poor substitute for the real life history lessons we learned from our grandparents!"

"In 1949 no one had a television set," an observer noted of the remote St. Martin community of Catahoula in 1960, "but since 1955 the number of antennae has grown like mushrooms so that one is attached to the humblest home." This held true for all of Acadiana: in 1950 less than 1 percent of its households had television, but about 80 percent had it by the end of the decade, when at least seven stations were beaming signals across the region. Two of those stations were located in Acadiana, KLFY Channel 10 in Lafayette and KPLC Channel 7 in Lake Charles. In 1962 KATC Channel 3 in Lafayette went on the air; its call letters stood for Acadian Television Corporation.

Oddly enough, a Cajun actor appeared regularly on the most popular television show of the medium's golden age. Although it was unknown to millions of viewers, the drumming prodigy who played Little Ricky on the 1956–57 episodes of *I Love Lucy* was a Cajun from Bunkie named Keith Thibodeaux. Born in 1950, Thibodeaux was a product of Americanization: not even his Cajun surname betrayed his ethnicity, for producers replaced it with an Anglo-American stage name, Richard Keith. Thibodeaux was too difficult to pronounce or remember, they explained. The experience confused the young south Louisianian, and when French actor Maurice Chevalier asked, "Your name is really Thibodeaux? Are you French?" he could only reply "I don't know."

National programming dominated the airwaves, but like elsewhere, television stations in south Louisiana provided a few shows aimed solely at local audiences. Shortly after KLFY began broadcasting in June 1955, it offered viewers a weekly half-hour Cajun music program featuring accordionist Aldus Roger and the Lafayette Playboys. Dixie 45 brand beer sponsored the program, and so successfully did Roger market the beverage that even non–French speakers were known to refer to it offhandedly as "Dixie *quarante-cinq*." His popularity bolstered by television, Roger paid tribute to the medium by composing "La valse de KLFY" (KLFY Waltz). KPLC also offered a Cajun music show, hosted by performer Jimmy C Newman. Later, KATC aired its own Cajun music programs as well as syndicated French-dubbed episodes of *Gunsmoke* titled *Police des plaines* (The Plains Police). Ultimately, French-language shows comprised only a fraction of local programming because they did not attract sufficient advertising dollars. English-language shows, on the other hand, appealed both to bilingual viewers and to the increasing number of south Louisianians who spoke only English. This latter group included children growing up on a steady diet of *Howdy Doody, Lassie,* and *World of Disney.*[30]

Cajun children who came of age during the postwar period stood uneasily between two worlds: one was familiar, rural, French-speaking, the other was mysterious, urban, English-speaking—and more enticing to many than the seemingly outmoded world inhabited by their forebears. Most south Louisiana youngsters emulated young Americans elsewhere. "They read comics about Archie and Jughead and Reggie and Betty and Veronica," a Cajun from Ville Platte recalled of his teenaged peers during the 1950s, "and in dress and liking for hamburgers were very much like . . . all-American teenagers." Another Cajun from Erath recalled, "It wasn't cool to speak French. . . . I wanted to get into the American way of life."[31]

Many young Cajuns nonetheless felt anxious about the changing world around them, as reflected in surveys taken of more than one hundred rural and small-town Lafayette Parish teenagers between 1951 and 1953. These youths generally expressed discontent with their surroundings, complaining about the scarcity of jobs, poor road conditions, and the "snoopy people and gossiping" that existed in small communities. Some offered complaints unique to their locales. In Carencro, for example, teenagers derided the presence of "cows in the street." In Duson they deplored the overabundance of "old people," signaling a divergence from their traditional culture, which revered community elders. More than half of Cajun teenagers said they planned to leave their hometowns after graduation, prompting the surveyors to observe, "They want good jobs. They are not afraid of leaving home to find them. . . . They are following the modern trend of society to move from rural to urban areas."

The same surveys provided a snapshot of the typical Cajun teenager during the 1950s. Of those surveyed, 55 percent worked at home doing housework or farm chores or outside the home at drive-ins, restaurants, filling stations, and grocery stores. Among their pastimes they listed sports (particularly baseball), dancing, and movies as well as reading, skating, and listening to the radio. About 75 percent sought amusement outside their hometowns. Youngsville teenagers, for example, traveled between five and twenty-five miles for their recreation, indicating access to automobiles. Most of the teenagers were active in extracurricular groups such as the 4-H, Future Farmers of America, Home Demonstration Club, Glee Club, Teen-Age Literary Club, and the Scouts, which, with its patriotic tenets, acted as a strong Americanizing agent. (In 1959 there were roughly forty-three thousand Boy Scouts and seventeen hundred Girl Scouts in central Acadiana.) Catholic groups such as the Holy Name Society, the Altar Boy Society, and the Sodality were also popular among these youths. After examining their data, the survey teams concluded that Cajun teenagers in rural and small-town Lafayette Parish were "an active, normal, fun-loving group, concerned with their future, but living in the present." In other words, "They seem pretty normal, well-adjusted Americans."[32]

During the 1950s a distinct youth culture developed throughout the nation, fueled by disposable incomes many baby boomer teenagers acquired from after-school jobs and their aspiring middle-class parents. Young people had money to spend on clothes, comic books, fast food, and music, particularly rock 'n' roll records. Like their peers elsewhere, Cajun teenagers listened with fascination to such new musical artists as Fats Domino, Little Richard, and Elvis Presley, whose exotic sounds invaded Acadiana through radio programs and inexpensive 45 RPM records. As Terry Gene DeRouen, a typical Cajun teenager in the 1950s, recalled, "I'd find myself getting back from school and turning on the Big Bopper. . . . That's when I started gettin' to moving, man! I wanted to be like them guys." One Iberia Parish youth asked in his local newspaper, "Is 'rock and roll' music undermining the morals of the modern teenager?" It was a question parents were asking nationally, and the youth's response demonstrated a growing generation gap. "The answer is an emphatic NO!"

Cajun teenagers not only listened to rock 'n' roll but created their own rock 'n' roll idiom. Eventually known as swamp pop, the sound revealed the extent to which they had been Americanized. Swamp pop resulted from colliding cultural elements—folk and mainstream, rural and urban, French and English. The genre's golden age stretched from 1958 to 1963, during which it yielded dozens of regional hits and sixteen national hits, including Dale and Grace's number-one single, "I'm Leaving It up to You." ("Grace" was Grace Broussard of Ascension Parish.) Swamp pop musicians played modern rock 'n' roll instruments, used standard pop music chord progressions, and sang primarily in English. The sound was typified by highly emotional lyrics, tripleting honky-tonk pianos, undulating bass lines, bellowing horn sections, a strong rhythm and blues backbeat, and mournful, lovelorn lyrics, exemplified by compositions such as "Mathilda," "This Should Go on Forever," and "I'm a Fool to Care." A typical swamp pop ballad thus gave little or no hint of its composer's ethnicity. The following lyrics, for example, were composed by John Allen Guillot in 1958:

> *Lonely days and lonely nights, dear,*
> *I cry myself to sleep,*
> *Thinking how much I love you,*
> *Wondering why I want you near.*

Guillot's case demonstrates how rock 'n' roll served as a powerful Americanizing agent in south Louisiana. Like many swamp poppers, Guillot was bilingual, originally performed traditional Cajun music, and reached adolescence in the 1950s. Then, at age seventeen, he experienced an intense musical awakening when he witnessed a live performance by Elvis Presley. "You could wring my neck right now," recalled Guillot, "but I don't believe I could remember who else was on that show except Elvis Presley, because he just stole the show from everybody. . . . He just blew everybody off the stage." Inspired by Presley, Guillot convinced the other teenaged musicians in his Cajun band to switch to rock 'n' roll, a move that required the ouster of their fifty-year-old bandleader, accordionist Lawrence Walker. "So that's what happens when you put an old horse out to grass," lamented Walker on learning that his Wandering Aces had renamed themselves the Rhythm Rockers.

Young Cajuns lost interest in their musical heritage and created a new musical style that reflected the realities of their changing world. Instead of playing "Jolie blonde," "Allons à Lafayette," and "Les flammes d'enfer" on the accordion, fiddle, and iron triangle, they began to play their own songs on the electric guitar and bass, upright piano, saxophone, and drumming trap set. Furthermore, swamp pop musicians often adopted Anglo–American stage names. Guillot, for example, became Johnnie Allan; Robert Charles Guidry became Bobby Charles; Joe Barrios became Joe Barry; Elwood Dugas became Bobby Page; and Terry Gene DeRouen became Gene Terry. Some no doubt changed their names because they were ashamed of their Cajun heritage, a feeling shared by a segment of the entire Cajun population. But economics motivated most swamp pop musicians: they wanted to sell records not only at home but beyond, where the pronunciation of names like Guillot, Barrios, and DeRouen eluded promoters, deejays, and consumers. And they did sell records, by the millions: Rod Bernard, for example, received two gold records for his national hit "This Should Go on Forever," the popularity of which propelled him onto the *Alan Freed Show* and Dick Clark's *American Bandstand* and into road shows with Jerry Lee Lewis, Frankie Avalon, Chuck Berry, B. B. King, and Roy Orbison. Meanwhile, Warren Storm had a national hit with "Prisoner's Song" and hung out with Elvis at Graceland, while Bobby Charles composed rock 'n' roll classics like "Later Alligator" for Bill Haley and the Comets and "Walking to New Orleans" for Fats Domino.

Despite its rock 'n' roll influences, swamp pop was not entirely devoid of Cajun content. Bobby Page and the Riff Raffs recorded "Hippy-Ti-Yo," a bilingual rock 'n' roll version of the traditional Cajun French song "Hip et taïaut," and Rod Bernard did the same with "Allons danser Colinda." Joe Barry rerecorded his swamp pop hit "I'm a Fool to Care" in French under the title "Je suis bêt pour t'aimer." Randy and the Rockets issued "Let's Do the Cajun Twist," a remake of the local classic "Allons à Lafayette." For their version, the Rockets composed new English lyrics with local-color references, including one to *Jolie blonde,* the blonde-haired, blue-eyed rustic maiden (not all Cajuns have dark hair and dark eyes) who personified Cajun culture as a sort of workingman's Evangeline. Significantly, the Rockets depicted her as an Americanized teenager who danced the Twist, a national craze in the early 1960s.

> *Let's go to Lafayette*
> *And do the Cajun Twist.*
> *We'll twist with* Jolie blonde
> *And twist all night long.*
> *We'll go to Grand Coteau*
> *And eat some good gumbo*
> *Then go to 'tit Maurice*
> *And do the Cajun Twist.*[33]

While many imbibed swamp pop, others continued to listen to traditional south Louisiana music. A handful of talented folk musicians such as Shirley Bergeron, Austin Pitre, Nathan Abshire, and Iry Lejeune took advantage of western swing's declining national and local popularity to revive the accordion around 1950. The boisterous instrument had disappeared from Cajun music during the 1930s and 1940s, when local Texas-style string bands, such as the Hackberry Ramblers and the Rayne-Bo Ramblers, dominated Acadiana's music scene. These accordionists were not resistant to change, however, for they retained instruments borrowed from western swing during the string-band era, such as the drums, bass, and steel guitar, and for inspiration they often drew on popular music, especially the country-and-western sound.

Other south Louisianians experimented with a heavily Americanized strain of Cajun music that lent itself to mass consumption. Cleveland Crochet's accordion-driven hit "Sugar Bee," for example, was performed in English and became the first Cajun song to make the Billboard Hot 100. Al Terry (real name Allison Theriot), Jimmy C Newman, and Rusty and Doug Kershaw all left south Louisiana for Nashville and became stars by performing Cajun-themed songs, usually in English but sometimes bilingually. Terry, for example, hit with a bilingual tune called "Good Deal Lucille," prompting readers of *Country and Western Jamboree* to choose him over Elvis Presley as best new singer of 1955. Newman eventually recorded more than twenty hits, including "Alligator Man," "Bayou Talk," and "Louisiana Saturday Night." The Kershaw brothers yielded the classics "Diggy Liggy Lo" and "Louisiana Man" and joined the Grand Ole Opry. Doug eventually went solo, showing off his dynamic fiddling style on national television programs like the *Ed Sullivan Show* and the *Tonight Show.*

As some Cajun musicians entered the mainstream, their music became part of popular culture, influencing other performers. Country pianist Moon Mullican rewrote "Jolie blonde" in English using Cajun-tinged clichés; it became one of the period's best-selling records. Hank Williams composed "Jambalaya (on the Bayou)," a country classic based on the Cajun song "Grand Texas." Louisiana's singing governor, Jimmie Davis, recorded a largely English version of "Allons danser Colinda." The sound even influenced rock 'n' rollers: Jackie DeShannon, best known for her 1960s pop hit "What the World Needs Now Is Love," recorded a song titled "Cajun Blues" in 1958 with a Cincinnati-based group called the Cajuns. That same year future country-and-western star Waylon Jennings released a rock 'n' roll version of "Jolie blonde" produced by music legend Buddy Holly.[34]

Like Acadiana's music, tourism helped to introduce mainstream Americans to Cajun culture—and to introduce Cajuns to mainstream Americans. The Great Depression and World War II had stunted the tourism industry's growth until the coming of peace and good economic times in the late 1940s and 1950s, when tourism experienced a national boom. Americans then flocked to exciting destinations, including south Louisiana, where they visited Grand Isle's bird habitats and sports fishing grounds; the annual pirogue race on Bayou Barataria; New Iberia's Shadows-on-the-Teche plantation manor; Jungle Gardens, Bird City, and the Tabasco sauce factory at Avery Island; the Azalea Trail in Lafayette; elegant waterfront homes and gardens in Lake Charles; and the Evangeline oak and shrine in St. Martinville. Such harvest celebrations as the Rice Festival in Crowley, the Sugar Cane Festival in New Iberia, and the Yambilee Festival in Opelousas also attracted thousands, including politicians stumping for office. Senator John F. Kennedy appeared at the Yambilee, and his glamorous wife, Jackie, accompanied him to the Rice Festival, where she endeared herself to older locals by addressing them in French.[35]

National magazines reflected the growing interest in Acadiana as a tourist destination, even if their depiction of the region gravitated toward the unusual and exotic. *Travel* magazine visited south Louisiana in 1957 and called the region "as 'foreign' a country as any to be found on another continent . . . where Main Street may be a bayou, and the postman must be a motorboat pilot," while *American Heritage* asserted that "nearly every Acadian earns his living trapping, fishing or farming." Cajuns usually laughed off such misrepresentations—but not always: when in 1954 a writer from *Collier's* magazine depicted residents of rural Vermilion Parish as backward swamp dwellers prone to drunkenness and violence, the Abbeville Chamber of Commerce convened a special meeting, condemned the article, and called on Louisiana politicians to express their outrage. Some travel writers, however, made keen observations about postwar Cajun culture. *Holiday* magazine, for example, noted that "the world of the 20th Century has finally battered its way into the region," and a writer for the *Christian Science Monitor* confessed in 1955 his futile search for "real dirt-floor, slab-shack, mink-trapping Cajuns." Instead, he found that "all along the Bayou Teche, up and down Bayou Lafourche, modern, mechanized civilization is moving in, rapidly displacing the easy-going ways that have grown up over two centuries."[36]

Whether lured by fantasy or reality, an estimated three and a half million tourists visited Louisiana in 1954, spending some $290 million. By the end of the 1950s, tourism ranked as the state's largest industry. Although it would eventually fall behind agriculture and petrochemicals, tourism continued to spark economic growth as well as to erode cultural barriers by exposing Cajuns to curious outsiders. "The Cajuns are more than friendly," observed one travel writer. "And they will come more than half way toward seeing that you enjoy your trip and get the most out of their country."[37]

Tourism fueled the commercialization of Cajun culture, as visitors demanded souvenirs ranging from postcards to ceramic Evangeline statues to cookbooks teaching them how to prepare the region's delicacies. Although Cajun cuisine had attracted attention before World War II, it was only after the conflict that it became the region's primary cultural export, a role it later shared with Cajun music. In 1946, for example, a popular Lafayette restaurant included on its menu several dishes now considered standard Cajun fare: fried oysters and shrimp, soft shell crabs, frog legs, turtle stew, shrimp remoulade, fish courtbouillon, shrimp and oyster gumbo. These and other exotic dishes appealed to tourists and locals alike, prompting chefs to create new recipes using traditional and nontraditional ingredients. One of these inventions, crawfish étouffée, a rich stew of seasoned onion, bell pepper, celery, and crawfish tails served with rice, quickly displaced crawfish bisque as the exemplar of Cajun cuisine.

According to Cajun chef Dickie Breaux, crawfish étouffée was originally known as crawfish courtbouillon. It was served as early as the 1930s by Yolie and Marie Hebert, whose mother, Mrs. Charles Hebert, ran the Hebert Hotel in Breaux Bridge. During the mid- to late 1940s, the Hebert sisters gave the recipe to Aline Guidry Champagne, owner of the local Rendezvous Restaurant, who prepared a batch for herself. When a well-to-do customer asked what she was cooking, Champagne answered, in French, "I'm smothering some crawfish"—*étouffée* being French for "smothered." The customer returned shortly with a group of friends and ordered "crawfish étouffée," coining the name by which the dish became famous. This recipe probably did more than any other to popularize Cajun cooking as a commercial product, and it appeared in the earliest Cajun cookbooks, one of which in 1955 hinted at the dish's newfound status: "Restaurants proudly proclaim that crawfish étouffée or crawfish bisque is available."

Cookbooks played a major role in commercializing Cajun culture and introducing it to the rest of America. Perhaps the earliest explicitly Cajun cookbook was the annual *Creole Cajun Cookery,* first published by the *Daily Iberian* newspaper in 1952. In 1954 the Les Vingt Quatre Club of Lafayette published the aptly titled *First—You Make a Roux.* (Roux is a browned mixture of flour and cooking oil used as a base in gumbos and other south Louisiana dishes.) Next year the Acadian Handicraft Museum of Jennings published the official *Acadian Bi-Centennial Cook Book,* while St. Martinville resident Carmen Bulliard Montegut issued *Recettes (Recipes) du petit Paris de l'Amérique.* Among more cosmopolitan white French Creole dishes, the latter included several rural Cajun staples like "la gelée ou fromage de tête de cochon" (hogshead cheese) and "boudin rouge," which called for a "quart of fresh pig's blood," an ingredient later excluded for sanitary reasons.

Some businesses used Cajun cookbooks as promotional tools, further demonstrating the commercial appeal of south Louisiana cuisine. In 1955 the I-Ron Pot Roux Company of Ville Platte issued *Recipes Fit for a King,* a collection aimed at advertising a new culinary concept, canned instant roux. Similarly, in 1956 Don's Seafood and Steak House in Lafayette issued *Don's Selected Recipes for Fine Food,* a cookbook geared toward uninitiated tourists. "A word of advice about buying crawfish," it noted. "Do not buy just 1 or 2 pounds. Most Acadian recipes call for from 5 to 10 pounds of crawfish. Season highly." Don's also offered canned crawfish bisque and crawfish étouffée by mail order. "Can be shipped anywhere," it advertised. "Send some to a friend today!"[38]

In 1955 the commercialization of Cajun culture merged with the growing tourism industry in the Acadian Bicentennial Celebration (ABC), a ten-month commemoration of the Acadian expulsion from Nova Scotia and the largest expression of Cajun ethnicity to date. Because the event took place at the height of the Cold War, however, the ABC's organizers assumed the seemingly paradoxical task of celebrating their distinctive French-Catholic heritage without appearing to question mainstream American values. As a result, the ABC did not celebrate genuine "Cajun" culture but a mythical "Acadian" culture drawn from the flowery hexameters of Henry Wadsworth Longfellow's 1847 epic poem *Evangeline,* about an Acadian maiden who searched patiently for her lover, Gabriel, after being separated during the upheaval.

Evangeline naturally appealed to the ABC's leadership, which consisted of wealthy or upwardly mobile Cajuns who entertained strong Anglo-Saxon pretensions. Known later as genteel Acadians, these elite members of south Louisiana society found in Longfellow's verses an enticing alternative to reality as well as to the stereotype of the drunken, indolent, swamp-dwelling Cajun. In addition, the poem had been written in English by an Anglo-American educator from that bastion of Anglo-Saxonism, Harvard University. Who better to invoke, then, when presenting Cajun culture to the rest of America? "Beautiful is the land, with its prairies and forests of fruit trees," Longfellow wrote. "They who dwell there have named it the Eden of Louisiana!"

Led by Thomas J. Arceneaux, SLI's dean of agriculture, the ABC's organizers quickly adopted two policies that reflected their elitism and

Anglo-conformism (the tendency to adopt Anglo-American values and customs). First, the term *Acadian* would be used in preference to *Cajun,* which the ABC regarded as lower-class slang, a corruption of the proper term, *Acadian.* Second, the ABC would characterize the Acadians' brutal mass dispersal as a "migration," presumably because "expulsion" sounded too negative and because the ABC feared that this term would embarrass or offend Anglo-Americans in both the U.S. and Canada: after all, it was their British ancestors who had orchestrated the forced removal of the Acadians from Nova Scotia.

The ABC started with the arrival of over a hundred delegates from Canada, many of whom represented French cultural organizations, including Le Conseil de la Vie Française en Amérique, Le Comité Permanant de la Survivance Français en Amérique, Action Catholique, and the ABC's Canadian counterpart, La Société National de l'Assomption. These delegates toured central Acadiana, receiving honorary citizenships and French greetings from local schoolchildren despite the ban on French imposed by educators. (The students evidently had been coached in Parisian French for the occasion.) Over the next several months, ceremonies sponsored by the ABC praised the virtues of "outstanding Acadians," most of whom were local blue bloods and a few of whom were not even Cajuns. Guests were entertained with opera instead of genuine Cajun music, while U.S. President Dwight Eisenhower, whose administration exhibited little concern for minorities, sent official greetings, remarking that the Acadians have "maintained a way of living which has uniquely contributed to the variety and richness and interest of life in America."

The ABC's progression of ceremonies, plays, concerts, and pageants drew media attention from across the nation and beyond. A young Cajun woman dressed "like Evangeline" in a Norman milkmaid's costume (Acadian women never wore such apparel) appeared on NBC's *Today Show* and *Matinee* to promote the event to potential tourists. A *New York Times* headline read, "200 Years in the Bayou Country," and *Time* magazine declared, "On the farms and along the bayous of Louisiana the bicentennial visitors danced the Acadian 'Fais Do-Do,' sang *Evangeline,* and chatted in their special brand of French." Montreal's *La presse* reported, "Acadiens de Louisiane et du Canada réunis sous le chène d'Evangeline, sur la rive de célèbre bayou Tèche

[Acadians from Louisiana and Canada reunite under the Evangeline Oak, on the banks of the celebrated Bayou Teche]". Even the *Guam Daily News,* published some seventy-five hundred miles from Cajun country, reported, "Louisiana Re-Enacts Longfellow's 'Evangeline.'"

The ABC peaked in August 1955, when 165 south Louisianians made a pilgrimage to Canada. There they offered a public toast to the queen of England, who ruled Canada as a dominion, even though she also represented the government that had unapologetically expelled the Cajuns' ancestors. The south Louisianians joined nearly ten thousand Acadians from Canada and the northeastern U.S. for a Mass at Grand Pré Memorial Park. A holy site for many, it was at Grand Pré two hundred years earlier that British soldiers seized some of the first Acadians for deportation. "If the expulsion of the Acadians and burning of Grand Pré was an attempt at genocide," observed the *Toronto Star Weekly* that summer, "it was a failure. They're returning in their thousands." One was Lurnice Begnaud of Lafayette, who described the scene at Grand Pré in almost spiritual terms. "I had a feeling of peace and serenity," she recalled. "As I looked out over the prairies, I could almost see the Acadians being driven into exile 200 years ago. . . . I feel as though all of us on the trip were one big happy family going back to the land of our ancestors."

When the ABC ended, organizers congratulated themselves on what appeared to be an unqualified success. The event had heightened ethnic pride and awareness among a segment of the Cajun population. It had convinced the state Department of Education to place more emphasis on French-language education in high schools and to publish a surprisingly open-minded teacher's guide titled *Our Acadian Heritage: Let's Keep It!* The ABC brought positive attention to an ethnic group previously disregarded or maligned. It contributed to the establishment of other south Louisiana festivals, such as the popular Breaux Bridge Crawfish Festival. Finally, for good or bad, it boosted the commercialization of Cajun culture, with its promotion of "Evangeline Country" tourism and its creation of official ABC history books, cookbooks, doubloons, and other ephemera.

But the deference that Arceneaux and his supporters manifested toward all things Anglo-Saxon suggested an ironic conclusion: the ABC was less about celebrating Cajun culture than about seeking the validation of mainstream America. The ABC impressed outsiders with its tales of the devoted

Evangeline, but it failed to gain the support of most ordinary Cajuns, who had never read Longfellow, had no appreciation for *Evangeline,* and had been excluded from the event because they supposedly did not represent "real" Acadian culture. More than another decade would pass before these Cajuns, inspired by the civil rights movement, would organize to preserve and promote their culture.[39]

Prior to the civil rights movement, however, segregation made up an integral part of everyday life in Acadiana. About 28 percent of the region's population was black in 1960, and nearly one-third of its twenty-two parishes belonged to the South's Black Belt, a sociological term used to denote parishes or counties in which at least 33 percent of inhabitants are black. These parishes were Assumption (41 percent black), Iberville (49 percent), Pointe Coupée (54 percent), St. James (49 percent), St. John the Baptist (52 percent), St. Landry (43 percent), St. Martin (37 percent), and West Baton Rouge (49 percent). Although many south Louisiana blacks shared with Cajuns a French-Catholic heritage, Acadiana was nonetheless firmly entrenched in the racism found in the surrounding Anglo-Protestant South. Whites throughout the former Confederacy, including Cajuns, kept blacks one step removed from slavery, using a variety of dubious legal acts known collectively as Jim Crow laws. These regulations forced blacks to use separate water fountains, phone booths, and bathrooms and barred them from restaurants, hotels, swimming pools, and other public facilities. Blacks had their own sections in movie theaters, courtrooms, hospitals, churches, and prisons and attended their own schools, which were dilapidated, staffed by low-paid teachers, and lacking decent textbooks. In some parts of the South, blacks by law could not swear on the same Bible as whites, could not engage in games of checkers with whites, or, oddly enough, patronize the same brothels as whites. Those who dared to cross racial barriers faced harsh extralegal penalties: between the 1880s and the 1950s, more than thirty-eight hundred blacks were lynched in the South.[40]

Louisiana institutionalized segregation as early as 1724, when as a French colony it adopted the *Code noir,* or Black Code, a series of laws governing race relations that remained in effect for more than a century. Slavery flourished in Louisiana from the colonial era to the 1860s, when the state joined others in the South to secede from the Union. Although the South's defeat during

the ensuing Civil War, the passage of federal civil rights laws, and the ratification of the Thirteenth, Fourteenth, and Fifteenth Amendments to the U.S.
Constitution ostensibly gave freedmen equal rights, Louisiana, like other
southern states, created new Black Codes designed to circumvent these federal acts and to preserve white supremacy. As a result, Jim Crow existed in
Louisiana well into the post-World War II era and thrived in Acadiana. When
in 1949 *Holiday* magazine published a snapshot of a quaint Cajun eatery in St.
Martinville, the words "Whites Only" showed clearly on its plate-glass window, just below signs advertising French drip coffee and seventy-five-cent
crawfish bisque. This photograph betrayed the legacy of white supremacy and
racial segregation that lurked behind the region's popular image as a semitropical Eden.[41]

As elsewhere in the South, the issue of black voting rights strained race
relations in Acadiana, causing racial incidents in Ascension, Avoyelles,
Calcasieu, Iberia, Lafayette, St. John the Baptist, and St. Landry Parishes,
among others, no doubt. Blacks who failed impromptu and often spurious
history, civics, and literacy tests found it galling that registrars allowed non-
English-speaking Cajuns to vote. As one black activist recalled, "A white person entered the office and said, 'Je m'enregestrais pour voter' [I want to register to vote], and he was allowed to register, no questions asked."[42]

In addition to subterfuge, whites in south Louisiana used intimidation
and violence to prevent blacks from voting. In Ascension Parish, blacks
were allowed to register but were attacked and robbed of their ballots at the
polls. In St. Landry, which according to one historian practiced "white
repression at its most brutal," deputies under Sheriff Clayton Guilbeau
jailed and beat several blacks from Lebeau and Eunice who tried to register; one of the activists is said to have died from his wounds. St. Landry
police also arrested and roughed up two French-speaking blacks who mis-
takenly entered the registrar's office. (They had only intended to sign up
for the military draft.) Guilbeau's successor, Sheriff D. J. "Cat" Doucet, supported black voting rights in St. Landry, but only because black votes
enabled him to remain in office and skim revenues from the parish's many
illegal gambling joints and whorehouses. When segregationists in the state
legislature implied that Doucet genuinely sympathized with blacks, the
outspoken Cajun sheriff bluntly declared, "I'm not a 'nigger lover.'"

Doucet's enemies publicized the statement in a full-page newspaper advertisement intended to alienate his black supporters.[43]

Sexual relations between blacks and whites, either real or imagined, triggered south Louisiana's most virulent racial incidents, even though mixed-race relations had been rare since the antebellum period. Black musicians performing in Cajun nightclubs were particularly susceptible to sex-related violence, a danger that predated the tensions of the civil rights era: according to some sources, for example, legendary black accordionist Amédé Ardoin was badly beaten around 1940 when at a Cajun dance he wiped away his sweat with a handkerchief offered by a white female. Ardoin eventually died from his wounds, physical and emotional. During the 1950s and early 1960s, Huey "Cookie" Thierry of swamp pop group Cookie and the Cupcakes similarly entangled himself in racial trouble by dallying backstage with adoring Cajun females. "In Lawtell they'd got the rope to hang him and everything over there one night," recalled a nightclub owner. "He was messing around with a white gal." It "really wasn't his fault," however, because while females would throw themselves at him, either out of genuine affection or to incite white males. A backlash occurred as word spread of Cookie's affairs: in Lake Charles, whites attacked the group, flipping over its station wagon and trailer; in Eunice, racists blocked Highway 190, preventing the group from reaching a nightclub in nearby Lawtell. "It got so bad," recalled the band's pianist, "that when we'd get ready to go into St. Landry Parish we had to have a state deputy to meet us in Basile to go all the way with us into Lawtell and Opelousas." Cookie eventually left for the West Coast and would not reside again in south Louisiana for more than a quarter century.[44]

Another black musician who experienced racial trouble was Gabriel King, a saxophonist from Opelousas who performed with local bandleader Good Rockin' Bob. In the summer of 1956, King kissed a Cajun female behind a Ville Platte nightclub fittingly called the Rendezvous. When their tryst came to light, police arrested King, and as a fellow band member recalled, "We went to court, man, the courthouse was on fire. There was six black people in there—me, his daddy, his mother, his lawyer and him and Good Rockin' Bob. Man, they was hollering '*Hang him! Hang him! Hang him! Hang him!*'"

Twenty-two-year-old King did in fact kiss his white admirer, who happened to be a minor, aged sixteen. The court therefore accused King of indecent behavior with a juvenile, but it was clearly race that made his infraction a small-town scandal. The saxophonist understood the volatility of the situation, for in a letter to his admirer he lamented, "What a fool I was to think you could love me. After all, I know the condition. You hate me just as the others do. . . . I didn't think you was like the rest of the people." King stood trial in a packed Evangeline Parish courthouse. Stirred by the scene, Ville Platte's *Weekly Gazette* waxed Shakespearian, declaring, "Friday morning the harsh sword of court procedure ripped open the belly of the drama, laying bare the dark and quivering flesh whose ancient and primitive yearnings do on occasion make poor, miserable sinners of us all." After examining the evidence, Judge J. Cleveland Frugé sentenced King to a one-year jail term. Using the musician as an example, the court handed down a clear message: sexual relations between blacks and whites would not be tolerated in south Louisiana.[45]

As oppressive as these incidents seem, there was a strong influence at work in Acadiana that tended to mollify racial tensions: Catholicism, which preached toleration and condemned racism and hate crimes as sinful. Indeed, during the mid-1950s, Bishop Jules B. Jeanmard excommunicated two white parishioners in Erath who had assaulted a female religious instructor for integrating her catechism class. "This act of violence," declared the bishop, "committed within the very precincts of the church itself, is a scandal to the church, a scandal to the community, and a strong indictment of the public officials whose sworn duty it is to uphold law and order." Catholicism also precluded Klan activity in Acadiana, because the Klan was anti-Catholic as well as antiblack.[46]

In addition, Cajun culture by its nature fostered attitudes more laissez-faire than found elsewhere in the South, and Anglo-Protestant enmity toward both Cajuns and blacks created at least a modicum of compassion between the two minorities. Most Cajuns therefore accepted advances in racial equality, albeit with some reluctance. For example, despite initial efforts to curb black voting, by 1956 twice as many blacks were registered to vote in the state's French-Catholic parishes as in its Anglo-Protestant ones. About a third of Lafayette and Lake Charles voters rejected a state amendment designed to block *Brown v. Board of Education,* the 1954 Supreme Court case that declared unconstitutional the doctrine of separate-but-equal accommodations and ordered the desegregation of public schools. When white supremacist legislator Willie Rainach of north Louisiana visited SLI campus to drum up support, white student leaders confronted him, saying, "Senator Rainach, we would like you to leave the campus. . . . Please go. We don't need you here."[47]

Acadiana's reaction to integration at SLI demonstrated its more tolerant racial environment. In summer 1954, only weeks after the *Brown* decision, SLI became the South's first previously all-white state college to admit blacks as undergraduates when four local blacks filed suit against the school. They claimed the right to enroll because the region had no separate college for blacks, and they could not afford to attend black institutions elsewhere. Known as *Constantine v. SLI*, the suit was spearheaded by a team of noted NAACP attorneys, including future Supreme Court Justice Thurgood Marshall. Days after the court ruled that SLI had to open its doors to local blacks, a black Arnaudville resident enrolled without incident; by the end of the month, nearly seventy other blacks had registered. Two years later, SLI graduated its first black student.[48]

Compared to the debacles that would occur over integration at Ole Miss, Alabama, and other southern universities, the peaceful integration of SLI seems almost surreal: no angry white mobs, no federal troops, no showdown between national and state politicians. The restraint exhibited by SLI's white student body and the region's white community in general partly explains why Senator Rainach decried Acadiana whites for being lax on segregation. Jim Crow would nonetheless persist in Acadiana into the early 1970s. It finally would be put to rest during the administration of the state's first Cajun governor, at a time when Cajuns looked to the civil rights movement as well as to other liberation and empowerment movements for inspiration in fostering their own cultural renaissance.

THREE

CAJUNS AND THE 1960S

We're slaves to a system. Throw away the shackles . . . and be free with your brother.

—Cajun student protester, 1968

The only LSD we need is Love, Sincerity, and Dedication.

—Cajun politician Roy Theriot, 1971

In June 1971 as many as one hundred thousand hippies invaded Acadiana to attend the Celebration of Life rock festival at Cypress Point, a two-hundred-year-old sugar plantation in rural Pointe Coupée Parish. The concert was envisioned as a recurrence of the 1969 cultural phenomenon called Woodstock, a three-day concert that featured more than two dozen bands and drew more than four hundred thousand hippies. But the Celebration of Life would be even more grandiose: it promised more than sixty acts over an eight-day period. Among the artists scheduled to perform were Canned Heat, Country Joe and the Fish, Quicksilver Messenger Service, Sly and the

Family Stone, Ravi Shankar, and the American Rock Opera Company, presenting *Jesus Christ Superstar.*

Hippies poured onto the seven-hundred-acre plantation, imbibing the music, dancing, getting high, meditating, and rapping with locals. One reporter watched as long-haired youths introduced a nearby farmer to marijuana. He puffed on the joint curiously but decided to "stick to beer." "Keep music in your soul and the music will follow," advised Maharishi Mahesh Yogi, the Beatles' former spiritual guru, who appeared on the bandstand. Thousands of hippies ignored safety warnings from wildlife and fisheries agents, skinny-dipping in the dangerously turbulent Atchafalaya River. As the semitropical summer heat and humidity swelled, nudity seemed to be everywhere. An astonished journalist witnessed "a teenaged Lady Godiva riding nude on a motorcycle through rural Louisiana, waving to deputy sheriffs who did nothing to stop her." Another reported, "Sexual intercourse became public."

So did drug use: a straw poll found that at least 90 percent of festival goers cited drugs as a major reason for attendance. They were not disappointed, for large quantities were readily available. While Point Coupée's sheriff assured the media, "We have ways of finding out who's doing what," a reporter saw "Dozens of vendors with signs advertising marijuana, hashish, LSD and other illegal drugs." "Lids, lids, lids, get your marijuana here!" cried one dealer, while another openly peddled "electric watermelon," watermelon laced with LSD.

Like Woodstock and other rock festivals, little at the Celebration of Life went as planned. A hot-air balloon crashed into a tent; numerous musical acts canceled; security guards scalped tickets; the IRS showed up to impound gate receipts; part of the main stage collapsed, injuring two people; and everyone suffered from poor sanitary conditions and a scarcity of food and water. Dozens overdosed, causing one death, and two hippies drowned in the Atchafalaya. Violence also marred the concert. Bikers armed with shotguns, knives, and chains roughed up hippies, and police accidentally shot a bystander after a mob shouting "Get the pigs!" attacked officers making a drug arrest. The final setback came when medics, lacking necessary supplies, quit in protest. Four days into its eight-day schedule, the festival closed amid chants of "Rip-off!"

Organizers blamed the fiasco on the local establishment, which followed the national trend of hippie bashing instigated by President Richard M. Nixon. Alarmed by the thousands of "freaks" swarming into Pointe Coupée, parish authorities had passed an emergency ordinance only three days before the event's opening; it banned large gatherings unless a permit had been secured at least ten days in advance. Armed with this last-minute edict, police moved in with riot guns and barricades, causing a six-mile traffic jam on the usually tranquil Atchafalaya levee. "This is an illegal assembly," explained the sheriff. "We have a law which forbids such a gathering."

While organizers hurriedly sought a restraining order, police barred anyone from setting up food, sanitation, and medical facilities. When the concert inevitably failed, it merely confirmed the local establishment's view that the counterculture—which eventually consisted of a nebulous mixture of hippies, activists, students, minorities, and feminists—was not only self-destructive but a serious threat to the American way of life. "I wish they would go home and take a good bath," scoffed a deputy as he surveyed the horde of dejected flower children.[1]

The 1960s had come to Cajun country, and as elsewhere in the nation it signaled a time of "tumult and change," as *Life* magazine remarked in 1969. Political, social, and cultural upheaval characterized the period, transforming America from a WASP vision of stability into a chaotic, multicultural amalgam that espoused "doing your own thing." In the process, the nation lost three vital leaders to assassins' bullets, wandered into a military quagmire in Vietnam, and watched as the struggle for black equality became more confrontational, inspiring other ethnic groups to organize for their own special interests. America saw the rise of protest movements, the hippie counterculture, the sexual revolution, casual drug use, and the evolution of romantic rock 'n' roll dance music into socially conscious rock music that sought to change the world. It launched a war against poverty, enacted laws to protect civil rights and the environment, expanded the welfare state, and sent astronauts to the moon. America had changed significantly in only a few years: "That is the legacy of the 1960s," observed one historian, who aptly noted that the issues and values that defined the period continued throughout the first half of the 1970s. In a broad sense, therefore, the term *1960s* can be applied not only to a precise decade but to an era of remarkable events that occurred roughly between Kennedy's assassination in 1963 and the loss of the Vietnam War in 1975.[2]

Like other Americans, Cajuns were caught up in the period's turmoil. In general, they adhered strongly to the values they had recently adopted from mainstream America. They believed in the government, the military, and the American Dream. Conversely, they rejected hippies, protesters, and political radicalism. The era "left a lot of us wondering what this world was coming to," recalled Zilda Hebert. By aligning themselves with Nixon's "great silent majority," the Cajuns allowed themselves to be further assimilated into Anglo-American culture.

Some Cajuns, however, identified with the counterculture. They were found among the first wave of Cajun baby boomers, whose members began to reach adulthood in the mid-1960s. Many of these youths sensed not only a generation gap between themselves and their parents but also a culture gap. They spoke English and, like young people across the nation, they listened to the Beatles, the Rolling Stones, and Bob Dylan; wore long hair, blue jeans, and loud T-shirts; and used slang such as "groovy," "cool," and "far out!" A few went further and became "Cajun hippies," smoking dope, listening to acid rock, and rejecting the American establishment. So numerous were young baby boomer Cajuns that advertisers targeted them as a distinct demographic group by the late 1960s. "Evangeline Maid goes mod with a twist in a swinging new wrapper," a Lafayette bakery declared, addressing youthful consumers who "dig fresh bread."[3]

But the 1960s were not entirely about chaos and counterculture: they were a period of economic prosperity for America, including south Louisiana. As a result, Cajuns continued their pattern of shedding traditional ways to embrace the materialism of mainstream society. At the same time, the coming of a new means of transportation, the superhighway, further eroded the insularity of "Acadiana"—a word popularized during the 1960s for economic reasons—and led to increased commercialization of south Louisiana culture.

The election of President John F. Kennedy offered Americans renewed hope and idealism at the dawn of the 1960s, challenging them to awaken from the previous decade's complacency. His assassination shattered this promise and anticipated the nation's chaotic transition over the next several years. The new president, Lyndon B. Johnson, assumed Kennedy's agenda, pushing through Congress numerous important reforms, including the Civil Rights Act, the Voting Rights Act, the Immigration Act, the Economic Opportunity Act, the Elementary and Secondary Education Act, the Higher Education Act, the Wilderness Act, the Water and Air Quality Acts, Medicare and Medicaid, the establishment of the National Foundation for the Arts and Humanities, and the creation of the Corporation for Public Broadcasting, to name only a few "Great Society" programs. LBJ's attempt to restore hope and idealism to America, however, was eventually eclipsed by two issues that would define the period, race and war.

U.S. race relations degenerated suddenly in August 1965, when a routine traffic stop of a black driver by a white policeman in Los Angeles spiraled into looting, arson and street fighting. More than fifteen thousand soldiers and police officers were called in to quell the violence, resulting in nearly four thousand arrests, over one thousand injuries, and thirty-four deaths. The Watts Riot and its aftermath demonstrated how differently blacks and whites perceived America: blacks saw it as a nation filled with hatred; whites saw it as advancing equality through the Civil Rights and Voting Rights Acts, both recently signed into law by LBJ. "What do they want?" asked the president, puzzled by the rage he witnessed on television.[4]

The riot marked the beginning of a more confrontational phase of the civil rights struggle. The entire nation soon plunged into unrest over the struggle for black equality, and with it went Cajun Louisiana. While race relations in Acadiana remained less virulent than elsewhere in the South, the region continued to be segregated. Blacks who spoke out against the status quo were branded unpatriotic troublemakers or worse, communist sympathizers. When civil rights activists interrupted a community action meeting in St. Landry Parish, one editorialist condemned them as "hate-mongering agitators," remarking, "The idea of a young Opelousas Negro . . . screaming threats of 'Burn, baby, burn' . . . is not only disgusting but is completely self-defeating, to put it mildly." As Ben B. Babin, a typical white south Louisianian, confided, "We as Cajuns had a little problem understanding the civil rights movement. . . . We thought the black folks were exactly the way they wanted to be."[5]

Because of their less virulent racial attitudes, Cajuns reluctantly accepted the social changes forced on them by the federal government, and there were no major civil rights clashes in Acadiana. This did not mean, however, that all Cajuns were content with desegregation. Leroy "Happy Fats" LeBlanc and Clifford "Pee Wee" Trahan, for example, vented their frustrations through protest songs that reflected the thoughts of many white south Louisianians. LeBlanc had performed Cajun music as early as the 1930s, when he fronted the popular Rayne-Bo Ramblers. He later formed the equally successful Happy, Doc, and the Boys, and he emceed the *Mariné* Cajun music program on KLFY-TV. But in the mid-1960s the usually gleeful LeBlanc issued a series of political recordings on Crowley's Reb Rebel label that took issue with LBJ's inability to win in Vietnam, the outcry of war protesters, the expense of Great Society programs, and especially the civil rights movement.

LeBlanc's anti–civil rights recordings were a product of the white backlash occurring throughout America. Incited by black militancy and the federal government's efforts to desegregate society, this backlash manifested itself most evidently in 1968, when archsegregationist George Wallace of Alabama ran as an independent candidate for the presidency. He received 13 percent of the national vote and 50 percent of the Cajun vote, a protest against growing federal interference in south Louisiana, especially in regard to elementary and high school desegregation. Unlike the peaceful enrollment of a few black students at SLI in the mid-1950s, the forced mixing of thousands of black and white minor students, at a time when the nation already seemed in upheaval, outraged white south Louisianians. LeBlanc and other Cajuns therefore saw a champion in Wallace, and after his defeat they looked to a second chance for victory in the next presidential election. "Vote Wallace in '72," urged LeBlanc in one of his Reb Rebel recordings. LeBlanc's most popular anti–civil rights recording, however, was "Dear Mr. President," which expressed a Cajun farmer's confusion over the impact of civil rights legislation. "My white coon dog won't hunt with my black bird dog," he complained to LBJ over a country-and-western soundtrack. "Could I get an injunction to make them hunt together?"[6]

LeBlanc's recordings were innocuous compared to those of "Johnny Rebel," identified by John Broven as the pseudonym of Cajun musician Clifford "Pee Wee" Trahan. Although Trahan was known for writing jovial tunes like "Lâche pas la patate" and "South to Louisiana," these Reb Rebel recordings were anything but jovial. Rather, they exhibited overt racial hatred that promoters marketed dubiously as "subtle, rib-tickling satire." Song titles alone indicated the vulgarity of Johnny Rebel's compositions: "Who Likes a Nigger?" "Nigger Hatin' Me," "Some Niggers Never Die (They Just Smell That Way)." In "Kajun Klu Klux Klan," for example, he sang approvingly about Cajuns lynching a black sit-in protester. "You niggers listen now," he warned, "the Cajun Klu Klux Klan is going to get you bye and bye." Unsurprisingly, LeBlanc and Johnny Rebel's recordings were advertised in the *Fiery Cross,* a Klan magazine based in Alabama.[7]

Regardless, there was no Cajun Ku Klux Klan. Cajuns had always shunned the white supremacist group because of its blatant anti-Catholicism. Thus, in 1965 the state's Joint Legislative Committee on Un-American Activities disclosed that of four Klan groups operating in Louisiana, none were based in Acadiana. A Cajun politician assured the south Louisiana public that there were "no Klans in our area, period."[8]

Racial tensions nonetheless flared in Cajun Louisiana during the mid- to late 1960s as blacks demonstrated boldly for civil rights. In St. Landry Parish, for example, blacks empowered themselves by registering voters and picketing segregated businesses like the Opelousas Inn, a hotel and popular dinner club. "We went into the Inn," recalled one of the picketers, "and that shocked the living hell out of them." St. Landry blacks also abandoned their paternalistic white champion, Cat Doucet, and supported one of their own for sheriff in 1968; they lost, but without black support, so did Doucet. "Our purpose in running was to destroy the illusion that Cat was the savior of the black man," one activist recounted.[9]

As elsewhere in south Louisiana, blacks in St. Landry also sought to end public school segregation, fifteen years after the U.S. Supreme Court declared the practice unconstitutional through *Brown v. Board of Education.* They received their wish in 1969 when a federal judge ordered St. Landry and other parishes to desegregate their school systems. In response, many Cajun parents in St. Landry formed white supremacist groups aimed at preserving separate but equal schools. These parents participated in mass rallies, marches, and picket lines, threatened to establish all-white private schools, and declared legal "guerrilla warfare" on federal agencies like the U.S.

Department of Justice. Some lashed out at anyone who supported integration: blacks who wanted to attend historically white schools were called "animals"; whites who wanted mixed-race schools on moral grounds were slandered as "socialistic, communistic, and atheistic."

Cajun parents also boycotted, keeping their children at home instead of sending them to school. On the first day of the 1969–70 school year, more than eighty-three hundred St. Landry children did not show up for class, about one-third of the parish's student population. Integration caused boycotts, rallies, marches, and other forms of protest among whites in other south Louisiana parishes, including Acadia, Ascension, Calcasieu, Iberia, Evangeline, and West Baton Rouge. In Calcasieu, for example, about twelve thousand whites held a fiery rally at which many attendees displayed shotguns and rifles. In Evangeline, loudspeaker trucks roamed white neighborhoods and called for a boycott; as a result, Ville Platte High School had "more federal agents than white students" on the first day of class, an eyewitness noted. It was an amazing understatement, for only one white student, a minister's daughter, showed up with her 168 new black classmates. In Pointe Coupée, St. Landry, and Evangeline Parishes, white parents formed private schools, called segregation academies, attracting a substantial number of students who had formerly attended all-white public schools.

By the mid-1970s the effort to integrate Louisiana's public elementary and high schools was floundering as resistance to federal intervention led to widespread resegregation. Although some progress had been made in Acadiana, the issue would remain largely unresolved for decades. As late as 2000, for example, a federal judge sparked controversy when he boldly enforced a thirty-year-old court decree, ordering Lafayette Parish to desegregate its schools.[10]

During the mid- and late 1960s a growing militant black power movement swept the nation, rejecting Martin Luther King Jr.'s message of nonviolent activism. Huey Newton, Bobby Seale, and Eldridge Cleaver organized the Black Panthers to fight "pig" brutality, while H. Rap Brown echoed assassinated militant Malcolm X by proclaiming that "violence is necessary" to achieve equality. Black power soon came to Acadiana: in 1969, for example, local black activist Marion Overton White called white males "violent beasts," according to a south Louisiana newspaper, and urged a gathering of

NAACP members in Opelousas to "take control . . . by whatever means possible." He further advised, "If you think whites are going to attack you, you attack first."[11]

By the late 1960s blacks in south Louisiana no longer yielded to the Cajun establishment. They spoke out, protested, boycotted. When the parish courthouse in Lafayette refused to lower its flag to half-mast after Martin Luther King's assassination, black marchers pulled it down themselves. Learning that it had been raised again, they returned to the courthouse shouting "Riot, now!" and "Violence!" Whites booed and hissed. One onlooker cursed the crowd and made obscene gestures. Police stood by armed with riot guns. Faced with an increasingly hostile crowd, parish officials advised deputies to remove the flag completely. The marchers finally dispersed after the president of the local NAACP chapter assured them he would make every effort to have the flag flown at half-staff.[12]

South Louisiana blacks also expressed resentment at the Cajuns' growing cultural hegemony: suddenly the word *Cajun* seemed to be everywhere—on license plates, T-shirts, billboards, and, most disturbingly, public buildings. In 1971 black students spoke out when the University of Southwestern Louisiana (USL, formerly Southwestern Louisiana Institute) dubbed its new football stadium Cajun Field. "We must take issue with the naming of the new stadium," explained a black student leader. "There are no blacks who would consider themselves 'Cajuns.'" This antipathy toward Cajuns extended back to the nineteenth century, when blacks tended to regard the ethnic group "as the darkies elsewhere look down upon 'poor whites.'"[13]

While blacks across the nation and south Louisiana struggled for equality, American troops in Vietnam waged a war against communist guerrillas and their North Vietnamese allies. During the eight-year conflict, about 22,700 Cajuns served in the military, but only 36 percent of them spoke French as their first language, about half the ratio for Cajuns who had served in World War II. As in previous conflicts, Vietnam introduced those who were less Americanized to "a real world outside of Louisiana," as W. J. Ducote recounted. Some were again ridiculed because of their ethnic peculiarities. Cajun veteran Paul Landry recalled meeting a career counselor who "made fun of my accent and said 'I have just the job for you.' Well, you can imagine, no one wanted that hot-as-hell job, and he had a quota, and me and my accent was selected." Even the nicknames imposed on Cajun GIs were the same. Other soldiers could not pronounce Wridley Fontenot's surname, so "I was known as 'Frenchy' because I was from Louisiana and spoke French."

And just as during World War II, Cajun GIs who spoke French sometimes found their linguistic skills useful, particularly because Vietnam had formerly been a French colony and protectorate. "I met Vietnamese officers who spoke English rather poorly," recalled Camille J. France. "Their French was impeccable, which enabled me to have conversations with them. When they experienced difficulty when speaking to English-speaking officers, I was able to step in and translate for them."

Cajun GIs in Vietnam went through the same grueling experiences as other American GIs, fighting in jungles and rice paddies and trying to survive what was becoming a bloody ordeal. "My attitude was just to stay alive and not be a dead hero," noted Paul A. Mire. Like roughly 58,000 other Americans, some Cajuns came home in body bags, perhaps as many as 150 during the entire conflict. Among them was Farrell J. Vice of Abbeville, aged twenty-one, who was killed in action during a search-and-destroy mission north of Lai Khe. "I'll tell you what the Army probably didn't," a combat buddy wrote to the Vice family back in Vermilion Parish.

> We were all nervous because we were supposed to go up north for a rough day. That morning Vice came up to me as he done every morning and shook my hand and said, "I'm scared." We were all that day.
>
> He left first on the helicopters, his [platoon]. Then we left. At about 2:30 I heard my radio man say that 3 men tripped a booby trap. They gave their numbers over the radio and I looked on my paper and I saw Vice's number. Ten minutes later I heard number 131 was K.I.A. and it was like a dream, I couldn't believe it. . . . Vice was 2nd in a file and the Lt. tripped it and all they heard was a flash. As soon as the medic could get there he went straight to Vice. He said he was dead before he hit the ground, so he didn't suffer.

"There's no doubt in my mind he'll go to heaven," concluded Vice's buddy, "because he spent his time in hell."[14]

Like most Americans, Cajun civilians back on the home front generally supported the war effort during the mid-1960s. "We were all extremely patriotic," recalled Ben Babin, "and had absolutely no use for any protester." Always outspoken, Happy Fats LeBlanc mirrored the feelings of many Cajuns in several political recordings, including "Birthday Thank You Tommy, from Viet Nam," "Veteran's Plea," and "What Has Happened to Old Glory?" His recordings extolled the lowly foot soldier, demanded swift victory, and excoriated LBJ for his ineffectual handling of the conflict. LeBlanc called demonstrators "slackers and cowards" and labeled draft dodgers and flag burners "scum." Swamp pop musician Rod Bernard added to the local antiprotest sentiment. A Marine Corps reservist, he told of a Cajun veteran returning home from Vietnam to witness protesters burning the flag:

> *What kind of an American*
> *Would set our flag afire?*
> *Is he what I've been fighting for*
> *And is he why men have died?*[15]

Some Americans regarded war protesters as traitors, discerning behind them the specter of communism. South Louisianians were not immune to this suspicion, despite the assurances of Cajun anticommunist E. E. Willis, chairman of HUAC, who in 1965 told an Acadiana audience, "In this area we have no communist organizations and we have no communist front organizations." Only a year later, the region experienced a miniature Red Scare, complete with McCarthy-style hearings, perhaps revealing (as with the earlier Sas-Jaworsky affair) an overzealousness among some Cajuns to prove themselves "good Americans." The incident stemmed from divisive national issues—civil rights, Vietnam, and particularly Johnson liberalism. In fact, the trigger was LBJ's "War on Poverty," launched in 1964 with passage of the Economic Opportunity Act, which funded community action groups aimed at fighting poverty. Civic leaders in Lafayette mobilized to take advantage of this funding, and in late 1965 they established their own community action group, Acadiana Neuf (Acadiana Nine), so called because it was to serve nine south Louisiana parishes. Ultimately, it served only Lafayette Parish and five adjacent parishes, whose poorest residents benefited from the group's supervision of Great Society programs such as Medicare, the Neighborhood Youth Corps, and Operation Head Start. "The nation's War on Poverty has moved into the Southwestern section of Louisiana," announced the Office of Economic Opportunity in Washington, D.C., which empowered Acadiana

Neuf to establish and oversee "a wide range of antipoverty programs in the low-income, French-speaking area."

Within two years of its founding, however, Acadiana Neuf came under fire for having an all-white directorship and for supposedly misusing federal funds by hiring whites over more qualified blacks. Activists from groups like the NAACP and the Congress of Racial Equality (CORE) complained to Acadiana Neuf's executive director, Roland Hebert, that his organization was controlled by "racists and enemies of the poor," by a "wealthy, sophisticated, lily-white board" less interested in helping the poor than in "helping them-selves maintain control of the poor . . . by preventing them from escaping from the camps of poverty." But the most serious threat to Acadiana Neuf came from the opposite end of the political spectrum, when prominent Cajun journalist Bob Angers Jr. alleged that the organization had been infil-trated by communist sympathizers.

A graduate of Louisiana State University's school of journalism and a World War II veteran, Angers gained a reputation as a fierce anticommunist by aiding exile groups from communist Cuba and by using his press creden-tials to expose "subversives" in Acadiana. "South Louisiana has been growing in 'popularity' as a center of communist and communist front organizations," he warned readers of Lafayette's *Daily Advertiser* in 1967 and 1968. "It's your country they're out to destroy!" The danger to the region was evident: "Red Penetration!" "Are there any communists in the Cajun Country," he asked rhetorically. "There are. . . . Are there any communists in the war on poverty in Louisiana? No doubt about it; the only question remaining: How many?"

When Angers accused Acadiana Neuf of employing communist sympa-thizers, Louisiana's Joint Legislative Committee on Un-American Activities traveled to Lafayette in 1967 to convene a two-day hearing. Serving as a key witness, Angers charged two Acadiana Neuf workers with "parroting the Red line." One worker, he asserted, had helped to organize a communist-sponsored world youth festival in Algeria and locally had established "vari-ous insurgent economic organizations," including the innocently named Sweet Potato Alert, an agricultural co-op designed to help impoverished St. Landry Parish farmers. The other worker, claimed Angers, was a convicted draft dodger who had recently urged a group of St. Mary Parish high school students to evade military service and whose wife had solicited donations at a local Lutheran church on behalf of the Viet Cong. The Lafayette hearings also revealed one more alleged subversive in the region's antipoverty movement: her image appeared in the *Advertiser* above the caption "COMMUNIST."

Already troubled, Acadiana Neuf collapsed amid the charges that it had been infiltrated by subversives. Angers, however, continued his high-profile campaign against "Cajun communists and their fellow traveling friends," exposing a Trotskyite revolutionary organization called the Spartacist League, which he asserted had infiltrated Louisiana's educational system, a major state newspaper, and even a space program facility. Spurred by Angers's frenzy, the *Advertiser* also took aim at suspected USL subversives, printing a letter that charged two professors with conspiring to deceive the public about the Vietnam War. Around the same time, USL's chapter of the American Association of University Professors accused the paper of trying to recruit a student to spy on faculty members with alleged leftist leanings, an accusation the paper did not deny when in response it defended the public's right to know.

Lafayette was abuzz with rumors of subversive activity during the late 1960s. Even a prominent USL administrator believed that a cadre of Cuban-trained communist agitators had infiltrated campus. Some citizens thus expressed gratitude to the *Advertiser* for "seeking out a . . . realistic danger to the community." But others grew impatient with the paper's McCarthyist overtones. One reader sarcastically congratulated it for exposing USL as a "headquarters of subversion," another pointed out that the number of leftists in the area could be "counted on two hands," and another accused the paper and the community of "intellectual sickness," commenting, "Lafayette has more right-wing nuts than any comparable town I have experienced." USL's student newspaper lampooned the *Advertiser,* linking the ritual of campus panty raids to a subversive conspiracy. "IT'S ALL A BIG COMMUNIST PLOT!" proclaimed the *Vermilion.* "The dirty Reds started panty raids and . . . are destroying the morale of our generation."[16]

Despite their unruly reputation, most college students never engaged in antiwar protests and actually backed the war effort until 1968, when the Tet Offensive dealt the U.S. a major psychological defeat. Prior to this reversal, pollsters discovered that more students than parents favored sending troops to Vietnam. As a result, prowar demonstrations occurred on campuses across America as thousands of students signed petitions endorsing LBJ's military policy. Other students sent giant telegrams of support to the White House, or held "bleed-ins" to collect blood for wounded servicemen. Circumstances were no different in Acadiana, where most Cajun students remained firmly behind the president and the military. In 1966, for example, more than five thousand USL students signed a petition informing LBJ of their support. "You have made 'us Cajuns' proud," an air cavalryman wrote home to the students on learning about the petition. Even after Nixon's expansion of the war and the shooting of four students at Kent State University by National Guardsmen, 66 percent of USL students voted to "earnestly support the President's decision to send the military into Cambodia and hope that other Americans likewise do the same." This support defied national trends but reflected the conservatism found on many southern campuses.[17]

A small number of Cajun youths, however, spoke out against the war and the U.S. establishment that engendered it. "A peace movement has begun at USL," the school newspaper observed in 1969 as students created a Stop the War committee. More than a hundred USL students held a quiet all-night vigil after the Kent State incident. Not all protest at USL was peaceful: four days after Kent State, three USL students, two of them Cajuns, firebombed the campus ROTC building. Their Molotov cocktail caused such minor damage that some on campus referred to it jokingly as a "Boudreaux cocktail," a quip that others found offensive because it implied that Cajuns were natural bunglers, even when it came to arson.[18]

A few young Cajuns went beyond mere protest to embrace the counterculture that blossomed throughout the nation in the late 1960s, turning their backs on mainstream America but not necessarily on the Cajun way of life. "We still ate crawfish, enjoyed fishing in the bayous and swamps, and speaking with a Cajun accent," noted Bob Duet, a former hippie who attended Nicholls State University at Thibodaux. "I still liked French Cajun music and was still proud to be a coonass. Most of my Cajun friends were hippies as well. It was a generation thing more than a Cajun/non-Cajun culture thing." Like other areas of the nation, Acadiana even had its own underground counterculture magazine, aptly named *Undercurrents,* which urged young Cajuns to mobilize for self-preservation. "The fight is for the survival of a people," proclaimed one contributor, writing under the French pseudonym LaVoix (The Voice). "And right now, the fight is being lost."[19]

As occurred among young blacks, Hispanics, and American Indians during the period, some young Cajuns freed themselves to reevaluate their ethnicity by rejecting the establishment and its Anglo-conformism. Among these youths was a Tulane student named Zachary Richard, who would become a major figure on south Louisiana's music scene. "The summer of love, Woodstock, the war in Vietnam are part of the cultural matrix from which my political conscience sprung," he recalled. "I do not know what I would have done had I been drafted, but I would not have gone to Vietnam." So disturbed was Richard by events in the United States that he went into self-imposed exile in Britain. "This departure allowed me to distance myself from what had become a difficult situation in the USA," he recounted. "I had friends, war protesters, who were in jail. Others had fled to Canada. Getting out of the situation was for me a lifesaver."

Richard soon transferred his militancy from protesting the Vietnam War to saving Cajun French culture. "Réveille! Réveille!" he sang, combining traditional Cajun and modern rock music elements.

C'est les goddams	*[The goddams (British*
qui viennent	*soldiers) are coming*
Voler les enfants.	*To steal your children.*
Réveille! Réveille!	*Awaken! Awaken!*
Hommes acadiens	*Acadian men*
Pour sauver l'héritage.	*To save our heritage.]*

Richard's lyrics were not merely about the Acadian expulsion that began in 1755; they were a cultural call to arms, advocating a new militancy (later dubbed *cadjinitude*) against the Anglo-conformism that was destroying traditional Cajun culture. "I had just discovered my Acadian heritage, and I had a fever," recalled Richard. "At that point, I wanted to turn the world around. It was the naïveté of a young militant." That militancy would remain with Richard for decades, manifesting itself in his music and poetry. "Je voudrais planter une bombe à Lafayette Electric, brûler l'Oil Center," he penned. "Parle français, ou crève maudit"—I want to plant a bomb at Lafayette Electric, burn down the Oil Center. . . . Speak French, or die and be damned.

Disturbed by American society, Richard immersed himself in his francophone heritage. He traveled to Quebec and New Brunswick, forged relationships with French speakers outside the United States, and refused to speak English even when at home in Louisiana. "I would insult people who spoke to me in English, whether they were Cajun or not. It made no difference to me," he recounted. "The whole period was a natural succession to my experience during 1968 and '69, when I was a revolutionary, or when I played at being a revolutionary."[20]

Around 1970 another Cajun hippie, Benny Graeff, formed a musical group called Rufus Jagneaux, a name he and other band members chose because it alluded to their Cajun ancestry (*Jagneaux* is a Cajun surname) and because it suggested their admiration for the Rolling Stones (*Jagneaux* implied *Jagger*). Like swamp pop groups in the 1950s and early 1960s, Rufus Jagneaux combined rhythm and blues, country and western, and Cajun and black Creole elements. It also drew on other, more recent sounds, including rock and folk-rock music. In 1971 the group issued a major regional hit, "Opelousas Sostan," a composition that featured a harmonica mimicking the sound of an old-time Cajun accordion.[21]

Despite the enormous talent demonstrated by Rufus Jagneaux and Zachary Richard, the older, genteel Acadian establishment scorned their raucous music and counterculture values. Richard, for example, angered upper-class preservationist Jimmy Domengeaux at one festival by raising a defiant clenched fist and parading homemade flags emblazoned with the motto "Solidarité—Fierté" (Solidarity—Pride). Like other elites, Domengeaux frowned on radicalism, associating it with dirty, ill-mannered hippies and fearing it might spark ethnic discord such as that raging among Anglos and French speakers in Quebec. "Domengeaux was furious that we had made what we all considered a political statement during the performance," noted Richard. "He vowed never to let me play the festival again." Genteel elitists reacted similarly to Rufus Jagneaux, even though the band was nonmilitant. "Some of the more-Cajun-than-thou people . . . thought that we were ridiculing Cajuns," noted the group's leader, "and that we were prostituting [Cajun culture] and all this stuff. And that couldn't be further from the truth." Like Richard, Rufus Jagneaux found itself blackballed from cultural events because of its mixing of traditional Cajun elements and modern counterculture values.[22]

Genteel or ordinary, most Cajuns detested the youth culture of the 1960s and everything it represented, real or perceived. A year after the Celebration of Life fiasco in Pointe Coupée Parish, the Evangeline Parish police jury (Louisiana's equivalent of county government) quashed a similar rock festival slated to occur in the countryside north of Ville Platte. Sheriff Elin Pitre and Police Chief Audley Vidrine informed the concerned jurors that "such a festival would wreak havoc with law enforcement in the parish." This view mirrored attitudes about rock festivals throughout the nation after Altamont, a sequel to Woodstock that resulted in violence and the murder of a black concertgoer by motorcycle gang members.[23]

Politician C. J. "Bobby" Dugas of Baton Rouge summed up the views of many Cajuns when he lashed out fiercely at "hippie power . . . student power, arson power, gun power, flower power, sex power, black power," all of which he equated with "power to create fear, power to dominate, power to defy courts of law and constitutional authority, power to destroy, power to break laws, power to rape, power to kill à la Charles Manson and his 'family,' power to blame the ills of society on order, affluence, the establishment, conformity, and the status quo." Dugas also decried other traits he associated with the counterculture, including poor hygiene, androgynous clothing and hairstyles, casual sex, obscene language, pornography, recreational drug use, and even the fledgling gay pride movement. "Common sense dictates that homosexuals and lesbians are abnormally sick people," he remarked, "and need some kind of treatment."[24]

The Cajuns' traditional views about gender and family caused them to frown not only on homosexuality but also on the women's liberation movement, which grew out of the civil rights movement and the counterculture. Feminists had established the National Organization for Women (NOW) in the mid-1960s, but it was not until 1968 that they attracted national attention by disrupting that year's Miss America pageant. Outside the competition, activists ripped up *Playboy;* trashed girdles, bras, hair curlers, and false eyelashes; and shouted "Liberation Now!" These extreme actions shocked the nation and seemed particularly alien to south Louisiana's strictly male-dominated society. As a folklorist noted in the 1940s, Cajun males "make good husbands, so long as their wives behave." Attitudes had changed little by the 1960s, when an observer recorded, "Papa is head of the household. . . . There is no question who wears the pants because he is *the boss.*" Cajun males carried their views on gender into the workplace, from oil rigs in the Gulf of Mexico to Capitol Hill in Washington, D.C., where in 1972 Congressman F. Edward Hébert refused to give freshman Representative Patricia Schroeder her own chair when she joined his formerly all-male Armed Services Committee. Instead, he made her share a seat with a black congressman, explaining that women and blacks were worth only half of one "regular" member.

Regardless, the notion of women's rights trickled into south Louisiana during the late 1960s and early 1970s. Protest was uncommon, but it did occur, as when in 1970 USL's Association of Women Students demanded equal treatment in cafeteria serving lines, better dorm conditions, and the abolition of dorm curfews. The latter issue not only took exception with greater freedoms afforded male students, but with the unpopular national practice called in loco parentis, the system of university codes that regulated students' personal lives, including how late they stayed out at night, "in the place of parents." "How long do you intend to be 'mothered' and protected?" the association asked fellow coeds. "Life has no permission cards or housemothers. Are you afraid of your parents?"

Employment trends reflected more subtle changes in the region's views toward women: in 1970 about 28 percent of Acadiana's white females worked outside the home, roughly 12 percent less than the national average; by 1980 the number had risen to about 36 percent, still below the national average but nearly triple the number for south Louisiana since World War II. "Life experiences outside of the domestic realm," noted one historian, "armed women with a sense of independence that altered relations between husband and wife . . . bolstering the self-image of Cajun women." Even homemakers became more empowered: those married to oil-field workers, for example, reared children, balanced checkbooks, and made important decisions while their husbands labored offshore for weeks at a time. The role of the woman in Cajun society had been altered forever by outside influences.[25]

If south Louisianians generally held negative views of the counterculture, the counterculture at least had mixed perceptions about Acadiana. Some hippies regarded the Cajun way of life, even if stereotyped, as an appealing alternative to mainstream America. They saw it as a return to nature and simpler times, qualities many hippies across the nation sought at the time by joining rural communes. One of the most popular rock bands of the period, Creedence Clearwater Revival, reflected the antiestablishment interest in south Louisiana culture. The group actively fostered a "Cajun" image, even though its members hailed from the counterculture's epicenter, San Francisco. Creedence issued albums titled *Mardi Gras* and *Bayou Country* and in 1969 released the hit single "Born on the Bayou." "Wish I was back on the bayou," sang lead singer John Fogerty, "rollin' with some Cajun queen." The group's Cajun image promoted its members as rustic good old boys who, observed a British music writer in the early 1970s, seemed to come "from somewhere like Baton Rouge or Lake Charles." But as its bass player later confessed, "We wouldn't have known a 'Cajun vibe' if it had stopped to talk to us. None of us had ever been to Louisiana or the bayou in our lives."[26]

On the other hand, some hippies viewed the region as a backwoods overrun by intolerant, violent rednecks, a term often used negatively to describe benighted, working-class Anglo-Protestant whites in the South. It was an ironic misconception, for actual rednecks in the nearby Bible Belt tended to regard Cajuns as inferior and to make them targets of ridicule. Regardless, in the classic 1968 movie *Easy Rider,* hippie bikers Captain America (Peter Fonda), Billy (Dennis Hopper), and their ACLU lawyer tagalong (Jack Nicholson) were brutalized and murdered by rednecks in Cajun Louisiana. "I don't think they'll make the parish line," remarked an antagonistic local to a law officer, portrayed in the film by a real Pointe Coupée deputy wearing his actual uniform. Nearly all the other rednecks in the film were portrayed by south Louisiana extras with Cajun surnames, including Robillard, Lafont, Guedry, Hebert, LeBlanc, Billodeau, and David.

Art mimicked reality: the longhaired stars of the movie were taunted when they arrived in Morganza to shoot the film's southern café scene. "I kin smell 'em!" a local man remarked. "Kin yew smell 'em? I kin smell 'em!" Actor-director Hopper defused the situation by tricking the unfriendly locals into appearing in the movie as themselves. "Just say things like you were saying when we came in," he coached. Tensions nonetheless remained high during the shooting. The café evicted the movie crew from a room used only for serving black customers (a violation of the Civil Rights Act of 1964). A fight broke out when Fonda openly used coarse language. And the deputy refused to cooperate further with the film after grasping its antiestablishment message.[27]

As shown by the deputy's reaction, some south Louisianians viewed the counterculture as a threat to traditional American values. A few even regarded hippiedom as an insidious Soviet plot, aimed at undermining democracy by hooking America's youth on psychedelic drugs. "I'm worried about the infiltration of dope into this country," Cajun politician Roy Theriot commented in the early 1970s, reflecting Nixon-era paranoia. "What is happening today is part and parcel of Marxism," he warned. "Weren't we told that the communists would take America from within and not from without?"[28]

Despite this warning, capitalism flourished during the prosperous 1960s, one of the best periods in history for the U.S. economy. Boosted by a 1964 tax cut, incomes rose, inflation dropped, and jobs were plentiful for high school and college graduates alike. South Louisiana did not miss out on these economic good times. Cajuns continued to pursue the American Dream, departing even further from the antimaterialistic values of their ancestors. Their desire for luxury goods attested to this trend: by 1970, the percentage of Acadiana dwellings with clothes dryers was 43 percent, while 84 percent had at least one automobile and 96 percent had televisions, all corresponding closely to national figures. Moreover, because of the semitropical climate, 86 percent had clothes washers, 55 percent had air conditioners, and 43 percent had home food freezers, numbers that cumulatively averaged 17 points above national figures.[29]

This consumerism was fueled partly by the demise of small farming in south Louisiana. The massive flight from farms to towns that began during World War II became complete during the early to mid-1960s, as stragglers gave up folk occupations to take better paying blue-collar jobs in more urban settings, whether cities such as Lake Charles and Lafayette or smaller communities such as New Iberia, Morgan City, and Houma. Some of these blue-collar jobs were created by the region's oil industry, still a booming source of revenue that contributed immensely to the growth of consumerism. By the mid-1960s Louisiana's oil industry was expanding faster than that of any other state and ranked second only to Texas in production. Significantly, Acadiana yielded 60 percent of the state's total mineral wealth—worth about $1.7 billion in 1965—including nonfuel minerals (clay, gravel, lime, salt, sand, shell, and sulfur) and more lucrative fuel minerals (liquid petroleum, natural gas, natural gas liquids). Most drilling occurred along or off the marshy coastline, where Cajun oil-field workers battled adverse conditions to maintain what one journalist called "a vast array of floating towns" extending more than a hundred miles into the Gulf of Mexico.[30]

Meanwhile, transportation improvements eroded barriers between Cajuns and other Americans. Commercial air travel became available across the nation after World War II, and by the late 1940s airliners were arriving at Lafayette and Lake Charles. Air travelers to the region increased notably in coming decades, especially after the advent of the jet age. But the superhighway made a deeper impact on south Louisiana. Because of defense concerns, economic prosperity, and the proliferation of automobiles, President Eisenhower signed into law the Federal Highway Act in 1956. An outcome of this legislation was Interstate 10, about two hundred miles of which bisected Acadiana. This superhighway opened gradually to traffic, segment by segment, between the mid-1960s and mid-1970s, when workers finally completed the Acadiana stretch.

South Louisianians were fascinated by the construction of I-10, particularly an eighteen-mile section known as the "Atchafalaya Expressway." The monumental elevated causeway cut directly through the Atchafalaya Basin, a vast, snake-infested wetlands that to many symbolized south Louisiana's cultural isolation. "They said it could not be done—building a highway over the swamps," mused a journalist. The engineering feat so impressed one south Louisiana musician that he composed "Cajun Interstate," a rock 'n' roll paean to the structure that also manifested a growing grassroots ethnic pride movement:

> *Here comes the superhighway,*
> *That superhighway boss,*
> *But it's gonna take a Cajun crew*
> *To get that road across.*
> . . . .
> *Mama make a gumbo*
> *Tonight we'll celebrate*
> *And sing about your Cajun boy*
> *That built that interstate.*

Eventually, the interstate ran nonstop from Florida to California, connecting towns such as Lake Charles, Jennings, Crowley, Rayne, Lafayette, Breaux Bridge, and Gonzales to New Orleans, Houston, and beyond. With I-10 came more commerce and more non-Cajun transplants. It also provided a convenient route of departure for Cajuns leaving south Louisiana for better opportunities abroad. "If U ♥ N.Y., Take I-10 East," read a derisive bumper sticker in central Acadiana.[31]

The coming of I-10 bolstered Louisiana's tourism industry, which in 1968 generated more than five hundred million dollars statewide. Wanting their share of this wealth, Cajuns encouraged "cultural tourism" by packaging their ethnicity as a commercial product. "We can publicize that there does exist in the United States a region in which French is spoken and in which there is a distinct culture . . . different than the stereotypical homogenous U.S. culture," proposed one civic leader. "Right in our own backyard is a goldmine tourist attraction," echoed a south Louisiana newspaper. "That is, our Acadian culture." Ironically, by packaging their culture for mass consumption, the Cajuns further demonstrated their adoption of mainstream American values, which viewed almost everything as a commodity.[32]

Indeed, the popularity of the word *Acadiana* stemmed chiefly from economic motives. An unknown New York typist supposedly created the word by accident around 1963, adding an extra *a* to *Acadian* when addressing Lafayette's Acadian Television Corporation, parent company of KATC-TV 3. But the *Crowley Daily-Signal* newspaper had used *Acadiana* in print as early as 1956, when it simply meant "things pertaining to Acadia Parish." It was KATC, however, that rediscovered the word and recognized it as a catchy new way to describe its broadcast area. The station promoted the word "strictly as a sales decision," according to former general manager William A. Patton, instilling it with a new, broader meaning: it would describe the greater Cajun homeland, stretching "from Texas to the Mississippi and from the Piney Woods to the Gulf."

Although KATC adopted Acadiana as a marketing gimmick, the word nonetheless appealed to a growing sense of ethnic pride, which, as will be seen, mirrored a national trend affecting many ethnic groups. Because of this twofold attraction, the word's popularity spread quickly throughout south-central Louisiana during the mid-1960s. Other media outlets repeated the word, while businesses began using it as part of their corporate names. The general public also began to use the word. As KATC observed in a 1967 company newsletter (aptly titled *Acadiana*), "Since its first usage by Channel Three, the name has caught hold to the extent that it is used extensively throughout the Cajun Country. . . . Our people have come to think of themselves as residents of Acadiana."

As ethnic pride blossomed across the nation and in south Louisiana, the word assumed a life of its own, and in 1970 a new Lafayette-based economic development group, The International Relations Association of Acadiana (TIRAA), convinced state legislators to define the region by concurrent resolution. TIRAA envisioned Acadiana as a twenty-two-parish economic district united by its common Cajun heritage. These parishes would extend from Lafourche and St. Charles in the east to Calcasieu and Cameron in the west and from the Gulf Coast in the south to Evangeline, Avoyelles, and Pointe Coupée in the north. At its heart sat Lafayette, the self-proclaimed capital of Cajun Louisiana.

TIRAA's choice of parishes for inclusion in the region was somewhat arbitrary, for it excluded a few that boasted notable Cajun populations, particularly Allen and Jefferson Parishes. Apparently to appease these and other border parishes, the legislature designated the twenty-two core parishes as the "Heart of Acadiana," thereby implying the existence of a larger, more nebulous "Acadiana." The legislature further clouded the region's makeup by including an unspecified number of other, unnamed parishes "of similar cultural environment" in the Heart of Acadiana.

Regardless, once the resolution had been approved in 1971, the twenty-two core parishes immediately shortened their designation to Acadiana and ignored the legislative clause including other parishes in the region. This de facto exclusion had more to do with economics than ethnicity, for the region's creation would publicize "on a national and international level the beauty of Acadiana," as the resolution itself asserted. Furthermore, the region would be "so designated by the U.S. Travel Service and by other maps and publications for international distribution." Legislative sponsors required copies of the resolution to be sent to the U.S. Travel Service and all international airlines servicing the United States as well as to the National Geographic Society and other cartographic organizations.

Not all south Louisianians were pleased with the resolution. According to former station manager William Patton, KATC complained that the legislature had interpreted *Acadiana*—the word the station had popularized—too broadly by extending the region across the Mississippi River. In addition, the resolution sparked a minor backlash against the growing Cajun-pride movement: some local Anglo-Americans resented the imposition of a blanket geographic term that strongly identified them with Cajuns. One complained that she was "sick and tired of having the other states . . . looking down on us as a place of swamplands with uneducated, backward people who live in shacks, go barefooted, and speak a broken French and English dialect."[33]

In 1974 Cajun legislators pushed through a resolution adopting an official flag for Acadiana, "le drapeau des acadiens louisianais," the flag of Louisianian Acadians. Again, the motivation was primarily economic, although not entirely devoid of ethnic pride. The flag nonetheless would help to "encourage the development of tourism in Louisiana," as a legislative cosponsor explained, suggesting the marketing savvy that underlay the resolution.

Although it became a tourism advertisement in the 1970s, the Acadian flag was created a few years earlier purely as a symbol of ethnic pride. It sprang from a 1964 visit to Canada by Lafayette lawyer, politician, and cultural activist Allen Babineaux, who noticed a colorful flag decorating the town of Caraquet, New Brunswick: it was the French Tricolor with a gold star adorning its blue field. "At every corner I saw this flag flying," he recalled, "it intrigued me." On inquiry, he learned that it was the flag of the Acadian people in French Canada.

Back in Louisiana, Babineaux suggested that the same flag be adopted for a modest 1965 sequel to the Acadian Bicentennial Celebration of ten years earlier. Others supported the idea, but Dean Thomas Arceneaux of USL suggested the creation of an entirely new flag that reflected south Louisiana's own history. Borrowing heavily from his university's seal and that of France-Amérique de la Louisiane-Acadienne, a small Lafayette-based French-preservation group, Arceneaux devised a flag bearing three silver fleurs-de-lis on a blue field, symbolizing the Cajuns' roots in prerevolutionary France; a gold castle on a red field, representing the Acadian exiles' settlement in Spanish colonial Louisiana; and a gold star on a white field, symbolizing Our Lady of the Assumption, patron saint of the Acadian people. Arceneaux drew the star and its religious symbolism from the Acadian flag of French Canada and from the local France-Amérique seal, but he infused it with new patriotic symbolism: it represented the participation of Acadian soldiers in the American Revolution under Spanish Governor Gálvez, indicating pride in his ancestors' contributions to U.S. history.

Arceneaux, Babineaux, and others introduced the flag at an ABC ceremony in 1965. Sanctioned by France-Amérique, the flag gradually appeared around south-central Louisiana, particularly during 1968, a year that would witness an outpouring of Cajun ethnic pride. Babineaux himself sponsored the flag's production, selling or giving away dozens, mainly in miniature to be flown from car antennas. Soon the flag waved over schools, businesses, and government buildings and appeared in decal form on the helmets of USL's football team. Ironically, the flag became so popular that even its creator complained it was time "to get the Acadian flag flying from flagpoles, where it belongs, and remove it from garbage trucks."[34]

Beckoned by Acadiana and its ubiquitous flag, tourists poured into the region in growing numbers. Many of these visitors wanted to see "real Cajuns," and for the sake of tourism dollars some Cajuns all too eagerly obliged. When an NBC television crew arrived in Breaux Bridge to film a Cajun *fais do-do*, more than a hundred locals showed up in costumes ranging from Little Bo Peep to Little Lord Fauntleroy. There were also southern belles and beaus, as well as the inevitable Acadian milkmaids, not to mention dancing girls in leotards and a man wearing a large plastic crawfish on his head. A self-proclaimed *fais do-do* expert insisted that everyone sing "the" *fais do-do* song, an archaic French lullaby unknown to the crowd, including the seasoned Cajun musicians secured for the filming. After some coaching everyone sang the tune in unison while the Acadian milkmaids danced for the cameras. So disgusted with the scene was cultural activist and attorney Paul Tate of Mamou that he threatened to sue NBC for airing the segment, which he characterized as "a great deception on the American TV audience and a crime against the living cultural remnant of Acadia in Louisiana."[35]

At the same time, some south Louisianians grew weary of inquisitive journalists who portrayed the Cajuns as a primitive, forgotten people. Even *National Geographic* fell for the myth of the primeval Cajun, depicting the ethnic group as solely "a rural people" who "hunt, trap, raise sugar and rice, and tend 380,000 head of cattle." The essay's opening photograph showed a group of costumed Cajun youths dancing under a moss-draped live oak "like phantoms out of the past"—more Acadian milkmaids! One south Louisiana editorialist took aim at these articles, which he regarded as "patronizing, condescending, and glazed with a gratuitous coating of feelings of superiority." He aptly summed up many of the hackneyed themes exploited by the media:

> Pierre and Marie on the ol' farm; the Saturday night fais do-do; the illiterate trapper in a cabin with a "cute" accent; Grandma Clotile at the loom; dancing in the streets because the shrimp boats is a-comin'; Jean, who is brave, him, and who drinks a pot of black coffee that is strong, strong, yes, before venturing out to the swamplands to Indian wrestle with alligators.[36]

At least a few Cajuns responded to the invasion of reporters by making them the butt of practical jokes. When a travel writer visited a Cajun barroom in 1970, locals duped him into believing they had no concept of the outside world. "Say you go from Belle River now," a young Cajun asked the cosmopolitan sightseer. "Would you be home in Washington by dark?" When the journalist answered, no, it would take more than thirty hours for him to reach home, barroom regulars reacted with "ill-disguised skepticism, muttering over their beer bottles and shaking their heads," as though no place could be so far from Belle River. Unaware of the joke that had been played on him, the journalist reported the experience as an example of the region's alleged cultural isolation.[37]

In fact, outside influences were increasingly wearing away at traditional Cajun culture, contributing to its Americanization. This disintegration was particularly evident among Cajuns born during the 1960s and early 1970s. Unlike previous generations, these youths had no reason to fear punishment at school for speaking French—because so few of them spoke French. Among Cajuns born between 1966 and 1970, for example, only about 12 percent grew up speaking French as their primary language; for those born between 1971 and 1975, the figure dropped to about 8 percent. A similarly dismal number spoke French as a second language. "The younger generation is so lacking in French," noted a journalist in 1968, "that the unique bilingual character of south Louisiana may soon die out."[38]

Americanization had resulted in Cajun children practically indistinguishable from Anglo-American children. They played with G.I. Joes and Barbies, watched *Gilligan's Island* and *The Brady Bunch,* and often spoke with neutral Midwestern accents or Texan twangs learned from the children of Anglo oilfield workers. Most were unaware of their ethnic heritage, while older college-aged siblings expressed apathy. In 1968 a *New York Times* reporter visited a nightclub near the USL campus to interview Cajun students; to his surprise he found shaggy-headed youths dancing to psychedelic music under flashing, whirling lights. "They could have been from Long Island's Stony Brook, or Kansas State, or the University of Oregon," he observed. A headline in Lafayette's daily newspaper aptly summed up the situation: "Young in Cajun Country Don't Dig French Language."[39]

After three decades of increasingly rapid, widespread Americanization, many observers proclaimed traditional Cajun culture on the brink of extinction.

FOUR

FROM *COONASS* TO *CAJUN POWER*

I believe that this effort must be made now; otherwise, the French language as a native tongue will be lost forever.

—Cajun activist leader James "Jimmy" Domengeaux, 1968

En 1968, la Louisiane a été officiellement déclarée un état bilingue.
Et quoi c'est que ça veut dire?
Ça veut dire que quelque part à Bâton Rouge,
Signé, timbré, enterré dans un dossier,
Il y a un papier qui dit
Qu'en 1968, la Louisiane a été officiellement déclarée un état bilingue.
[In 1968, Louisiana was officially declared a bilingual state.
What does that mean?
That means that somewhere in Baton Rouge,
Signed, sealed, and buried in a folder,
There is a paper which says
That in 1968, Louisiana was officially declared a bilingual state.]

—Cajun poet Jean Arceneaux, "Un état bilingue," 1978

On May 9, 1972, Edwin Washington Edwards went to morning Mass looking like "the best-dressed pimp to ever strut through a whorehouse," according to one observer. Afterward, Edwards reigned as grand marshal of his own Mardi Gras-style parade. Mobs cheered, marching bands strutted, beauty queens waved from colorful floats, and doubloons splashed on the pavement as the "Cajun Prince" smiled from a limousine's sunroof, gesturing V for victory. "I don't like playing turtle," he told his entourage. "Let's get out and walk!" Edwards worked the parade goers on foot, shaking hands, grinning, charming them as he so expertly did every crowd. A short time later, in front of the state capitol, jubilant thousands listened in anticipation as Edwards stepped forward, poised to speak on a decorated rostrum.

An explosion shook the grandstands. Spectators scattered. Aides drew handguns and shoved Edwards down.

The blast turned out to be only a barrage of artillery salvos, fired in honor of the occasion. Edwards regained his composure, stepped forward, and first in French, then in English, took the oath of office as governor of the State of Louisiana.

Louisiana had sworn in its first Cajun governor, an event that Edwards himself viewed as significant. "While we Cajuns as a group have prospered in Louisiana," he remarked in his inaugural address, "the myth existed that the governor's chair was not available to one of us—a subtle myth without substance and another barrier which this election has destroyed." Edwards had chosen "Cajun Power!" as his campaign slogan. The phrase adorned hats, buttons, banners, T-shirts, license plates, and bumper stickers. Next to it often appeared the image of a white clenched fist, adopted from the defiant gesture of the era's militant black power movement. But there was something oddly benevolent about this particular fist—its fingers were clasped tightly around a bright red crawfish, a jovial symbol of Cajun ethnicity. "'Cajun Power' is a half-jesting assertion of an accomplished fact, not a distant goal," a *New York Times* journalist observed from the inauguration. When the journalist asked Edwards what the average Cajun thought about his election, the governor answered, "They probably think 'He has proved that a Cajun is as good as anybody else.'"[1]

Only a few years earlier the notion of Cajun Power would have seemed laughable. "The term 'Cajun,'" noted a travel writer in 1957, "is used by some as a term of disregard, applied to the most ignorant of the lower classes." Aware of negative traits attributed to themselves, many Cajuns believed that they were indeed a backward people. Their ethnicity became a source of shame, something to conceal or discard in the rush toward Americanization and its promise of a better way of life.[2]

Clearly, however, something dramatic had occurred to reverse this trend and to spark the outpouring of Cajun pride and empowerment that manifested itself by the early 1970s. That something was the 1960s, which exerted a major impact on ethnic groups across America. A new "Age of Ethnicity" developed in reaction to the Anglo-conformism of previous times, as minorities demanded their rights and honored their heritage. This trend grew out of the civil rights and black power movements as well as the counterculture, all of which had declared war on traditional attitudes. Ethnic groups rebelled against the old melting pot idea, which held that a homogenous national ethnic group could be created from an amalgam of minorities, the outcome being distinctly WASP in character. By 1970 *Newsweek* declared "ethnic power" a "rising cry" among the American people.

Signs of this new Age of Ethnicity were visible across America. Blacks, Hispanics, Indians, and other ethnic groups formed organizations such as the Black Panthers, the Mexican American Youth Organization, and the American Indian Movement. These organizations sought to fight oppression through militant activism and sometimes through armed conflict. American Indian Movement members, for example, occupied Wounded Knee, South Dakota, site of a nineteenth-century Indian massacre. There they exchanged gunfire with federal authorities, leaving two activists dead and one police officer wounded.

Most expressions of ethnic pride and empowerment, however, were neither radical nor militant. Americans took up genealogy as a hobby, traveled to ancestral homelands, wore traditional clothing, or gave children names that reflected their heritage. Scholars founded academic centers to examine ethnic cultures, while universities offered courses in ethnic history, art, and literature. The federal government aided this move toward a multicultural society. The Immigration Reform Act struck down discriminatory quotas against non-Anglo immigrants. The Bilingual Education Act funded classroom instruction for minority students in their native languages, and the Ethnic Heritage Studies Act provided grants for the study of ethnicity in America.

For the first time the U.S. Census Bureau questioned Americans about their ethnic origins, while politicians increasingly appealed to minority voters.[3]

In south Louisiana this trend spawned two parallel ethnic pride movements, one organized, autocratic, elitist and the other, nebulous, egalitarian, grassroots. Colliding in the mid-1970s, the grassroots movement emerged triumphant. Ordinary Cajuns reevaluated their image as a people and proudly embraced their heritage. They mobilized to save their unique French culture and history—even as their Americanization became nearly complete.

Prior to the 1960s, the Cajun establishment had made several ineffectual attempts to preserve its heritage, such as when genteel Acadians founded France-Amérique de la Louisiane-Acadienne in 1951. Like other early preservation groups, this organization floundered because it was small, disorganized, and elitist, dismissing genuine Cajun culture in favor of a more ideal culture based on the Evangeline myth. In 1968, however, these same Cajuns launched a more aggressive preservation effort: they established the Council for the Development of French in Louisiana (CODOFIL). Unlike its predecessors, CODOFIL was a large organization that received wide exposure, even internationally. It was chartered by the state of Louisiana and funded by sizable government grants. It also had a clear agenda, which was to restore French in Louisiana by teaching it in schools at all grade levels. In addition, the 1960s social movements offered powerful new elements that boosted CODOFIL's viability, including open resistance to assimilation, a radical intellectual base, and the advent of ethnic pride and empowerment.[4]

Ironically, a thirty-one-year-old non-Cajun, Raymond Spencer Rodgers, more than anyone introduced these counterculture values to the French-preservation movement. Born in Britain, adopted by his American stepfather, and living most of his adult life in Canada, Rodgers held a masters in international affairs and a doctorate in public law and government from Columbia University. Despite his Anglo-Protestant heritage, he cultivated a strong interest in minority rights, a trait reflected in his marriage to a wife of mixed French-Canadian and American Indian ancestry. In 1966 the University of Southwestern Louisiana hired Rodgers to teach in its political science department. Soon after his arrival in south Louisiana, he became intrigued by Cajun culture and its evident waning. Although his knowledge of French was admittedly "lousy," Rodgers concluded that the survival of the culture depended on preserving the Cajun French dialect. Indeed, in September 1966, less than a month after moving to Lafayette, he informed USL's administration that he wished to explore "the problem of French-language survival in the Southwestern Louisiana region."

A few weeks later Rodgers published two articles in the *Daily Advertiser* titled "Is French Dying in State?" and "Community Action Needed to Preserve French in Area." "The schools and colleges of Louisiana are doing nothing to preserve French," complained Rodgers. "Louisiana should fight to preserve the French language. But unless the fight starts now . . . all is lost." Rodgers encouraged closer ties with French Canada in a 1967 article published by the Louisiana Academy of Sciences, and he was formally appointed by Louisiana Governor John McKeithen to negotiate the Quebec-Louisiana Cultural Agreement, which called for artistic, educational, and economic exchanges. Rodgers viewed the relationship as crucial to French preservation: if French died in Acadiana, he asserted, it would disappear in Quebec and the Maritime Provinces, and hence in North America entirely. Metaphorically evoking the Cold War "domino theory," which held that one government's overthrow by communism inevitably caused the downfall of neighboring governments, Rodgers proclaimed Cajun Louisiana the "South Vietnam of French Canada."

Unlike restrained genteel Acadians, Rodgers made little effort to temper his words with diplomacy. Armed with a caustic wit that nettled south Louisiana's French-speaking elites, he mocked USL for choosing the English bulldog as its mascot and for dressing its band like British redcoats. After all, he observed, the British had expelled the Cajuns' ancestors from their home-land. Noting that Cajun children had been "thoroughly coca-colized and hamburgerized," Rodgers excoriated the Acadian establishment for its lack of vision, energy, and courage. "Its 'leaders' are mostly interested in having their pictures taken handing out honorary Acadian citizenship scrolls," he told the media. "Preservation of a minority language takes more gutsy effort."[5]

Rodgers's call to arms prompted Cajun civic leaders to mobilize. In early 1967 several Lafayette political, business, and educational leaders came together at Rodgers's urging to establish the French Heritage Committee (FHC), a branch of Lafayette's Chamber of Commerce. Recognized by the local media only two years later as "a catalyst in the Acadian renaissance," the organization encouraged French architectural designs, sponsored French entertainment events, and promoted French culture as a means of drawing tourists and businesses to Lafayette. The FHC also supported French instruction in schools, working with state and local officials to introduce teacher workshops, adult education courses, and a four-year French program for high school students.[6]

What the FHC proposed was revolutionary: although public and private high schools had previously offered French as a "foreign language" elective, educators would now teach children of all ages to speak French as a means of reclaiming their heritage. Influenced by the empowerment and liberation movements that started in the mid-1960s among other minority groups, Cajun educators responded enthusiastically, and when in early 1968 USL hosted a French-Acadian Conference, more than 150 teachers showed up to hear Rodgers and other speakers present lectures with such titles as "Bilingualism: An Asset, Not a Set-Back" and "Bilingualism: The Key to Inter-Cultural Understanding." French and English, they argued, could be taught side by side in south Louisiana schools, to the benefit of all, and they pointed to a similar project among Hispanics in Texas as a model to emulate.[7]

Two weeks later, four Cajun state legislators, Senator Edgar G. Mouton Jr. and Representatives J. Luke LeBlanc, O. C. "Dan" Guilliot, and Fredric G. Hayes, announced their support for a comprehensive French education program in southwestern Louisiana. "Bilingualism is a great economic asset," explained Mouton. "We should capitalize on this heritage in the future." When the Lafayette Parish School Board announced a special meeting to draw up plans for such a program, these four legislators invited all state representatives in the region to attend the brainstorming session. "Push Begins for Bilingual State," noted the *Advertiser*.

A few weeks later, twenty-two legislators signed a petition, suggested by Rodgers and sponsored by Mouton, calling on the governor and the superintendent of education to offer French courses from elementary to university levels. "If this is done," asserted the petition, "there will be a complete renaissance of the French language and customs, which will be a source of great pride and satisfaction to the entire state of Louisiana."[8]

This petition directly inspired State Act 409, passed July 20, 1968.

Apparently using Lafayette's FHC as a model, the legislation established the Council for the Development of Louisiana-French, an organization "empowered to do any and all things necessary to accomplish the development, utilization, and preservation of the French language as found in the State of Louisiana for the cultural, economic, and tourist benefit of the State." The council would consist of a chairman and an advisory committee of no greater than fifty members, all appointed by the governor. It would be authorized to cooperate with and advise other state agencies as well as to receive donations and grants from individuals, corporations, and governments. After experimenting with a new name, the Council for the Development of French-Speaking Louisiana, the organization settled in December 1968 on a third name, the Council for the Development of French in Louisiana.[9]

Governor McKeithen chose a genteel Acadian, James "Jimmy" Domengeaux, to chair CODOFIL. A newcomer to the preservation movement, Domengeaux was born in 1907 to a wealthy Lafayette family, graduated from Tulane with a law degree, and soon entered political life. He served in the state legislature and in Congress until 1949, when he left office to resume his Lafayette law practice. In 1968 the sixty-one-year-old attorney could have retired comfortably; instead, he took on the biggest challenge of his career—saving French in Louisiana. "The preservation movement has come to life," he explained shortly after CODOFIL's founding, "because of the belief in the necessity of doing what must be done to save the French language." The typical south Louisiana family, he noted, was losing the Cajun way of life—its traditional customs and, most alarmingly, its ability to speak French—and therefore CODOFIL had to "create interest in the children, also the parents; teach them that it is 'chic' to know French. And above all, we must interest our educators; they must lead the movement."[10]

That year, 1968, was remarkable nationally and internationally. The Tet Offensive marked a turning point in the Vietnam War. LBJ announced he would not seek reelection to the presidency. Martin Luther King Jr. and Robert Kennedy were assassinated. Campus rallies erupted into violence amid cries of "Revolution!" Police bullied protesters and innocent bystanders at the Democratic National Convention in Chicago. Meanwhile, the Soviet Union and its allies invaded Czechoslovakia to quell democratic reforms, while two nations that would shortly assist south Louisiana's ethnic revival, France and Canada, respectively witnessed mass civil unrest and the rise of an organized Quebec separatist movement. Eventually, France would look to south Louisiana as an American foothold in which to spread its political, economic, and cultural influence, while Quebec would view Acadiana as a satellite community in need of educational assistance—even while using it as a worst-case example of what could happen to the French language in Quebec under Anglo-Canadian rule.[11]

Acadiana also witnessed incredible events of its own during 1968. Besides the creation of CODOFIL, it saw the passage of several laws that bolstered the status of French in Louisiana. The state legislature mandated that public elementary schools offer at least five years of French instruction and that public high schools offer the subject for at least three years along with at least one course on the history and culture of French America. The legislature required state colleges and universities to offer teacher certification in elementary school French and approved the publication of legal notices and other public documents in French. It also demanded that state-funded educational television be bilingual, showing French programming in equal proportion to its French-speaking viewers. Finally, the legislature authorized the establishment of a nonprofit French-language television corporation in conjunction with USL, to be called Télévision-Louisiane.[12]

Other events contributed to making 1968 an astounding year for the French-preservation movement. USL committed itself to becoming a "world linguistic center" by establishing an Institute of French Studies and by expanding its role in training French educators. Civic leaders opened cultural exchanges with other French-speaking regions, symbolically pairing Lafayette with the city of Longueuil, Quebec, in what became known as a *jumelage* (twinning). Business leaders conducted a trade mission to Quebec to develop commercial ties. Educators started a summer student exchange program, sending Cajun children to Quebec and hosting French-Canadian children in south Louisiana. An International Acadian Festival took place in Lafayette, attracting more than one hundred governmental and media visitors from Canada and France for two days of receptions, lectures, exhibits, films, tours, and other events that highlighted the region's French heritage.

Cajuns quickly grasped the significance of this amazing period.

"Historians will circle calendar year 1968," announced *Acadiana Profile*, a new bilingual magazine, "as the time when the . . . French Renaissance took form and shape and direction in Louisiana."[13]

Of all these events, however, CODOFIL's founding most visibly demonstrated Cajun pride and empowerment. Domengeaux wasted no time in mobilizing the organization. Appointed chairperson in early September 1968, he convened CODOFIL's first meeting the next month and vowed to establish bilingual education in elementary and secondary schools by the 1972–73 school year. The task would be daunting, for Domengeaux intended to create the program from scratch, even revamping preexisting high school conversational French courses, which he deplored as a "criminal waste of time and money" because of their mediocre results. Domengeaux argued that French should be part of the regular curriculum for all grades and that children should be able to study the subject for at least half an hour daily. The cost of implementing this plan throughout Acadiana and the state in general would be enormous. Domengeaux estimated he would require more than one million dollars and nearly two hundred teachers merely to begin the program.[14]

Energetic and politically connected, Domengeaux solved the problem of where to find both teachers and funding. The funding would come primarily from the federal government through Title VII of the Elementary and Secondary Education Act, known as the Bilingual Education Act (BEA), which President Johnson had signed into law in 1968 as part of the Great Society. Although designed solely to assist non-English-speaking schoolchildren, such as Hispanics in the American Southwest, to become proficient in English by using bilingual teachers, textbooks, and other educational tools, the BEA nonetheless gave the state of Louisiana more than six hundred thousand dollars in 1970–71 for pilot programs aimed at teaching standard French to fluently English-speaking children. Eventually, the federal government spent millions on French education in Louisiana, not only through the BEA but also through Title VII of the Emergency School Aid Act, also known as the Bilingual/Bicultural Act, signed into law in 1972 by President Nixon.[15]

Convinced that local teachers were insufficiently trained as French instructors, Domengeaux imported low-salaried teachers from Canada, Belgium, and France. The first of these instructors, thirty from France, arrived in autumn 1970 and taught in the state's elementary schools for two years in lieu of French military service. Domengeaux called their arrival "probably the most important single event that has occurred in the French movement since CODOFIL was created."[16]

CODOFIL expanded quickly under Domengeaux's dynamic leadership. It hosted hundreds of French-speaking visitors, including educators, exchange students, businessmen, diplomats, journalists, filmmakers, and celebrities. It put up roadside billboards announcing "Ici on parle français" (We Speak French Here), and it convinced local businesses to display French placards bearing this and other messages: "French in the Schools, French in the Home," "Be Proud to Speak French," "French, Now or Never." It attracted the attention of the American media, from the *New York Times* to *Life* magazine to the *CBS Evening News*. Within a few years CODOFIL had recruited nearly three hundred instructors and administered language programs in more than half the state's parishes.[17]

CODOFIL under Domengeaux's leadership seemed indefatigable. It successfully backed a provision in the state's new constitution that guaranteed linguistic and cultural pluralism in Louisiana. It published a bilingual journal, *La révue de Louisiane,* and established a French theater company, Le Petit Théâtre Français. It handed out scholarships to local children for studying French abroad. It petitioned the North Vietnamese government, in French, asking Ho Chi Minh to treat American POWs humanely. It inspired spin-off organizations, including CODOJEUNE (a branch for teenagers), CODOSIL (Council for the Development of Spanish in Louisiana), CO DE SPAN (another Spanish group based in Louisiana), CODOFIM (Council for the Development of French in Manitoba), and CODOFINE (Council for the Development of French in New England).[18]

In addition to reviving the French language in Louisiana, CODOFIL advocated unabashed ethnic pride. "A social phenomenon is sweeping the lush bayou country," observed the *Philadelphia Enquirer.* "A million and a half 'Cajuns' are learning not to be ashamed of their heritage." Closer to home, CODOFIL member Roy Theriot declared, "Apologize to no one for your heritage."[19]

Along with pride came empowerment, as Domengeaux himself demonstrated by attacking perceived affronts to his heritage. Influenced by the national backlash against ethnic jokes, for example, he launched a public cam-

paign against Cajun humor that he deemed offensive. Joke telling was a popular oral tradition among Cajuns, providing entertainment at social gatherings
and helping to define the ethnic group by reflecting its worldview. What
Domengeaux sought to discredit, however, was "Cajun dialect humor," a particular joke-telling genre performed by a handful of professional humorists
that relied on the frequent misuse of standard English for comedic effect.

Walter Coquille first popularized Cajun dialect humor as early as the
1920s with his portrayal of Telesfore Boudreaux, "de mare of Bayou Pom
Pom fo' de tent' conservative time." Justin Wilson and Bud Fletcher later
refined the genre, and Domengeaux targeted them more than anyone for
criticism. Also known for his culinary skills, Wilson told his otherwise
innocuous jokes with an exaggerated south Louisiana accent and coined the
catchphrase "I GAR-RON-TEE," a cliché associated ever since with Cajuns.
(Wilson's birthplace and ethnicity have been subjects of debate for decades.
Before his death in 2001, Wilson informed the author that he was born in
Roseland, Louisiana, northeast of Baton Rouge, not in Texas or Mississippi,
as often rumored. "I am part Cajun and proud of it," he asserted, noting that
his mother was of French heritage and that she and a neighbor taught him
French as a child.) Fletcher's humor, on the other hand, was risqué if not
downright vulgar, as demonstrated by his series of "Outhouse" recordings. In
one instance, the comedian told of meeting a "big Cajun boy" at the entrance
to a gas station restroom equipped with a condom dispenser. "Mah frien', you
fixin' to go in dat res'room dair?" the Cajun boy asked. "Well, yeah, I tought
about dat," answered Fletcher, "how come?" "Cot blass!" swore the boy.
"When you got in dair, man, don' bought no gum outta dat machine, no!"

While many laughed at Wilson and Fletcher's jokes, Domengeaux deeply
resented their misrepresentation of Cajuns. "The Cajuns have their own
wonderful humor," Domengeaux told the *Times-Picayune.* "Why should they
then be expected to applaud imposters who are trying to wring out a living
by using not Cajun humor but jokes that make Cajuns look backwards, dull-
witted and stupid?" Domengeaux found an ally in fellow activist Paul Tate,
who described Cajun dialect humorists as "redneck bigots and racists."
Because of this criticism, many south Louisianians turned away from Wilson
and Fletcher and instead embraced more folksy comedians like Revon Reed,
known in character as Nonc Helaire (Uncle Helaire), and Marion Marcotte,

who performed their good-natured jokes in Cajun French. A joke that typified this more acceptable genre concerned a young Cajun who went off to college and returned home after a semester haughtily pretending to have forgotten French. "What's that?" he asked his parents. "Une chaise," they answered. "And what's that?" "Une table." "And that?" "Une porte." His parents soon tired of this game, but the young man continued to demonstrate his newfound inability to speak French. Later, just as he was pointing to a rake on the lawn to ask, "What's that?" he accidentally stepped on its teeth, causing the handle to pop up and smack him painfully on the forehead. "Mon maudit, sacré tonnerre de rateau!" he instinctively cursed. "Ah," said his father with a smile, "Je vois que ça commence à te revenir" (I see it's coming back to you).[20]

Domengeaux launched a more sustained crusade against the word *coonass*, which he considered the supreme ethnic slur against the Cajun people, a term used only "to humiliate, embarrass and degrade." At the heart of Domengeaux's drive to stamp out *coonass* was its alleged etymology: the word, he asserted, derived from the standard French *conasse*, meaning a "stupid person" or a "prostitute without medical papers" (essentially, "dirty whore"). According to Domengeaux's research, disdainful Frenchmen applied the word to Cajun GIs serving in France during World War II. He never explained why native Frenchmen would have slandered their Cajun liberators: perhaps it was because French males regarded the Cajun dialect as inferior, because they resented the cushy jobs some Cajun GIs found as translators, or because Cajun GIs used their linguistic skills to woo Frenchwomen. Regardless, other U.S. soldiers supposedly could not understand *conasse* but decided it sounded like *coonass*, a term they continued to apply to Cajuns after wartime.

Other amateur linguists have proposed their own etymologies. One traced the term to the devastating flood of 1927, when rescuers noted a resemblance between half-drowned Cajuns drooped over limbs and raccoons sleeping in treetops. Another asserted that "uncouth Texans" introduced the word to south Louisiana during the Great Depression, reflecting the traditional animosity between Cajuns and nearby Anglo-Americans. Yet another proposed that it came from a Spanish word, *cuñaso*, meaning "native born of European stock." Many believed that it came from Acadian soldiers wearing coonskin caps during the War of 1812 or the American Revolution. "A 'Disgusting' Prostitute or a Davy Crockett Hat?" asked the *Times-Picayune* in 1972, reflecting the uncertainty over the epithet's origin. Professional linguist Barry Jean Ancelet has dismissed all these theories—including the *conasse* theory, which he has called "shaky linguistics at best"—and instead has more convincingly suggested that *coonass* was coined in or near Acadiana and derived from the Cajuns' occasional habit of eating raccoons or, more likely, from the "doubly racist notion that Cajuns were even lower on the social scale than 'coons,'" a derogatory term for blacks.

Although Domengeaux's etymology sounded convincing, it was in fact wrong: *coonass* existed prior to the arrival of Cajun GIs in France during World War II. The earliest known use of the word can be traced to April 1943, when U.S. military photographers in the South Pacific captured the image of a C-47 transport plane nicknamed the Cajun Coonass, more than a year before the first Cajun GIs landed in France on D-Day. Furthermore, Lafayette educator Richard Nunez distinctly remembered being called a *coonass* in his youth during a 1937 visit to east Texas, ironically by another Cajun, who used the term jokingly.

Although the word's origin remains a mystery, Domengeaux used his flawed etymology to campaign against *coonass*. He began the effort as early as 1971, when he criticized a Lafourche Parish songwriter for composing "Coonie Moon." ("In this land of happy Cajuns / Keep on shining coonie moon.") Domengeaux then challenged Governor Edwin Edwards to stop using the word in reference to himself and other Cajuns. Domengeaux complained to the Federal Communications Commission in Washington, D.C., when the word appeared in a TV documentary about oil-field workers, and he criticized USL scholars for using the term in an early study of Cajuns.[21]

While Domengeaux provoked heated debates over Cajun dialect humor and the word *coonass*, CODOFIL became mired in negative publicity that eroded its support among the general public. Only two months after CODOFIL's founding, a dispute erupted when George Dupuis, a Lafayette school official and cultural activist, argued that Domengeaux did not deserve to chair the organization because he was a newcomer to the French-preservation movement. The office should have gone to a more seasoned preservationist, Dupuis asserted, such as Dean Thomas

Arceneaux, Judge Allen Babineaux, or Mrs. C. E. Hamilton, whose "contributions far surpass Mr. Domengeaux's." Dupuis also attacked Domengeaux's choice for CODOFIL's executive director, Raymond Rodgers. Dupuis characterized Rodgers as "uncooperative" and "lacking in stability," but the actual reason for Dupuis's objection was probably because Rodgers was "not a native of our area, or even of our state or nation." In response, Domengeaux implied that Dupuis was "trying to sabotage the movement," but the Lafayette Chamber of Commerce backed Dupuis's opposition to Rodgers, informing Governor McKeithen that Rodgers was "not qualified by training to lead our Acadian population in their dedicated efforts to preserve their French-Acadian culture and the French language."[22]

The Rodgers debate was moot: the young professor had already returned to Canada after USL declined to renew his teaching contract. The university gave no explanation for this decision, but rumors had circulated on campus for months that Rodgers's home had hosted "integrated orgies" (actually meetings of the Human Relations Council, a local civil rights group), that he had participated in a wild drinking party at the campus radio station (he merely delivered some audiotapes while the party was in progress), and that the administration was displeased with his public criticism of local conservatives. "By pushing 'too hard' for the Acadian revival," Rodgers observed at the time, "and to a lesser extent because of my racial liberalism, I have seemingly earned the extreme enmity of certain persons." He left Lafayette in 1968 just as CODOFIL came into being, "absolutely astounded," he confessed, "at the ingratitude and dishonesty of the community."

Oddly, some cultural activists have insisted that Rodgers exerted little or no influence on the French-preservation movement. A significant body of historical evidence, however, indicates that he had a major impact. For instance, not only did Domengeaux nominate Rodgers as CODOFIL's first executive director, but Governor McKeithen concurred, petitioning the University of Winnipeg to release Rodgers from a new teaching contract so that he could assume the directorship. "Dr. Rodgers has been very active during the past few years in the public affairs of this state," wrote the governor, noting that "persons at the heart of the movement" to save Louisiana French had "expressed a strong sense of loss" at Rodgers's departure.

McKeithen forwarded copies of his petition to the premier of Manitoba and to the prime minister of Canada, further attesting to Rodgers's prominence.

But the best evidence for Rodgers's importance to the French-revival movement came from Domengeaux himself, who stated during CODOFIL's first meeting, "One who has been of tremendous help and shown devotion to the cause, and in my judgment, has contributed greatly in wisdom, understanding and [has been] very active in working for this movement, is Dr. Raymond Rodgers and I want to publicly express my appreciation to him." Moreover, Domengeaux advised the media, "I must credit [Rodgers] with many of the original actions taken in the last two years [1966–68] in furtherance of the French movement. . . . As an illustration . . . it was he who suggested the organization of the French Heritage Committee. . . . He likewise suggested and put into effect the original idea of exchange of students between Canada and Louisiana. It was he who suggested the adoption of bilingual street signs in the city of Lafayette." And on learning that USL had declined to renew the professor's contract, Domengeaux futilely informed its administration, "I want to do everything to help keep Rodgers at work in this state and particularly in coordinating the movement to revitalize and extensively pursue the French language. . . . We just cannot afford to lose a man of this caliber."[23]

Following the spat between Domengeaux and Dupuis over leadership posts, other problems attracted further negative publicity for CODOFIL, the least of which was a legislative auditor's charge that the organization had misappropriated state funding. More hurtful was growing public resentment, especially among elementary and high school educators, concerning the authority invested in Domengeaux, who had no teaching experience and yet who wielded his academic power imperiously. "I just shoved the damn program down their throats," he boasted to a reporter. Furthermore, Domengeaux's reliance on imported teachers, most of whom had no classroom experience, aggravated ill will among local educators, who feared displacement by lower-paid foreign recruits. They were also insulted by Domengeaux's claim that native teachers were inadequate and that Cajun French was inferior to standard French. The general public concurred with local educators. "I can't think of anything that is needed less," complained one south Louisianian, "than imports from France or other sources to teach the

French language to Acadians." "Mr. Domengeaux," voiced another, "has been reluctant to help promote the Acadian culture. . . . If we do not revive fully our pride in being Cajuns, we will never regain our pride in our language." Even a fellow genteel Acadian, Rousseau Van Voorhies, condemned Domengeaux's imported teachers as "educational mercenaries" and coined the term *codofilism* to describe the campaign to impose standard French on Acadiana. Meanwhile, several of the imported teachers complained about lack of benefits and went on strike against CODOFIL. Domengeaux responded by firing strike leaders but denied that his actions were retaliatory.[24]

By the early 1970s many ordinary Cajuns questioned the organization's commitment to preserving their culture. "CODOFIL is a phony," declared an Abbeville educator, while an editorialist called it "a farce . . . a ridiculous sham." Activists in Church Point responded to CODOFIL's elitism by forming their own group, Présence Francophone Amérique (PREFAM), a self-described grassroots organization aimed at usurping the French revival movement. More democratic and radical than its Lafayette rival, PREFAM claimed all persons of French heritage as members and audaciously declared that CODOFIL was therefore a PREFAM subsidiary.[25]

Meanwhile, children enrolled in CODOFIL programs received only a half-hour of French instruction daily, which left virtually no impression on the English-speaking youths. When a *New York Times* reporter visited a classroom in St. James Parish, he witnessed Cajun children struggling with basic conversational French. "Qu'est-ce que c'est?" asked their instructor. "Souris," the students replied uncertainly, with conspicuous American accents. Later a teacher patiently coached a young girl on the correct pronunciation of *au revoir*, but the student "finally left without really getting it right." Observed a south Louisiana newspaper, "French Language Instruction Falters in South Louisiana."[26]

Indeed, French continued to disappear in south Louisiana at an alarming rate despite CODOFIL's efforts. "The carefully cultivated impression of a French-speaking populace dissolves when a visitor is on his own," noted a Canadian reporter who in 1973 peeked behind the facade of orchestrated ceremonies, receptions, and press conferences. "In fact," he concluded, "the Cajun French language is dying in southwestern Louisiana." The reporter was correct, for during CODOFIL's first seven years of operation, the number of young Cajuns who spoke French as their first language dropped by about 35 percent; in another decade it would plummet by nearly 75 percent. The percentage of young Cajuns who spoke French as a second language is unknown, but impressionistic data revealed an equally dismal situation. "The children eat, play, and have all their other classes in English," complained a language instructor from Quebec, making it nearly impossible to teach the students French. Another teacher lamented that her students were "not really concerned about learning French."[27]

Despite these failings, CODOFIL could point to at least a few accomplishments during its first years of operation. It convinced the state to expand French education in public schools. It forged stronger cultural and economic relations with Quebec, Belgium, France, and other francophone regions. It bolstered Acadiana's economy by promoting the region as a tourist destination. And it attracted positive media attention, both in the United States and abroad. Finally, CODOFIL served as an effective Cajun watchdog group, responding harshly to perceived ethnic slurs and stereotypes.

The organization also boosted Cajun ethnic pride and empowerment, but these elements already existed in south Louisiana prior to CODOFIL's genesis. Indeed, a strong but ill-defined grassroots pride and empowerment movement ran parallel to (and sometimes contrary to) CODOFIL's elitist, organized agenda. While CODOFIL sought to impose ethnic pride from the top down, the grassroots movement drew its strength from the latent ethnic pride that always existed among some ordinary Cajuns. Only occasionally did this pride reveal itself, however, as during a 1941 defense rally, when a south Louisiana civic leader proclaimed, "When we get going and get to fighting side by side with those Yankees and rednecks against a common foe, by the living gods, the flag of the Cajun will fly as high as any in the land, and the bravery, daring, and downright hell-raising of the Bayou Blitz will be surpassed by none."[28]

Yet a genuine Cajun grassroots pride and empowerment movement did not exist until the 1960s. And if that movement had a symbolic beginning, it occurred more than a thousand miles from Acadiana, in Newport, Rhode Island, where three Cajun musicians appeared at the 1964 Newport Folk Festival as guests of prominent folk activists Ralph Rinzler and Mike Seeger. The south Louisianians performed with dozens of other obscure folk artists as well as with such renowned musicians as Joan Baez, Johnny Cash, Bob Dylan, and Peter, Paul, and Mary. One of those Cajun musicians, an insurance sales-man from Basile named Dewey Balfa, was astonished by the crowds of atten-tive listeners. As he later confessed, "I had no idea what a festival was. . . . I had played in house dances, family gatherings, maybe a dance hall where you might have seen as many as two hundred people at once. . . . And in Newport, there were seventeen thousand." The audience embraced the Cajun musicians, cap-tivated by their unusual strains and evident joy in performing. "The Cajun band . . . is truly wonderful to watch and hear," reported the *Newport Daily News,* which called the group's lively performance during the opening cere-mony "one of the best numbers of the program." Even the *New York Times* commended the group for its "exotic, flavorful sounds." Folk aficionados con-curred, offering the group a resounding ovation. In fact, they "wouldn't let us get off stage," recalled Balfa, who commemorated the experience in a song titled "Valse de Newport" (Newport Waltz).

Newport transformed Balfa into a cultural militant, igniting his dormant ethnic pride and inspiring him to mobilize other ordinary Cajuns. "When the echo came back," he observed, "I think it brought a message . . . that there were great efforts being made by people who were interested in preserving the culture. . . . *Mais il y a un tas du monde qui connaît pas qu'ils ont un bon pain de maïs sur la table avant que quelqu'un d'autre leur dit* [But a lot of peo-ple don't realize that they have a good cornbread on the table until somebody tells them]."

Charged with a sense of mission, Balfa worked tirelessly to preserve and promote Cajun culture. He joined the new Louisiana Folk Foundation, which operated out of the sleepy Cajun town of Mamou with funding secured from the Newport Folk Festival Foundation. He convinced Ville Platte recordman Floyd Soileau to release an album of traditional Cajun songs, which inspired other musicians to revive and record archaic folk songs. He encouraged fellow performers to appear with the Balfa Brothers band at festivals across the United States as well as in Canada and France. Many of these musicians would contribute immeasurably to the grassroots movement in coming decades. Balfa also helped to define the grassroots movement by making Cajun music and musicians its focal points. While genteel Acadians stressed the primacy of standard French and appointed lawyers, politicians, and other wealthy professionals as cultural spokespersons, grassroots activists saw Cajun music as a unifying element—because of both the sound's mass appeal and its reliance on the local French dialect—and they cast working-class musicians in the role of cultural ambassadors.[29]

During the late 1960s and throughout the 1970s, the explosion of ethnic pride and empowerment among ordinary Cajuns manifested itself in other ways besides the revitalization of traditional music. Genealogy became a popular hobby, fueled by the publication of such books as Bona Arsenault's *Histoire et généalogie des acadiens* (1965), its abridged English version *History of the Acadians* (1966), Dudley LeBlanc's *The Acadian Miracle* (1966), and Father Donald Hébert's *Southwest Louisiana Records* (1974–98) and *South Louisiana Records* (1978–85), compilations of church and civic records that eventually spanned sixty volumes. At the same time Robert Olivier published his first novels in more than three decades, *Tidoon: A Story of the Cajun Teche* (1972) and *Tinonc: Son of the Cajun Teche* (1974). Both works examined the Cajuns amid a rapidly changing world. As Olivier's character Tidoon complained, "The great American melting pot . . . is making white-gravy rednecks and green-coffee Yankees of all the Cajuns." According to *Tidoon*'s book jacket, the author "deplores the Americanization of the Cajun, the mechanization of his environment and the homogenization of his speech and manners."[30]

Other Cajuns penned cultural manifestos, such as Pierre V. Daigle's *Tears, Love, and Laughter* (1972), which sought to awaken Cajun pride with a blend of history, genealogy, and biography. "Never, never be ashamed of your name, language, or your heritage," asserted Daigle. "Let's make Cajun a name of which to be proud. Then we can brag about being Cajun." Revon Reed soon contributed his own manifesto, *Lâche pas la patate* (1976), literally "Don't Drop the Potato," a Cajun expression translated more accurately as "Don't Give Up." A cultural primer aimed at French speakers abroad, Reed's book nonetheless was written in Cajun French. In doing so, Reed not only published the first book composed in the dialect but demanded that Cajuns be accepted into the international French community on their own terms.[31]

Meanwhile, visual artist George Rodrigue developed his trademark paintings of Cajuns posing under murky, moss-draped live oaks, while Floyd Sonnier perfected his pen-and-ink drawings of rural Cajun life, evoking, as one observer admired, "The same cry of history that I hear in Iry LeJeune's music." Cartoonists Earl Comeaux and Ken Meaux created "Bec Doux et ses amis" (Bec Doux and His Friends), a bilingual comic strip that appeared in several south Louisiana newspapers. "Bonjour, mes amis, ca ici c'est Bec Doux [Hello, my friends, this here's Bec Doux]," announced the strip's title character, a mustachioed Cajun with a prominent Gallic nose and cleft chin. "I'm bilingual, you know, . . . and real proud of it." On local TV actor John Plauché portrayed an avuncular Cajun fisherman named Polycarp who brought to life a world of Cajun-themed characters "as familiar to the children of Acadiana as Mickey Mouse and Donald Duck." Children also read about Clovis Crawfish in a series of illustrated books by Mary Alice Fontenot, and during the holiday season they enjoyed *Cajun Night before Christmas* (1967), a local-color version of the classic yuletide poem that substituted flying alligators named Gaston, Pierre, Alcée, Ninette, and Renée for St. Nick's reindeer. During the same period, USL officially renamed its football team the Ragin' Cajuns, a name it had informally adopted in 1963, when the school's student newspaper noted, "USL football fans are coining another nickname. . . . Instead of the official Battling Bulldogs, Southwestern boosters have started referring to Coach Russ Faulkinberry's squad as the Raging Cajuns" because nearly all the players were south Louisianians. The school's other athletic teams soon were donning the name on their traditional red and white uniforms. At sporting events, students cheered in rudimentary French, "Yea rouge, yea blanc, yea Cajuns, allons!" while waving signs that exhorted "Geaux Cajuns" ("Go Cajuns," a play on the pronunciation of the letters *eaux*, found in many local surnames).[32]

The grassroots movement also affected the state's political arena. When Dudley LeBlanc died in 1971, congressman Edwin W. Edwards became the leading grassroots politician among Cajuns. Like LeBlanc, Edwards stressed his impoverished rural childhood, wooed older Cajun voters in French, and ruffled the sensibilities of genteel Acadians with his *bas-clas* (low-class) manners. As governor, Edwards contributed significantly to the state's welfare, overseeing the ratification of a new state constitution that streamlined government bureaucracy, protected civil rights, and ended Jim Crow in Louisiana. He also imposed a severance tax on crude oil that dramatically increased state revenues. Finally, Edwards supported the French-preservation movement, backing a constitutional clause that guaranteed

Cajun GI Ralph "Frenchie" LeBlanc of Breaux Bridge, standing in the foreground next to a wounded soldier, surveys the aftermath of the Japanese attack on Pearl Harbor. (U.S. Navy photo, National Archives and Records Administration)

Rural Cajuns check out books from the Louisiana Library Commission's "Traveling Library." (U.S. Office of War Information photo, National Archives and Records Administration)

Dudley LeBlanc poses with President John F. Kennedy at the White House, flanked by Evangeline lookalikes from across Acadiana, August 1963. (John Fitzgerald Kennedy Library)

A horse and buggy travel down a rural south Louisiana highway near Maurice in 1947, far in the wake of a modern automobile. (Standard Oil [New Jersey] Collection, Special Collections: Photographic Archives, University of Louisville)

Swamp pop duo Dale and Grace, backed by Randy and the Rockets, perform before a crowd of Cajun teenagers in New Iberia, ca. 1963. (Huey Darby)

Zachary Richard raises a defiant clinched fist at the 1975 Tribute to Cajun Music while his retinue displays flags reading SOLIDARITÉ—FIERTÉ (Solidarity—Pride); as a result, Richard was banned from the festival for several years. (Elemore Morgan, Jr.)

Cajun activists Judge Allen Babineaux, at far right, and James "Jimmy" Domengeaux, fourth from right, display the Acadian Flag in downtown Lafayette, ca. 1968. (Raymond Spencer Rodgers)

The "Cajun Coonass" C-47 transport plane in the South Pacific, April 1943, shown with its crew, including Cajun pilot Lt. Albert Burleigh of Sunset, at far left. The photo is significant not only because it documents the earliest known use of the word "coonass" but also because Burleigh clearly used the word as a badge of ethnic pride. (National Archives and Records Administration)

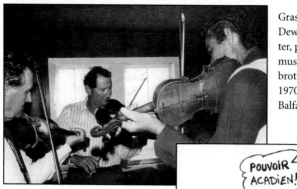

Grassroots activist Dewey Balfa, at center, performs Cajun music with his brothers, ca. early 1970s. (Christine Balfa)

Cajun cartoon character Bec Doux raises a crawfish in his clenched fist and shouts, "Cajun Power." (Earl Comeaux)

POUVOIR ACADIEN!

— CAJUN POWER —

A capacity crowd attends the first Tribute to Cajun Music, Lafayette, 1974. (Elemore Morgan, Jr.)

linguistic pluralism and encouraging the use of French as a means of every-day communication. As he pleaded somewhat mawkishly after his 1972 victory, "Let us all speak French at home and with our family, as I do at home, particularly with my dear mother." Despite his infamous weakness-es for gambling, womanizing, and questionable business dealings ("There is a big difference," he often jested, "between what's illegal and what causes you people to raise your eyebrows"), Edwards retained his Cajun voting bloc. As a result, he won the governor's office four times in two decades, a feat that epitomized Cajun Power. (Edwards's downfall finally came in early 2001, when a federal court found him guilty of extorting funds from Louisiana casino license applicants.)[33]

But Cajun music remained the medium through which the grassroots pride and empowerment movement expressed itself most vibrantly. Filmmakers fea-tured the sound in documentaries such as Les Blank's *Spend It All* and Paul Goldsmith's PBS production *The Good Times Are Killing Me.* Cajun-country artist Jimmy C Newman scored an international hit with "Lâche pas la patate," the first Cajun release to earn a gold record. Apollo 12 astronauts enjoyed Doug Kershaw's "Louisiana Man" while en route to the moon. Not to be out-done, Lesa Cormier and the Sundown Playboys of Lake Charles released "Saturday Night Special," a traditional Cajun French recording, on the Beatles' Apple label of London.[34]

In 1974 Cajun activists staged the first Tribute to Cajun Music, an event that became a milestone in Cajun history. More than any other factor, Dewey Balfa's activism brought about the Tribute. Despite warnings that Jimmy Domengeaux disliked Cajun music, Balfa attended a CODOFIL meeting in late 1973 and proposed that the organization sponsor a concert. He assured Domengeaux that the event would attract thousands of ordinary Cajuns to his cause. "You've got the power," Balfa asserted. "If you put on a festival here, you'll see what the music can do for our people." Domengeaux dismissed the idea, but as folklorist Barry Jean Ancelet observed, "the seed had been sown."

A few months later Ancelet became a key player in the grassroots move-ment. Hailing from a working-class family, he had shown little interest in his native culture until he visited France in 1973. At a café in Nice, the homesick USL undergraduate heard a folk musician perform a Cajun instrumental titled "The Crowley Two-Step." The melody transported Ancelet back to south

Louisiana, and after the show he thanked the musician, who identified several Cajun musicians as major influences, including Dewey Balfa. "I didn't know
any of them," confessed Ancelet, "and it occurred to me that something was
wrong. . . . I knew about the châteaux along the Loire in France but virtually
nothing about the cultures along the Bayou Teche in my native state."

Balfa became Ancelet's mentor, encouraging him to compile a personal
folk archives and to join the campaign for a Cajun music concert. In early
1974 the two activists sensed an opportunity to reintroduce the concert proposal: Domengeaux had invited a group of French-speaking journalists to
Acadiana and required an event that would showcase the vitality of Cajun
culture. Frustrated by CODOFIL's declining popularity, Domengeaux agreed
to sponsor the concert for his international guests and the general public. As
he once stated, "I don't like it. But if they want music, we'll give them music."

Domengeaux appointed a blue-ribbon panel to coordinate the event, but
the group soon became mired in abstract debate about what constituted genuine Cajun music. As a result, Balfa, Ancelet, and a few volunteers hurriedly
organized the event on their own for CODOFIL. Sensing tremendous public
interest, they moved the venue from USL's student union to Lafayette's
largest indoor arena, Blackham Coliseum, which seated eight thousand.
Meanwhile, folklorist Ralph Rinzler agreed to host the event with USL professor of French Hosea Phillips. Rinzler's involvement attracted the attention
of the Smithsonian Institution, which became a cosponsor with CODOFIL.

Balfa's original idea of a modest concert was unfolding into a major celebration. But when violent thunderstorms drenched south Louisiana on
March 26, 1974, the day of the Tribute, organizers wondered if anyone would
show up, including the musicians, none of whom were being paid. The musicians arrived, however, and so did concertgoers, young and old—so many
that several hundred were left outside, stranded under umbrellas.
Disregarding fire codes, someone threw open the arena to the rain-soaked
crowd, filling the coliseum beyond seating capacity. Perhaps as many as
twelve thousand people turned out for the event. "It was obvious to everyone
that this was a magic moment," recalled Ancelet. "We all felt it, organizers,
musicians, audience, and journalists alike."

Presented entirely in French, the concert was designed to demonstrate
Cajun music's evolution from the colonial era to the present. Inez Catalon

and Marcus Landry opened the program, performing a cappella folk ballads traceable to medieval France. Dennis McGee and Sady Courville appeared next with fiddle instrumentals that reflected early Cajun music. Accordionist Marc Savoy and Don Montoucet, backed by fiddlers Lionel Leleux and Varise Connor, reconstructed the sounds of early-twentieth-century *bals de maison* (house dances). The Balfa Brothers played family-style Cajun string band music. Nathan Abshire and his Pine Grove Boys performed selections evoking the accordion's postwar resurgence, while Blackie Forestier and his Cajun Aces played modern Cajun music. Jimmy C Newman even rendered his peculiar blend of traditional Cajun and modern country music, while Bois-sec Ardoin, Canray Fontenot, and Clifton Chenier demonstrated the relationship of black Creole sounds to Cajun music.

The coliseum echoed with animated music and heartfelt ovations. "If we had told our grandparents this was going to happen," declared a joyful musician, "they would have laughed at us. I can't believe it." "This is great," Balfa informed a reporter. "I've been working towards this for twelve years now." Amid national reports about Watergate, economic stagflation, and long gas lines, Lafayette's newspaper declared, "Coliseum Is Full of Cajun Spirit."

The impact of the Tribute was manifold. By presenting Cajun music in a formal concert setting under the aegis of CODOFIL and the Smithsonian, the event legitimized the music of ordinary Cajuns as a means of cultural expression. It also made heroes of previously obscure folk musicians, who now became role models for young Cajuns, some of whom would act as cultural ambassadors in coming decades. The Tribute also led to the formation of the Center for Acadian and Creole Folklore on the USL campus, an idea proposed by folklorist Rinzler. The center's archives would eventually contain hundreds of recorded interviews and musical performances in French and English, the largest collection of its kind in the world.

Most significantly, the Tribute to Cajun Music represented the victory of the grassroots Cajun movement over the genteel Acadian establishment. "It was a lesson for the cultural authorities," observed Balfa. "At the time, I wanted for those people who held the reins of the culture to be exposed to the Cajun music experience so that they could see what the people felt about their own music." Stunned by the public's exuberant reaction to the program, Domengeaux conceded his error in dismissing Cajun music as a unifying force. "I don't get on my knees for anybody," he told Balfa and Ancelet backstage, "but I will admit that I was wrong about this."[35]

By the mid-1970s the Cajun people had crossed a major threshold in their ethnohistory. They reevaluated their image and worth as a people, professed ethnic pride openly, and became personally involved in the preservation of their heritage. At the same time, a new generation of young Cajun activists rose to positions of authority, including Ancelet, historian Carl A. Brasseaux, linguist Richard Guidry, attorney David Marcantel, and musicians Michael Doucet and Zachary Richard. These and other important baby boomer activists shared a few common characteristics: they generally hailed from working-class backgrounds; grew up in the 1950s and 1960s, suspended between traditional and mainstream cultures; and, significantly, underwent what Ancelet has called an "exile experience." By leaving their homeland and exposing themselves to new ideas and surroundings, these Cajuns were either inspired to become activists or, if already activists, were energized with a renewed sense of mission. As shown, Ancelet had his exile experience while studying in France, converting him into an activist-scholar. Richard, however, was already an activist when he underwent his experience in Quebec in the mid-1970s. It was at this time that he discovered "radical francophone political philosophy," which changed the direction of his activism. Eventually, all these baby boomers would play pivotal roles in the campaign to save Cajun culture as well as in legitimizing the culture as a field of academic inquiry.[36]

From this grassroots pride and empowerment movement rose a vague philosophy that might be called Cajunism—the feeling that the Cajun lifestyle was the best way of life. As with black power, brown power, and similar movements, Cajunism nurtured a sense of ethnic pride and self-confidence, wiping out the former notion that Anglo-American culture was superior and should be emulated at all costs. For most Cajuns, this new attitude did not entail questioning their American patriotism; it simply meant attending regional festivals, enjoying traditional Cajun music and cuisine, maintaining close family ties, making occasional fishing expeditions to the Atchafalaya, or declining to leave south Louisiana for better jobs abroad. To a handful of radical activists, however, Cajunism meant a rejection of American culture and values. It embodied an alternative to what they perceived as the increasingly impersonal, homogenized, and decadent way of life engulfing the mainstream. "American cultural rot is everywhere," proclaimed a Cajun extremist. "I strive for a modern Acadian society in Louisiana, one with head and shoulders planted firmly above the American melting toilet."[37]

Shifting attitudes about the culture sparked an accompanying change in iconography. The word *Acadian,* for instance, regarded by genteel elites as the only proper name for the ethnic group, experienced a decline in popularity. Meanwhile, the allegedly low-class word *Cajun* became the term of choice among most south Louisianians. Legislators officially sanctioned the word through concurrent resolution, and even Jimmy Domengeaux went on record as approving the label. To the dismay of some, the period also saw a rise in the use of *coonass* as a badge of working-class ethnic pride. "I'm a coonass and I'm proud of it," proclaimed one Cajun. The word appeared on decals, bumper stickers, license plates, baseball caps, T-shirts, and even whiskey glasses. A Louisiana Air National Guard squadron dubbed itself the Coonass Militia, while in 1976 a south Louisiana audience cheered when Republican presidential candidate Ronald Reagan suggested his own appointment as an "honorary Cajun coonass." During the same period, the quasi-religious cult of Evangeline, so vital to the genteel Acadian perception of south Louisiana culture, practically ceased to exist outside of St. Martinville, where her shrine remained a profitable tourist attraction. With Evangeline's decline, the patiently devoted milkmaid became the subject of ridicule among some Cajuns. "Gabriel, il etait pas beau," sang Alex Broussard, "Evangeline ne se valait pas mieux" (Gabriel wasn't handsome, Evangeline didn't look any better).[38]

Ultimately, the rise of grassroots Cajun pride and empowerment did not stop Americanization. Primarily French-speaking elders died off while mainly English-speaking youths made little effort to learn traditional ways, even while professing their newfound ethnic pride. This trend suggested a consensus among younger Cajuns that their ethnicity did not require the French dialect, a notion strongly rejected by most cultural activists. Ancelet, for example, complained about "the many wishful thinkers who would like to believe that Cajun culture will survive even without the French language." He urgently asserted, "It is simply not enough to drink beer, eat crawfish, cook gumbo and say 'Poo-yaie!' With this kind of 'commitment,' we will soon have only enough culture to fill the pages of a tourist brochure."[39]

National events conspired against saving the French dialect in south Louisiana. The coming of economic bad times, for example, distracted Americans from altruistic causes, as taxes, inflation, interest rates, and fuel costs rose in the mid-1970s. More importantly, the social movements that fueled the ethnic revival of the late 1960s and early 1970s lost their cohesiveness once the Vietnam War ended and the civil rights movement achieved many of its goals. In addition, after Vietnam, the Pentagon Papers, and Watergate, Americans learned to question authority and became skeptical about institutions, organizations, and mass movements. Instead, they focused on the individual and on self-fulfillment. The popular phrase "Do your own thing" summed up the nation's prevailing attitude during the mid-1970s, when the activism and idealism of the 1960s transformed into the self-absorption of the "Me Decade."[40]

Local factors also contributed to public apathy about French preservation. These included CODOFIL's failure to reach out to ordinary Cajuns, the organization's use of imported French teachers, and its emphasis on standard French. As a result, many Cajuns associated CODOFIL with snobbism and turned against both the organization and its crusade for bilingualism. In addition, the public was unimpressed with the scant amount of French learned by children enrolled in CODOFIL programs and expressed dislike for the teachers imported by CODOFIL, some of whom in turn made little effort to hide their disdain for Cajun French. At the same time, many parents viewed the traditional dialect as a dead language and saw no practical reason for handing it down to their children. Like newly arrived immigrants, they regarded the mastery of English as essential to success in modern America. Other parents simply were unable or unwilling to commit the time required to teach their children a second language.

These trends prompted many ordinary Cajuns to disregard Domengeaux and CODOFIL. Instead, they defined for themselves what it meant to be Cajun, and for most the definition did not include speaking French. Indeed, the public demonstrated its lack of interest in the subject by ignoring Act 714, a state law requiring schools to create a second language program when demanded by at least 25 percent of students' families. Only once did parents take advantage of the provision. The content of *Acadiana Profile* magazine also reflected the public's indifference toward French preservation. During the mid-1970s the journal dropped its subtitle "A Magazine for Bilingual Louisiana" and became a primarily English-language publication. Politicians responded to the apathy by refusing to implement the pro-French legislation they had approved so enthusiastically only a few years earlier. For example, they never enforced the state law requiring educational television to broadcast French-language programs in proportion to its French-speaking audience. Similarly, the state never funded Télévision-Louisiane, the nonprofit French-language television corporation it had authorized.[41]

By the mid-1970s the mass of ordinary Cajuns had redefined themselves in what amounted to a de facto cultural revolution. Dismissing the French-preservation movement as inconsequential to their ethnicity, most Cajuns perceived themselves as a primarily English-speaking ethnic group, albeit of French-speaking heritage. They had abandoned to history their traditional language, having already sacrificed their traditional values in pursuit of the American Dream. Paradoxically, at the height of their self-proclaimed ethnic revival, the Americanization of the Cajuns had become almost complete.

FIVE

EXPLOITATION AND REVITALIZATION

When I stir my gumbo with one of these spatulas, I feel like I'm stirring in three hundred years of Cajun history. . . . Could the blood, sweat, and tears of my ancestors be in this spatula?

—Advertisement for spatulas made from wood cut by seventeenth-century Acadians, 1998

By this document, we declare that our objectives are to support the French language in Louisiana, to establish its continuity, and to ensure that all Cajuns have the knowledge of their heritage.

—Manifesto of Action Cadienne (Cajun Action), cultural activist group, founded 1995

Something peculiar happened to Cajun culture in the late twentieth century. Once derided as backward, it suddenly became associated with words such as *hot, chic,* and *trendy.* Mainstream society not only discovered Cajun culture but embraced it, usurped it, and reshaped it almost beyond recognition into a highly marketable commodity. A soft drink company in north Louisiana hawked Cajun Cola. A condiment manufacturer in Arizona introduced Ass

Kickin' Cajun Hot Sauce. A mollusk farm in Oregon marketed "Cajun-Style" Kitchen-Sliced Slugs. Electronics giant Lucent Technologies manufactured a line of computer hardware under the trademarked brand name Cajun. A major theme park included a "Cajun Country" section featuring rides like the Cypress Plunge, the Gator Bait, and the Muskrat Scrambler. An inventor sold a battery-powered key chain called a "Cajun in Your Pocket" that played six "authentic" sayings, such as the decidedly unauthentic "Ooo, I love you like a pig loves corn."

Salesmen peddled California Cajun Pistachios, Cajun Kippered Beefsteak ("great for your Y2K stockpiles"), and an "Official 'Be a Cajun' Kit" that inexplicably included cigars and hot sauce made in Florida as well as a Jimmy Buffett CD. New Age gurus sold Cajun magic charm bracelets, Cajun mojo bags "blessed by the High Priestess," and a meditation CD that combined soothing Cajun-inspired music with natural swamp sounds. A professional wrestler named Lash LeRoux, also known as the Cajun Sensation, battled opponents before millions on national television. Country star Ricky Skaggs reached the Billboard Top Ten with "Cajun Moon," British pop band Adam and the Ants sang about "Cajun Twisters," and heavy metal rock group Exodus recorded a tune called "Cajun Hell."

Cookbooks appeared with such strange titles as *Microwave Cajun Country Cookbook, Cajun Vegetarian Cooking,* and *Kosher Cajun Cookbook,* the cover of which showed an Ultraorthodox Jew enjoying south Louisiana's spicy cuisine. Marvel comics added a Cajun superhero, Gambit, to its pantheon of crime fighters to go with Spiderman, the Incredible Hulk, and Captain America. Meanwhile, hack writers issued cheap romance novels with titles such as *Cajun Rose, Cajun Summer,* and *Cajun Caress.* Even the underworld of hardcore pornography exploited the Cajun frenzy. *Juggs* magazine featured a Cajun nude layout, and *Bear* magazine presented an entire "Special Cajun Issue" for its gay male readership. Not to be outdone, one entrepreneur printed up T-shirts reading "Cajun Style" that depicted pairs of cartoon crawfish engaged in various sex positions.

"Cajun is being so commercialized," fretted Dewey Balfa in the late 1980s. "Someday it's going to be too much, if it ain't already."[1]

The final two decades of the twentieth century saw Cajun culture simultaneously exploited and revitalized after a lull in the pride and empowerment

movement. The wild demand for south Louisiana cuisine heralded into existence a national Cajun craze. Beginning around 1980, this culinary phenomenon introduced the region's delicacies to the world, but it also led to a rash of
fake Cajun food products in grocery stores and restaurants. Meanwhile, the
media presented Cajun stereotypes in movies and on television, depicting
them as backward swamp dwellers. The nation's infatuation with Cajun culture, real or otherwise, also created a tourism boom that economically benefited Acadiana while disrupting its remaining folk rituals. The ethnic group's
dependency on tourism increased during the devastating oil glut of the 1980s,
which caused a mass exodus from south Louisiana. Exiles boosted the ongoing
craze by introducing others to their culture, but they also exposed themselves
to influences that further eroded the traditional way of life. Cajuns who
remained at home fared little better, as demonstrated by the proliferation of
strip malls, fast food restaurants, and other trappings of mainstream society.
Both elite and grassroots activists struggled with an apathetic south Louisiana
public, which viewed the French-preservation movement as a failure.

Paradoxically, just as Americanization reached a critical mass in Acadiana
and seemed poised to eradicate Cajun culture entirely, an amazing event
occurred: the Cajun pride and empowerment movement renewed itself after
years of stagnation. Still a cultural power broker, Jimmy Domengeaux helped
to spark this renaissance by abandoning his former anti-Cajun French pos-
ture and by embracing a new approach to language instruction called French
Immersion. The same period witnessed the rise of Cajun literary and artistic
movements. It also saw a resurgence in the popularity of Cajun music, as a
new generation of performers attracted young audiences by pushing the
genre's boundaries. Inspired by the culture's ongoing rebirth, activists took
legal and political action, threatening lawsuits and passing legislation aimed
at eliminating age-old ethnic discrimination. Cajun pride soared, as demonstrated by celebrations such as the Congrès Mondial, which reunited south
Louisiana families with French-Canadian cousins after more than two centuries of separation. By the end of the 1990s it seemed clear that despite predictions to the contrary, a strong Cajun identity would persist well into the
twenty-first century—albeit not without changing in the process.

During the second half of the 1970s America suffered a national malaise as
taxes, inflation, interest rates, and energy prices soared. In the Middle East,

oil supplies vital to the United States were threatened by a Soviet invasion of Afghanistan, while U.S. diplomatic officials were held hostage in Iran. President Jimmy Carter lamented the ongoing "crisis of confidence" that struck "at the very heart and soul and spirit of our nation." Despite high oil revenues, south Louisiana joined the rest of the nation in its discontent. Viewing Carter as an ineffectual leader, its residents denigrated him for proposing a tax on oil companies, whose profits had skyrocketed because of deregulation, and for refusing to support a bill that would have helped the region's sugar industry. As a result, in 1980 many traditionally Democratic south Louisianians became "Reagan Cajuns," embracing Republican presidential candidate Ronald Reagan's conservative message of old-fashioned family values, patriotism, small government, and lower taxes. Actually, this political shift had been under way since the mid-1960s, when many southern Democrats balked at their own party's support of liberal civil rights legislation. By 1980 many Acadiana residents were therefore ready to join the conservative movement, accounting for one of two major constituencies (the other being urban voters) that fueled the state's Republican surge. As a journalist accurately predicted weeks before the election, "Cajuns Can KO Carter."[2]

After a rough start, the Reagan administration's massive federal spending eventually improved the national economy, and by the mid-1980s it had given rise to a new demographic group known as Yuppies. These young, upwardly mobile professionals resided in urban areas, occupied professional or managerial positions, and made sizable incomes that they spent on leisure products. Among the consumer items they coveted most were sports cars, designer clothing, electronic gadgets, and exotic gourmet foods—including Cajun food, a strange new delicacy they discovered in their own American backyard along with other ethnic cuisines, such as Asian and Hispanic foods.[3]

By coincidence, about a year before Reagan's election, a rising Cajun chef from Opelousas named Paul Prudhomme opened his own restaurant, K-Paul's Louisiana Kitchen, in New Orleans. Born in 1940 to a large family, Prudhomme as a child helped in the kitchen and picked up cooking techniques born of necessity. He learned to use fresh ingredients, for example, not only because they improved meals but because his family's unelectrified house had neither freezer nor refrigerator in which to store groceries. Prudhomme drew on these improvisational skills when he opened K-Paul's.

Unable to afford a commercial grill, he experimented with cooking a well-seasoned fish fillet on a superheated iron skillet. The result was a new entrée called blackened redfish.

Bolstered by yuppyism and its demand for the new and exotic, Prudhomme's creation became a culinary phenomenon, spreading quickly from Louisiana to the East and West Coasts. So popular was it that the Gulf of Mexico's redfish population fell dramatically by the mid-1980s. Conservationists feared the species would be cooked into extinction, and in 1986 the U.S. Department of Commerce banned commercial redfishing in federal waters. Early the next year, the state of Louisiana banned commercial and recreational redfishing in its waters.

In the meantime, Prudhomme became "a culinary God," to quote one journalist, as well as the world's most visible Cajun. Responding to demand for his cooking, Prudhomme took his restaurant on the road, setting up eateries in San Francisco and New York City. Patrons stood in line up to four hours to taste his culinary delights, while his cookbook, named *Louisiana Kitchen,* after his restaurant, sold nearly a half-million copies and appeared on the *New York Times* best-seller list for thirteen weeks.[4]

Prudhomme's success sparked a Cajun food phenomenon that brought attention to other south Louisiana chefs, such as John Folse, whose restaurant in rural Ascension Parish attracted visitors from around the world. "It was worth crossing the ocean to eat here!" a diner from Milan wrote in Folse's guest book. Like Prudhomme, Folse served as a cultural ambassador, taking his cuisine to epicures in England, France, China, and Hong Kong. He became the first American to open a restaurant in the Soviet Union, cooking in Moscow during a Reagan-Gorbachev summit. Folse's "Cajun care packages" and spicy dishes proved so popular that Muscovite restaurateurs complained about losing customers. Soviet authorities responded by ordering Folse to stop cooking, but they relented when the audacious chef threatened to throw a free barbeque in Red Square.[5]

"The world is sitting at Louisiana's dinner table," reported a major state newspaper. Restaurants in Acadiana prospered from increased business, while those elsewhere included Cajun dishes on their menus. Entrepreneurs even started their own Cajun restaurants far outside south Louisiana. New York City, for example, boasted several Cajun or quasi-Cajun eateries, including the Barking Fish Café, Crawdaddy's, La Louisiane, the Gulf Coast, How's Bayou, and the Bon Temps Rouler. Predictably, most of these restaurants catered to a predominantly yuppie clientele. As one customer noted, "Everybody was twenty-nine and contemplating opening an IRA."

"New York Eats Boudin," ran a headline in the *Times of Acadiana,* which reported that Big Apple sophisticates had drooled when one of its journalists took an ice chest of boudin (sausage made of seasoned meat and rice) to a fancy literary soiree. "An editor of *The Nation* begged us to send a boudin recipe," the journalist recalled. "A writer for the *Village Voice* had us steer him to the few platters still holding a few pieces. . . . A columnist from the *New York Times* scribbled down our south Louisiana restaurant recommendations." This occurred despite the journalist's failure to warn the cosmopolites not to eat the disposable sausage casings. ("They seemed to like them.")

"Cajun food is hot these days," noted the *Times-Picayune,* observing that it was "being imitated, hyped, discovered, marketed, mangled, misinterpreted, and just plain adored all over."

Adored—but mangled and misinterpreted nonetheless. The paper had touched on a growing negative side effect of the Cajun food craze—vulgar commercialization. This trend exhibited itself in the deluge of dubious Cajun products that occupied supermarket shelves, including Cajun potato chips, pasta, taco shells, wine, and Milwaukee beer brewed "in the time-honored Cajun tradition" despite the fact that Cajuns had no beer-making tradition. Ersatz products also became common among "fast-casual" and "family dining" restaurant chains. Pizza Hut offered Cajun Pizza, for instance, while Bennigan's promoted Cajun Chicken Salad. Chili's sold a Cajun Chicken Sandwich, and TGI Friday's marketed Cajun-Fried Chicken, Blackened-Cajun Chicken, Cajun Chicken Fingers, and Spicy Cajun Chicken Pasta. Shoney's publicized a shrimp dinner called the Big Boudreaux and another featuring shrimp served in something called Cajun Ya Ya sauce. Fast-food giants followed the same trend. McDonald's offered the Cajun Crispy Chicken Deluxe, Cajun McChicken Sandwich, and Cajun Biscuits, while its chief rival, Burger King, countered with the Cajun Whaler, Cajun Chick'n Crisp, and Cajun Cheeseburger.

No fast-food chain capitalized on the Cajun theme more than Popeye's— a restaurant used by sociologist George Ritzer as an example of

"McDonaldization," the process by which fast-food principles came to dominate virtually every sector of American society, even the selling of ethnic cuisines, by the late twentieth century. Founded in the 1970s by New Orleans businessman Al Copeland, Popeye's became the subsidiary of an Atlanta-based corporation, AFC (America's Favorite Chicken). With more than fifteen hundred locations in twenty nations, the chain boasted itself as the "worldwide leader in the Cajun dining segment," with sales in 2000 equaling about $1.2 billion. Its menu offered such items as Cajun Popcorn Shrimp, Cajun Battered Fries, Cajun Rice, and Cajun Fried Turkey. A spin-off organization, Popeye's Cajun Café, serviced malls, food courts, and entertainment venues. The franchise also spawned the Cajun Kitchen, a fast-casual chain whose first location opened in a Chicago suburb. Meanwhile, the founder of Popeye's went on to create another fast-casual chain, Copeland's, whose menu included Cajun-themed items like the Bon Temps Burger, Catfish Acadiana, and Fettuccine Alfredeaux.

In response to the flood of questionable Cajun products hailing from around the country, Louisiana's Department of Agriculture campaigned aggressively against companies that manufactured "out-of-state, bad-tasting, red-pepper-hot, copy-cat Cajun" goods, which, it argued, were "causing serious damage to the Louisiana industry." The department accused many of these companies of stamping their products with fake Louisiana addresses and telephone numbers to deceive consumers. As a deterrent, the state authorized a "Certified Cajun Product" logo and empowered attorneys to threaten non-Louisiana companies with false advertising lawsuits. One targeted business defended itself by arguing that *Cajun* was a generic term, vindicating an editorialist who warned that Cajun food was "losing its identity." A Houston restaurant demonstrated the point, billing itself as "Cajun" without serving a single authentic dish. As a customer remarked, the food was "not in any way Cajun. It's Chinese, and so are all the workers and cooks."[6]

The Cajun food craze helped to create a demand for everything Cajun, real or perceived, and further transformed south Louisiana into a thriving tourism destination. Sightseers had already spent $275 million visiting Acadiana in 1980, just before the mania for all things Cajun caused a dramatic increase in travel-related income. While these revenues benefited the local economy, the tourism boom ultimately harmed Cajun culture by repackaging it in caricature for mass consumption. "There has been a casualty in this campaign to whip up excitement over south Louisiana's tourist attractions," asserted journalist Trent Angers, who criticized the travel industry's depiction of Cajuns as swamp-dwelling hedonists, obsessed with eating, drinking, and dancing. "Are these guys flying in for a day or two, taking in the swamp tour, hanging around a Cajun dance hall for a while, reading a few tourist brochures, and writing a story based on just that?" Cajun country often came across as a bizarre Third World country, an image reinforced when one popular travel magazine paired the region with Vietnam as a good place to visit on a shoestring budget. "Vacation for pennies, in Vietnam . . . and Cajun Country," it advised. "Ho Chi Minh City, then gumbo and jambalaya."

Tourists themselves endangered Cajun culture by disrupting already declining folk practices. This development was most evident during the rural *courir du Mardi Gras* (running of the Mardi Gras), when costumed horseback riders traveled from house to house collecting ingredients for huge communal gumbos. Tourists not only threatened to outnumber local Mardi Gras participants by the 1990s but increasingly became participants without understanding the event's cultural significance. The *courir* was not an excuse to drink, dance, and chase chickens; it was an important rite of passage for young males and a prelude to Lenten sacrifices. Some locals reacted to these incursions by withdrawing from the celebration, as demonstrated when a busload of tourists arrived in Mamou during its Mardi Gras festivities. The outsiders immediately took over the dance floor, finding it "odd that very few of the local people were dancing," as one of the tourists noted—never considering that their own unexpected arrival might have caused the locals' inhibition.

Tourists soon became a year-round problem as they invaded even the most obscure Cajun nightclubs, interrupting the weekly ritual of Saturday night dancing and *bourré* card games. "Regulars are pushed to the walls," observed folklorist Ancelet. "Next Saturday night, the tourists are gone, but things are not quite the same." As a result, a subtle backlash developed against tourists, prompting a Cajun musician who benefited from tourism to complain nonetheless that south Louisiana "wasn't intended to be a getaway for middle-class urbanites who want to escape the stress of a fast-lane life in the big city, and pretend that they are Cajun for a couple of weeks out of the year." A T-shirt sold in Ville Platte reflected a similar sentiment:

below the image of an alligator flashing razor-sharp teeth appeared the caption, "Send more tourists, the last one tasted great!"

Cajuns were partly to blame for the damage inflicted by the tourism industry. Having embraced the American view that everything had a price, an attitude reinforced by the Reagan era's materialism, some Cajuns accommodated tourists by showing them exactly what they wanted to see, often at the expense of reality. Staged cultural events thus assumed a new importance. "South Louisiana has become a tourist fiction," an observer noted in the mid-1980s. "Cajuns put on the requisite show to attract the money . . . but they give it up as soon as the audience leaves." Activists lamented the tendency among some Cajuns to behave like "court jesters," assuming the role of ethnic stereotypes when accosted by tourists or journalists. Cajuns also abetted their own exploitation by polluting the landscape with what one visitor described as "garish" tourist-trap billboards. Another expressed displeasure with the "shed casinos full of bused-in Texans" that lined Acadiana's westernmost highways "like a backwoods Vegas."

Significantly, the tourism industry used the media to create the myth that New Orleans not only was part of Cajun country but was the center of the Cajun universe, despite the fact that the city was distinctly non-Cajun and had traditionally viewed the ethnic group as backward. Notable Cajun populations resided in nearby Jefferson and St. Charles Parishes, but according to the 1990 U.S. census, only 1 percent of New Orleans residents identified their primary ethnicity as Cajun. For perspective, persons of Italian ancestry outnumbered Cajuns in New Orleans by nearly four to one, Irish outnumbered Cajuns by nearly six to one, and Germans outnumbered Cajuns by nearly nine to one. Furthermore, Houston, Texas, possessed nearly the same percentage of Cajuns as New Orleans—less than a quarter of a percent difference—and on a per capita basis Houston actually boasted 4.5 times as many Cajuns. The tourism industry nonetheless successfully convinced the media and the public that New Orleans was veritably oozing with authentic Cajun culture. As a result, countless journalists praised the virtues of "New Orleans–style Cajun food," while usually cautious *National Geographic* reported that Cajuns were "a key ingredient in the cultural gumbo that is New Orleans."[7]

Like the tourism industry, the entertainment industry sought to exploit the Cajun craze by producing films and television shows that featured Cajun characters, most of whom were ignorant, violent, oversexed swamp dwellers. This negative image was nothing new to Hollywood. Cajun stereotypes populated the 1944 B-movie classic *The Mummy's Curse,* in which Lon Chaney Jr. arises from the swamps to terrorize a rural Cajun community. This low-budget horror flick was perhaps the earliest film to depict modern Cajuns, along with that year's film noir thriller *Dark Waters,* starring Merle Oberon as a young heiress in the bayou country nearly driven to madness by con artists. Cajun stereotypes also appeared in the 1953 action drama *Thunder Bay,* starring Jimmy Stewart as an Anglo wildcatter who must fight "a hostile town of Cajun fishermen" in his search for oil. And in the 1956 film *Bayou,* rereleased tellingly six years later as *Poor White Trash,* Anglo outsider Peter Graves battles a villainous south Louisiana rival for a Cajun belle played by scantily clad Italian starlet Lita Milan. "In the Cajun country, when you're fifteen, *you're a woman!"* ran the movie's tag line, "and every bayou man knows it!"

While Cajun stereotypes were hardly new to Hollywood, the number of movies released in the 1980s and 1990s that featured Cajun characters was unprecedented. These productions included *The River Rat* (1984), *Down by Law* (1986), *Shy People* (1987), *Gator Bait II: Cajun Justice* (1988), *Ragin' Cajun* (1990), *Hard Target* (1993), *Dead Man Walking* (1995), *Heaven's Prisoners* (1996), *The First 9½ Weeks* (1998), and *The Green Mile* (1999). A handful of movies, such as *Belizaire the Cajun* (1986), *Passion Fish* (1992), and *Dirty Rice* (1997), presented Cajuns in a positive, accurate light, but most relied on the old stereotypes. In *Southern Comfort* (1981), for example, Cajun trappers brutally hunted down and killed a squad of National Guardsmen on a swampland training mission. "It portrays us as uneducated murderers," complained a local moviegoer. Cajun swamp dwellers also appeared in *No Mercy* (1986), discussing in French their preferred method of sexual intercourse with unconscious, half-drowned Kim Basinger. ("Dans la bouche.") In *The Waterboy* (1998) comic Adam Sandler, who earlier portrayed the laconic Cajun Man on NBC's *Saturday Night Live,* played a bungling character described by *Newsweek* as "a dimwitted Cajun" and by *Entertainment Weekly* as "an uneducated, emasculated, socially retarded Cajun."

No film did more to misrepresent Cajun culture, however, than *The Big Easy* (1987), which the nation embraced as an accurate glimpse into the ethnic group's mysterious folkways. Even discerning critic Roger Ebert praised the film as "the most convincing portrait of New Orleans I've ever seen." Meanwhile, south Louisiana viewers snickered at the film's cultural clichés, its placement of rural Cajuns amid metro New Orleans, and actor Dennis Quaid's mispronunciation of "chèr," a common term of endearment. One scholar thus aptly dismissed the motion picture as a "New Orleans–style Cajun pizza kind of a movie."

Television shows also relied on these stereotypes and sometimes exceeded movies in their misrepresentations. Cajun villains were especially popular on television. An episode of *FX* featured a Cajun heavy named Sid Thibodeaux, while a *Silk Stalkings* episode included a Cajun mobster named Bayou Boudreaux. The *Jeff Foxworthy Show* offered a weapon-toting Cajun female who looked back fondly on her career as a prostitute. *NYPD Blue* prepared a teleplay about a black "Cajun" criminal from north Louisiana, but fortunately the show deserted the project before production. The short-lived legal drama *Orleans* not only misleadingly associated Cajuns with New Orleans but depicted the ethnic group as perverse. When asked how viewers would receive the program, actor Larry Hagman, who played a Cajun judge, quipped, "If they like incest, I suppose they'll like it."[8]

While the Cajun craze swept the nation, an international oil glut ravaged south Louisiana, creating economic devastation unknown since the Reconstruction era. The crash came at the peak of Acadiana's prosperity, for what had been an energy crisis for most Americans during the 1970s had been a bonanza for the petroleum-rich region. Indeed, around 1980, all but one of the state's twenty wealthiest parishes, as determined by per capita income, were located in south Louisiana. Then came 1981, when the price of crude oil began to slide after reaching an unprecedented high of nearly thirty-two dollars per barrel. "I don't ever want to see another year like '81," commented an oil-field professional. But the glut worsened, and words such as *downsizing, layoffs,* and *shakeouts* became commonplace. By 1983 oil service companies in south Louisiana were "cut down to the bone and trying to hold on," as one manager described the situation. The glut hurt not only those employed directly by the oil industry but the entire state: a Louisiana State University economics professor found that for every terminated oil-field worker, two other residents also lost their jobs.

Formerly prosperous south Louisiana communities like Lafayette, the state's "oil center," reeled from the glut's impact. In 1980 *Money* magazine had named it one of America's ten richest small cities. Only three years later, the *Times-Picayune* described Lafayette as a "Cajun Camelot Running on Empty." To the west, Acadiana's second largest city, Lake Charles, staggered under the burden of a 15.5 percent unemployment rate. Low educational standards exacerbated the lack of jobs, for many younger Cajuns, expecting lucrative oil-field jobs after a few weeks of vocational training, had not been encouraged to excel in high school, much less to obtain college degrees. The consequence was a large population of poorly educated workers who now lacked marketable skills. Civic leaders nonetheless tried to remain optimistic. "I see a boom in 1985," predicted an Iberia Parish industrialist who fabricated offshore platforms and other petroleum equipment.

Instead, the glut increased: in 1986 the average price of U.S. crude oil nose-dived to less than thirteen dollars per barrel, nearly half the previous year's average price. What began as an oil recession had become an oil depression. As the economy collapsed and major oil firms left the region, Cajuns turned against the once sacrosanct industry, charging it with abandonment after ruining their homeland with a toxic mixture that included arsenic, asbestos, formaldehyde, carbolic acid, barium, chromium, mercury, radioactive isotopes, and caustic soda (the active ingredient in Drano), all drilling by-products. When a study ranked ten south Louisiana parishes among the top 5 percent nationally for cancer deaths among white males, the petrochemical industry fired back with a study of its own, blaming the Cajuns' poor health on their smoking, drinking, and dietary habits. Meanwhile, the Cajuns' hunting, trapping, and fishing grounds disappeared, poisoned not only by chemicals but by saltwater intrusion caused by an estimated twelve thousand miles of oil canals crisscrossing the region's coastal marshlands. "The fishing grounds have been destroyed," lamented seventy-six-year-old Severin Broussard, "and now the oil industry is folding up and leaving. I feel sad, very sad, because I sold my heritage to the oil industry and now it's gone."[9]

Faced with unemployment, mounting debts, and bankruptcy, Cajuns departed their homeland by the thousands, seeking better economic opportunities abroad. So pervasive was the exodus that U-Haul and other moving companies found it nearly impossible to provide enough vehicles to meet demand. Although self-imposed, the mass exile naturally begged comparison to the eighteenth-century Acadian diaspora, as Cajuns formed ethnic enclaves in metropolitan areas across America. According to the 1990 U.S. Census, these areas included Atlanta (which boasted 4,334 residents of Cajun ancestry), Austin (3,690), Chicago (1,489), Denver (1,357), Los Angeles (4,273), Nashville (1,325), New York City (1,245), Orlando (1,444), Phoenix (1,428), San Francisco (1,157), Seattle (1,536), Tampa (1,475), and Washington, D.C. (2,501), to name some of the most popular destinations. These exiles fueled the ongoing Cajun craze by serving as cultural ambassadors, introducing the uninitiated to the south Louisiana way of life. "I want to educate people up here about Cajuns," noted one exile who capitalized on his heritage by opening a Cajun restaurant in Nashville. Other exiles formed Cajun clubs, organizing crawfish boils, gumbos, and Mardi Gras celebrations in their adopted communities; those in Atlanta even formed an amateur baseball team called the CIA (Cajuns In Atlanta). In general, however, the exodus had a negative impact on the culture, immersing Cajuns far from home deeper in mainstream society. "You start missing the people, the food, the south Louisiana atmosphere," bemoaned one exile who had sought refuge in Colorado. "You start thinking, 'What am I doing?'"[10]

Meanwhile, outside influences continued to invade south Louisiana, bringing fast-food joints, cable television, cookie-cutter neighborhoods, traffic jams, suburban sprawl, and various strains of Protestantism that threatened the Cajuns' traditional Catholic faith. Among these spiritual interlopers were Bible Belt fundamentalists, whose numbers had expanded considerably during the 1970s because of the national revival of evangelical religion. By the late 1970s more than seventy million Americans considered themselves born-again Christians. Among this "Moral Majority" were Cajuns, who increasingly renounced their Roman Catholic faith to join Protestant churches.

Several factors accounted for this trend, but nearly all reflected the encroachment of mainstream culture. Cajuns wanted access to "the pill" and other contraceptives forbidden by the Catholic Church, and they wanted quick divorces and the right to remarry without dogmatic hassles, all benefits offered by many Protestant churches. Cajuns also gravitated toward the "Gospel of Wealth" message spread by many evangelical sects, which asserted that God rewarded the faithful with money and luxury goods. This promise enticed Cajuns who had already embraced the American Dream and who found unappealing the virtue of poverty taught by Catholicism. Furthermore, Anglo-Protestants in south Louisiana zealously sought out French-Catholic converts. Some fundamentalists distributed anti-Catholic videotapes and literature, even in obscure rural communities. One small-town Cajun priest was dismayed to learn that fundamentalists had circulated a flyer among his parishioners calling the Catholic Church "gruesome," "hateful," and "satanic" and accusing Pope John Paul II of being a "Nazi World War II criminal" who had personally sold cyanide to Hitler's death squads at Auschwitz.

Because of these influences, Cajuns by the thousands gradually left their traditional faith, a trend reflected by the growing number of Protestant churches in the region. For example, although the number of Catholic churches in greater Lafayette doubled between 1965 and the end of the century, the number of Protestant churches in the community nearly quadrupled, eventually outnumbering Catholic churches almost four to one. (The 1965 ratio of Protestant to Catholic churches in greater Lafayette was 29 to 14; the 1998–99 ratio was 107 to 28.) Jesse Duplantis, a Cajun televangelist with an international following, personified this movement toward fundamentalism. One of his books, *Jambalaya for the Soul,* combined evangelical sermons with south Louisiana recipes and humor. "Maybe it's time you got a hold of some Godly advice," he invited readers, "Cajun-style!"[11]

Many visitors to south Louisiana disappointedly noted the impact of mainstream culture. French exchange students, for example, complained that Acadiana was "too American." Meanwhile, CODOFIL, the organization mandated to combat assimilation, could barely save itself from extinction, much less the French language. "Au secours!" it exclaimed in a flyer issued when the state began slashing budgets in the oil glut's wake—Help! "We sound the alarm for emergency assistance! . . . CODOFIL's elimination is now imminent." Funding was hardly its only problem, for interest in the entire French-preservation movement had fallen dramatically. Most ordinary Cajuns had already redefined their ethnic group as English-speaking, a trend horrifying to those who argued that the Cajun lifestyle would perish without its dialect. Activist David Marcantel asserted that the culture was dying "due to the apathy and indifference of the Cajuns themselves."[12]

Long-time CODOFIL chairperson Jimmy Domengeaux seemed to be hastening the culture's demise, abetting its Americanization by alienating the mass of ordinary Cajuns. By the late 1970s it was clear to many parents and educators that his costly programs were failing to instill a basic knowledge of French among south Louisiana's youth. A review panel substantiated this opinion when in 1978 it found "considerable evidence of fundamental weaknesses" in CODOFIL's performance. These weaknesses ranged from excessive use of English in classrooms to poorly trained teachers to a lack of defined objectives. Armed with this evidence, several school boards revolted against CODOFIL that year. Acadia, Evangeline, Iberia, Jefferson Davis, and Terrebonne all terminated their programs, and St. Mary threatened to join the movement. Ultimately, all but two of these maverick parishes reinstated their CODOFIL courses, but the revolt underscored widespread dissatisfaction with the organization.[13]

Domengeaux apparently learned little from this criticism, for the next year he further alienated Cajuns by ardently opposing the first Cajun French textbook. Written by James Donald Faulk, a foreign-language teacher from Vermilion Parish, *Cajun French I* contained thousands of words and phrases culled from the Cajun lexicon, all rendered in a phonetic code devised by the author for his English-speaking students. "Il fait beau aujourd'hui" (It is a beautiful day today) thus became "Ee fe bo ojoordwee." As Faulk explained, "You can read the words in English, but it comes out in Cajun French."

Some educators criticized Faulk's method because it prevented students from reading and writing standard French. Domengeaux opposed it simply because he despised Cajun French, and a bitter public feud erupted when CODOFIL's leader dismissed the textbook as "a bunch of chicken scratches." Faulk fired back, "All the Cajun people are for me. They hate his guts." Domengeaux ultimately succeeded in blocking the use of Faulk's textbook in classrooms, but in doing so, Domengeaux caused a public relations disaster. The media depicted CODOFIL as an anti-Cajun Goliath, a charge that had been levied for years by some grassroots activists. Newspaper headlines reinforced this perception: "CODOFIL Chief Trying to Block Cajun French

Book," "CODOFIL Frowns on Cajun French Textbook," "CODOFIL versus Local Man."

Domengeaux further damaged the French-preservation movement when during the Faulk affair he told a United Press International journalist that Cajun French was "worse than redneck English." An Associated Press reporter attributed a similar remark to Domengeaux a year later, when esteemed Columbia University folklorist Alan Lomax criticized CODOFIL's use of imported French instructors. Moreover, Domengeaux defended his practice of hiring foreign instructors by asserting, "They can speak French better than any damn Louisianian." Newspaper headlines again seemed to confirm what many south Louisianians already suspected: "Attempt to Save Cajun Culture May Be Killing It."[14]

Not surprisingly, some observers pronounced the Cajun way of life moribund by the late 1970s. The rapid, widespread process of Americanization that began decades earlier seemed poised to crush the culture and with it the hopes of activists who had struggled so fervently to save it from annihilation. "I feel like the language is a cancer patient," confided one French instructor. "I want to hold out hope. If the best we can do is to hold onto it a little longer, then that's what we'll do." So apparent was the dialect's impending demise that Canadian Prime Minister Brian Mulroney used it as a metaphor to justify protecting French in Quebec. "French-Canadians will inevitably become Cajuns," he warned, pointing to south Louisiana as a worst-case scenario. "'Cajunization' Threat Looms over Quebec," warned an editorial cartoon in the *Toronto Globe and Mail.*[15]

Cajun French had virtually ceased to exist among younger generations. Outsiders had usurped the Cajun identity, warped it beyond recognition, and reduced it to a cheap marketing gimmick. The culture seemed to have reached its terminus: complete Americanization.

But four hundred years of history showed that Cajuns were survivors. Their ancestors' ability to endure genocide; to withstand disease, starvation, and exposure; and to adopt a new life on the semitropical frontier demonstrated this characteristic—one of the Cajuns' defining traits. "The most consistent element in Cajun country may well be an uncanny ability to swim in the mainstream," noted a team of scholars, "to reinvent and renegotiate their cultural affairs on their own terms." As folklorist Ancelet often jested, every time someone pronounced Cajun culture dead, the corpse sat up in the coffin. "On va les embêter," asserted cultural activist and musician Marc Savoy— We'll fool 'em, we'll survive.[16]

The culture did survive, despite widespread Americanization, because the Cajun pride and empowerment movement of the late 1960s and early 1970s resurrected itself in what the *Times of Acadiana* called a "second Cajun renaissance." The causes of this renaissance were several: frustration with CODOFIL's elitism and lack of success; belief that an immediate renewal of the movement was the only alternative to assimilation; and, significantly, the desire of Cajun baby boomers for their children to have what they had been denied as youths—the chance to embrace their heritage. "There's a new spirit fueled by this generation of baby boomers who've been educated and find something missing in their lives," observed one cultural activist. Echoed another, "I've noticed a certain amount of vindication by this generation of parents who say, 'I was deprived of my language because my parents were punished for speaking French, now I want it for my children.'"[17]

The revival of pride and empowerment began with a seemingly miraculous occurrence—Jimmy Domengeaux's sudden conversion to pro–Cajun French activist. A catalyst of this amazing turnaround was the publication of *Cris sur le bayou* (Cries on the Bayou), a collection of Cajun French poems by various contributors, including Zachary Richard and the enigmatic Jean Arceneaux, who appeared on the back cover of a subsequent volume disguised in a rural Mardi Gras costume. In *Cris sur le bayou*, Arceneaux anticipated the renewed fight against assimilation:

La marée américaine	[*The American marsh tide*
Commence enfin à baisser	*Is finally beginning to ebb*
Après tant d'années	*After so many years*
De nous avoir noyés	*Of drowning us*
Par les fossés dans nos levées.	*By the holes in our levees.*]

Arceneaux was none other than folklorist Ancelet, who has acknowledged that *Cris sur le bayou* came about partly in response to Domengeaux's claim that Cajun French was solely an oral dialect, that it lacked grammar and syntax, and that it therefore could not be written. When the book appeared,

Ancelet hid a copy behind his back and walked into Domengeaux's office. "I pulled it out and I slammed it on his desk," he recalled, "and I said: 'Now it is written.'" Domengeaux opened the book. "What the hell is this?" "It's written Cajun French," replied Ancelet. "Well, it looks like French." "That's because it is!" retorted Ancelet. Domengeaux kept the book and a few days later he called Ancelet. "Come over to my office," he said, "we're going to have to rethink this whole goddamn thing."[18]

A book of poetry alone, however, did not persuade Domengeaux to reconsider the value of Cajun French. The Faulk affair, for example, had forced Domengeaux to ally himself with pro–Cajun French activists like Ancelet, who for different reasons shared his disapproval of Faulk's textbook. Regardless, the alliance exposed Domengeaux to pro–Cajun French attitudes and forced him to see the issue from a new perspective. At the same time, several academic panels urged CODOFIL to include Cajun French in its programs—undoubtedly to Domengeaux's surprise, for he had expected the panels to vindicate his emphasis on standard French. A study by French, Belgian, and Quebecois educators called for Cajun French in the classroom, as did members of Projet Louisiane, a research project sponsored by three Canadian universities. Some of Domengeaux's imported French instructors also stressed the value of Cajun French, among them Philippe Gustin, a Belgian who eventually served under Domengeaux as CODOFIL's executive director. Meanwhile, scholars developed Cajun French textbooks that avoided Faulk's earlier mistakes, and both the University of Southwestern Louisiana and LSU used these books to teach Cajun French courses.[19]

All these factors contributed to Domengeaux's reversal, which brought about real changes at CODOFIL. It began to hire more local teachers, many of whom had been encouraged by the organization to obtain degrees certifying them as Second Language Specialists (SLS). Moreover, CODOFIL urged the state to hire one of those SLS teachers, Richard Guidry, to manage all foreign-language and bilingual education programs—a significant gesture, for Guidry was an outspoken grassroots activists who passionately supported Cajun French education. According to Guidry, CODOFIL's backing allowed him to "Louisiana-fy" the state's French programs. He published guides and textbooks that encouraged the use of Cajun French in classrooms, including *Le française louisianais,* a glossary issued by the state Department of Education that contained Cajun French words and phrases. Guidry also designed an orientation program for imported teachers that introduced them to south Louisiana culture and advised them to avoid terms such as "proper" or "standard" French, which implied that Cajun French was somehow improper or substandard.[20]

Domengeaux's reversal also forced him to concede that CODOFIL had grown "stagnant" and that it had failed to attain the primary goal it had established in 1968. "We have not rooted French sufficiently and adequately," he confessed, "although we probably did as much as we could." The organization, admitted his lieutenant, Gustin, "was not very effective. . . . We were not really producing young kids, bilingual children, in Louisiana." From this admission, however, sprang an idea that would profoundly influence French education in Louisiana. While in Montreal in the early 1980s, Domengeaux and a small group of Louisiana educators, including Gustin, state director of foreign languages Homer Dyess, and state superintendent of education Kelly Nix, visited schools for Anglo children whose parents wanted them to learn French, Quebec's dominant language. These schools had developed an effective program for achieving this goal, called French Immersion. It was a revolutionary venture, for it required students to be instructed in French throughout the school day, whether the subject was mathematics, social studies, or science. Domengeaux and his cohorts returned to Louisiana "extremely impressed" by the French Immersion method, which was clearly far more successful than CODOFIL's program of teaching French in daily thirty-minute increments.

Inspired by what they had witnessed in the Montreal schools, Domengeaux and his supporters pushed for the introduction of this approach in Louisiana. A pilot immersion program began in East Baton Rouge Parish in 1981. Two years later, Calcasieu Parish started the first immersion program in Acadiana. Ironically, Lafayette Parish, CODOFIL's home and the self-proclaimed capital of Cajun Louisiana, did not begin its first immersion program until 1992. The problem was partly one of funding, for the oil glut had resulted in educational budget cuts, and French Immersion was inherently more expensive than traditional schooling, requiring more teachers as well as new textbooks and other learning tools. Moreover, some Lafayette Parish school board authorities opposed the program because CODOFIL had shown poor management skills in the past, resulting in a largely ineffectual French education program.

But French Immersion worked. Children entered immersion courses no later than first grade, when their rapidly developing cognitive and language skills and their uninhibited curiosity made them highly receptive to learning a new language. "Words which take a high schooler a week to master are acquired by first- and second-graders in a day or so," noted one teacher. "The same is true for language structures and for accent." Admitted based on parental interest, teacher recommendation, and classroom size, children received French instruction in several subjects for about 60 percent of the school day. "French Immersion is marvelous," declared an instructor, "because now my students can do anything in French, whereas with the other program, the children might just learn a few basic words." Moreover, immersion students consistently scored higher than others on standardized tests, suggesting that the program had benefits beyond learning a second language and pursuing the lofty goal of saving the state's French heritage.[21]

Meanwhile, the publication of *Cris sur le bayou* enkindled the first Cajun French literary movement. Cajuns wrote the first fiction in their native dialect, such as Antoine Bourque's *Trois saisons* (1988), a collection of short stories comprising a novella, and Richard Guidry's *C'est p'us pareil* (1982), a compendium of autobiographical monographs written, for example, from the perspective of a French-speaking grandmother who laments her inability to communicate with her Americanized grandchildren. But the literary movement expressed itself most saliently through poetry. Notable works in this vein included the anthology *Acadie tropicale* (1981), Carol Doucet's *La charrue* (1982), Zachary Richard's *Voyage de nuit* (1987) and *Faire récolte* (1997), Jean Arceneaux's *Je suis cadien* (1994) and *Suite du loup* (1998), and David Cheramie's *Lait à mère* (1997). At the heart of these works lay the issue of language and the dilemma called "schizophrénie linguistique" by Arceneaux—the feeling of being torn between two languages, one spoken because it was the mother tongue, the other because it was necessary to survive in the modern world. Cajun poetry shared other common themes, such as anger toward Anglo oppression and toward Cajuns who had embraced assimilation. It dwelled on alienation caused by cultural rifts between the poets and the rest of society. Cajun poets also used their writings to motivate other south Louisianians to reclaim their heritage. One literary critic thus described the school as "Marxist" in its demand for radical change and its condemnation of American cultural hegemony.

A Cajun literary genre also developed among authors who wrote largely if not solely in English. These included the poet Darrell Bourque and fiction writers Tim Gautreaux and James Lee Burke. The latter, for example, achieved literary acclaim with his series of Dave Robicheaux detective novels, including *Black Cherry Blues, A Morning for Flamingoes,* and *Heaven's Prisoners.* He twice won the coveted Edgar Award for excellence in mystery writing and had his work adapted for the big screen, with actor Alec Baldwin portraying his rugged Cajun detective. "People from all countries come here specifically for him," noted a bookseller in New Iberia, where Burke and his fictional character resided.

Cajun nonfiction literature came of age during the same period, further reflecting the ethnic group's revitalized sense of pride and empowerment. A few tentative works had appeared during the 1970s, most notably the essay collections *The Culture of Acadiana* (1975) and *The Cajuns: Essays on Their History and Culture* (1978), as well as William Faulkner Rushton's journalistic *The Cajuns: From Acadia to Louisiana* (1979). The field remained virtually untouched, however, until the 1980s, when a new generation of scholars began to publish major works that appealed to academics and lay persons alike. James H. Dormon contributed *The People Called Cajuns* (1983), a primer covering four hundred years of Acadian and Cajun history. Carl A. Brasseaux penned the first academic works of early Cajun history, *The Founding of New Acadia* (1987) and its sequel, *Acadian to Cajun* (1992). Meanwhile, the indefatigable Ancelet published books on Cajun folklife, including *The Makers of Cajun Music* (1984), *Cajun Music: Its Origins and Development* (1989), and *Cajun and Creole Folktales* (1994). He also participated in the compilation of *Cajun Country* (1991), a survey of Cajun folklife and history based on research commissioned by the National Park Service. Other scholars followed, and suddenly no Cajun-related topic seemed too obscure for examination, from the depiction of Cajuns in books and movies to the role of the crawfish as a symbol of ethnic pride to the intricacies of social networks in south Louisiana neighborhoods.

At the same time, a Cajun visual arts scene developed in south Louisiana. Filmmaker Glen Pitre of Cut Off graduated from Harvard University and returned to his homeland to create several acclaimed dramatic and documentary films. These included *Good for What Ails You* (with Nicole Falgoust, 1998), which examined the *traiteurs* (faith healers) of south Louisiana. His most notable work, however, was the full-length motion picture *Belizaire the Cajun* (1986), which revolved around conflict between Cajuns and Anglo-Americans. Filmmaker Pat Mire of Eunice also made documentaries that examined present-day rural Cajuns, such as *Dance for a Chicken* (1993), about rural Mardi Gras traditions. Like Pitre, Mire released a full-length motion picture, *Dirty Rice* (1997), about a white-collar Cajun who returned from the big city to reclaim his heritage. Non-Cajun filmmakers also contributed important works, such as the music documentary *J'ai été au bal*, released in 1989 by renowned producers Les Blank and Chris Strachwitz.

Other visual artists, Cajun and non-Cajun, focused on south Louisiana culture. Greg Guirard documented south Louisiana swamp life in photography books such as *Cajun Families of the Atchafalaya* (1989). Elemore Morgan Jr. photographed Cajuns and contributed images for *The Makers of Cajun Music*. Philip Gould, a transplant from California, settled in Acadiana, photographed its people, and displayed his images in art books, including *Les cadiens d'asteur: Today's Cajuns* (1980) and *Cajun and Zydeco Music* (1992). Lafayette native Robert Dafford painted huge murals depicting the Acadians' expulsion and arrival in Louisiana and even the Americanization and commercial exploitation of their present-day descendants. Francis X. Pavy used symbolic imagery in his colorful paintings to reflect his heritage. Meanwhile, Floyd Sonnier continued to create his pen-and-ink drawings of rural Cajuns, while George Rodrigue turned his murky paintings of moss-draped live oaks into an international phenomenon by adding a strange yellow-eyed, blue-haired dog to his canvases.

The now famous Blue Dog originated when Rodrigue illustrated a book of Cajun ghost stories and transformed the likeness of a pet terrier-spaniel into a *loupgarou*, or werewolf in local folklore. Intrigued by the image, Rodrigue painted it repeatedly until he perfected its haunting, mesmeric stare. Displayed in his New Orleans gallery, the Blue Dog paintings quickly became as chic as Paul Prudhomme's blackened redfish, fetching six-figure price tags, attracting buyers such as Tom Brokaw and Whoopi Goldberg, and appearing in marketing campaigns for Absolut vodka and Xerox printers. According to some sources, Rodrigue's creation eventually lent itself to the

U.S. political lexicon, inspiring the term *Blue Dog Democrat* to describe con-servative party members who often supported Republican legislation. "It's not a dog anymore," explained the artist. "The image has evolved into the abstract; it's an object, a spirit, an entity that is my life."[22]

As in the late 1960s and early 1970s, however, Cajun music most embod-ied Cajun pride and empowerment. Veteran musicians such as Dewey Balfa, Nathan Abshire, and Dennis McGee continued to perform at dance halls, fes-tivals, and workshops into their twilight years, but by the early 1990s most of them had died, including Balfa. Fortunately, these musicians had conveyed their legacy to a younger generation, including Bruce Daigrepont, Wayne Toups, Zachary Richard, and Michael Doucet, who typified his contempo-raries by pushing the boundaries of Cajun music. As a founding member of the groups Coteau and Cajun Brew, Doucet mixed Cajun music with rock, blues, jazz, and even medieval styles, forms he continued to explore with his most popular group, BeauSoleil. Like Richard and other young musicians, Doucet attracted a youthful audience and kept the genre relevant in a rapidly changing world. "We turned young people on to what Cajun music could be," he observed. Those young people included the next generation of Cajun musicians, including Steve Riley and the Mamou Playboys, the similarly named Mamou, and Balfa Toujours, led by Dewey Balfa's daughter, Christine. Behind them came an even younger generation of performers, such as the all-child group La Bande Feufollet, as well as Hunter Hayes, who as a preschool-er in the 1990s amazed audiences with his mastery of the accordion.[23]

With the *fais do-do* extinct and most of the old rural nightclubs no longer standing, new venues sprang up to meet the growing demand for Cajun music. These included the *Rendez-Vous des Cajuns* weekly radio program, recorded before a live audience, and restaurants such as Randol's, Prejean's, and Mulate's, which combined Cajun food, music, and dance into a single experience. New celebrations like Festival International de Louisiane and especially Festivals Acadiens (which grew out of the milestone Tribute to Cajun Music) also provided forums for Cajun music. Radio and television stations served the same function. In the early 1980s, for example, USL's radio station, KRVS, changed from a rock format to one featuring cultural and ethnic music, including Cajun music with French-speaking deejays. Eventually, a half-dozen radio stations in central Acadiana offered at least a few hours of Cajun music weekly. At the same time, KADN-TV 15 in Lafayette aired *Laissez les Bons Temps Rouler,* a weekend Cajun music program reminiscent of earlier live television shows, while KLFY-TV 10 continued to feature Cajun music videos on its early morning *Passe Partout* program, a south Louisiana institution.[24]

Inspired by Cajun music's revival, enthusiasts formed the Cajun French Music Association, which sought to preserve the genre and to honor its performers. The same period saw the publication of important books about Cajun music. In addition to Ancelet's works, John Broven published *South to Louisiana* (1983), a detailed overview of Cajun music and other south Louisiana genres. Ann Allen Savoy, a respected performer, compiled *Cajun Music: A Reflection of a People* (1984), a collection of interviews, discographies, and sheet music, while another musician, Raymond E. François, issued *Yé yaille, chère!* (1990), an encyclopedic sheet music collection. Swamp pop musician Johnnie Allan published *Memories* (1988), a pictorial history containing hundreds of vintage music-related photographs. Cajun music also began to appear on the new medium of compact disc, issued not only by such local labels as Goldband, La Louisianne, Lanor, and Swallow but on larger labels, including Arhoolie, Rhino, and Rounder.[25]

Just as south Louisiana's cuisine became popular across the nation beginning in the 1980s, so did its music, helping to fuel the period's Cajun craze. The genre was especially popular on the East and West Coasts: from San Diego to Seattle and from Washington, D.C., to Boston, public radio stations, folk festivals, and nightclubs offered the sound alongside blues and other "root" genres, including Cajun music's black Creole sister genre, zydeco. So popular did Cajun music and dance become outside its homeland that country star Mary Chapin Carpenter immortalized the phenomenon in her Grammy-winning hit "Down at the Twist & Shout," named after a Washington, D.C., area nightclub (actually an American Legion hall) that sponsored monthly Cajun dances. "Wanna dance to a band from *Louisiane* tonight," sang Carpenter, accompanied by members of BeauSoleil, which itself won a Grammy in 1998 for its album *L'amour ou la folie.*[26]

A parallel cult following took shape overseas, particularly in Britain and northern Europe. British fans, for example, purchased imported Cajun music licensed to overseas labels including Ace and Zane and attended events such as the North Cornwall Cajun and Zydeco Festival, the Mid-Wales Cajun Zydeco Day, and the London International Cajun Music Festival. They published fan newsletters such as the *Cajun Users Manual* and the *Cajun Times* and established appreciation societies, including the Joli Catin Cajun Club in Exeter, the Oxford Cajun Club, and London's Filé Gumbo Cajun Music Club. They even formed their own Cajun bands, like the Balham Alligators, the Bearcat Cajun Playboys, and Andouille Louis and the Cajun Comets. "This is something the Louisiana Cajuns don't understand," a British fan noted. "They are always astonished at the scale of the enthusiasm here." More than one south Louisianian has noted the irony of Cajun music's popularity among the British, whose forebears, after all, expelled the Cajuns' ancestors from Nova Scotia.[27]

Cajun pride and empowerment expressed itself not only through a burgeoning literary, artistic, and music scene. It also evinced itself through legal and political activism that resembled 1960s militancy. This activism resulted in the federal government's official recognition of the Cajuns as a minority group through the landmark 1980 lawsuit *Roach v. Dresser Industrial Valve and Instrument Division.* The events that sparked this suit occurred four years earlier, when Calvin Joseph Roach, a World War II veteran born in the small Acadia Parish town of Mire and at the time a mechanical engineer in central Louisiana, attended a business meeting concerning the suspected theft of company property by fellow employees. During the meeting, two of Roach's superiors, both transplants to Louisiana, allegedly blamed the thefts on "cheap crooked coonasses" who were "unreliable" and "no good." "Bear in mind that this was done in my presence," Roach later pointed out, "they fully being aware that I was a Cajun," for Roach often spoke of his ethnicity at work. (His surname was originally spelled *Roche,* in the French manner, and his ancestry included Legers and Quebodeauxs, both of which are common Cajun surnames. In addition, French was the only language Roach knew until he attended school at age six.)

The situation degenerated when a supervisor turned to Roach at the same meeting and inquired, "Hey, Roach, you're one of them coonasses. How do you feel?" Roach testified, "I was so frigging stunned, I couldn't say anything. . . . I never expected to be the victim, and I said, 'Now wait awhile. . . . What you're doing is wrong.'" Roach suggested that his superiors remedy the theft problem without resorting to ethnic slurs, stereotypes, and groundless accusations. Later, he privately told one of the supervisors that "I was not a coonass and I was a damned proud Cajun and I didn't appreciate anybody, including himself, calling me a coonass."

A few months later Roach was fired, ostensibly because of unacceptable job performance, but he had no doubt about the actual reason for his termination. "I was fired because I, as a Cajun, took up for the Cajuns," Roach asserted. "Because I took the stand that I did, [because] I was trying to protect what they consider inferior second-class citizens . . . they chose to relieve me."

When Roach sued his former employer, Jimmy Domengeaux and Dean Thomas Arceneaux offered their support, countering the defendant's claim that the Equal Employment Opportunity Act of 1964 did not protect Cajuns because their ancestral homeland, Acadia, had never been an independent nation and thus could not have produced a bona fide minority. The judge, however, sided with Roach, declaring that Cajuns were indeed a minority and that the same antidiscrimination laws that applied to other ethnic groups also applied to them. As the judge ruled, "We conclude that plaintiff is protected by Title VII's ban on national origin discrimination" as found in the Civil Rights Act of 1964. Furthermore, the judge asserted, "By affording coverage under the 'national origin' clause of Title VII [the Cajun] is afforded no special privilege. He is given only the same protection as those with English, Spanish, French, Iranian, Czechoslovakian, Portuguese, Polish, Mexican, Italian, Irish, et al., ancestors." Before the case advanced to its next phase, however, Roach settled out of court and quietly disappeared from public. Regardless, *Roach v. Dresser* confirmed the Cajuns as a federally recognized ethnic group and reinforced the perception that *coonass* was an offensive term. Moreover, the case showed that Cajuns could stand up against and defeat Anglo-Saxonism, even when it was institutionalized in corporate America and defended by expensive Washington attorneys.[28]

The *Roach* decision inspired a subsequent effort to convince the state of Louisiana to recognize Cajuns as a minority. Sponsored by south Louisiana legislator Raymond "LaLa" Lalonde, the bill attracted national attention, but it encountered strong local resistance from black legislators who opposed sharing state affirmative action benefits with a group that was hardly an oppressed minority in its own homeland. "In what way have you been dis-criminated against?" demanded a black representative from New Orleans. Governor Buddy Roemer, an Anglo-American from north Louisiana, con-curred with the state's Black Caucus, promising to veto the "dysfunctional" bill. Lacking the required support for passage, Lalonde and his colleagues dropped the issue, vowing instead to launch an inquiry into the "plight of the Cajuns" and the culture's value to state tourism.[29]

Despite this setback, the *Roach* case probably influenced the U.S. Census Bureau's decision to include Cajuns for the first time among the various ancestry groups it would tally during the next census year. In addition, the case no doubt inspired Domengeaux to lobby state politicians to condemn the word *coonass,* another example of the new political and legal militancy. As early as 1974 legislators had discouraged the word's use in a roundabout way by identifying *Cajun* and *Acadian* as the only acceptable labels for the ethnic group. Urged by Domengeaux, however, State Senators Allen Bares, Armand Brinkhaus, and Ned Randolph introduced a more detailed, more assertive resolution in 1981 that explicitly condemned *coonass* as "offensive, vulgar, and obscene."

The resolution particularly targeted commercial items that used the con-troversial word, including bumper stickers, T-shirts, postcards, license plates, and whiskey shot glasses. "Eleven such items are sold in the gift shop atop the state capitol," complained Bares, who scorned *coonass* as a "nasty word." Not everyone agreed: a New Iberia legislator criticized the resolution as "stupid," while a straw poll by the *Daily Iberian* indicated that nearly 60 percent of local citizens opposed the term's condemnation. The resolution passed nonethe-less, but contrary to popular belief it did not ban the term or make its use ille-gal in Louisiana. By condemning the word, however, the legislature did pro-vide activists with a new moral weapon in their campaign to stamp out what they considered the supreme ethnic slur against the Cajun people.[30]

Domengeaux further demonstrated the new political and legal militancy when in 1983 he crusaded against Gulf Oil for distributing a promotional plastic cup that depicted the "Crawgator," a cartoon swamp-dwelling crea-ture from whose eggs sprang the Cajun people, or so claimed the cup's nar-rative. Domengeaux decried the cups as "childish, juvenile, and ridiculous." Others agreed, including Lafayette's *Daily Advertiser,* which berated the item as an "inane piece of stupidity," a "merchandising scam," and an "ill-conceived dollar-grabbing gimmick." Gulf finally withdrew the promotional cups, possibly in part because Domengeaux, ever the wily attorney, threatened to file a class-action lawsuit against the corporation demanding ten thousand dollars in reparations for every Cajun man, woman, and child.[31]

The Crawgator affair marked Domengeaux's last public controversy, as declining health robbed him of his characteristic vigor. Knowing the end approached, admirers overlooked Domengeaux's occasional foibles and heaped awards on the aging cultural activist. LSU bestowed on him an honorary doctorate. Governor Edwin Edwards, serving his third term as Louisiana's chief executive, declared a statewide "Jimmy Domengeaux Day." France declared him a commander of the Order of the Legion of Honor, its highest civilian award, while Belgium appointed him to its Order of the Crown. Six months later, Domengeaux died at age eighty-one, having dedicated the last two decades of his life to CODOFIL and its aim of making Louisiana a bilingual state.[32]

CODOFIL's chairmanship passed to Domengeaux's handpicked successor, John Bertrand, whose subtle management style contrasted sharply with his mentor's flamboyancy and outspokenness. According to Gustin, Bertrand steered through several reforms during his six-year tenure. For example, he convinced the state Board of Elementary and Secondary Education to require all public schools to offer language programs between fourth and eighth grades. At the same time, he transferred control of these programs from CODOFIL to local administrators, a move that furthered the organization's goals by placating educators who had resented CODOFIL's past omnipotency. School boards could now choose to take advantage of CODOFIL's programs or to devise their own, and they could offer other languages, not merely French, to fulfill state requirements. Bertrand also expanded French Immersion programs and appointed Earlene Broussard as CODOFIL's executive director, the first grassroots Cajun activist to hold the position. Like Richard Guidry's earlier appointment as manager of Louisiana's bilingual education programs, Broussard's hiring made the French-preservation movement more appealing to ordinary Cajuns.

In 1994 Bertrand handed over CODOFIL to a young Lafayette attorney named Warren A. Perrin. Born in rural Vermilion Parish to a working-class family, Perrin had expressed little interest in his heritage until the late 1980s, when a national event converted him into a militant cultural activist. That event was the passage of the Civil Liberties Act of 1988, which apologized for America's internment of about 120,000 U.S. citizens and resident aliens of Japanese ancestry during World War II. When Perrin tried to explain the internment to his six-year-old son by comparing it to the Acadians' expulsion, the son replied, "You mean, our ancestors were criminals?" The poignant question struck Perrin, moving him to research the expulsion, which he found not only had been illegal according to international law of the period but had never been repealed, meaning that Cajun tourists in Canada were technically defying a centuries-old military edict and were subject to prosecution. "We can't close that chapter of our history with this hanging over us," Perrin explained in 1995, "or we will live in exile forever."

Declaring the expulsion an overt case of "ethnic cleansing," Perrin used his legal skills to rectify a historical wrong: on behalf of the roughly one million living Acadian descendants in south Louisiana, Canada, and elsewhere, he prepared a class-action lawsuit titled *Warren A. Perrin et al. v. Great Britain et al.* Known by supporters simply as "the petition," the suit called on the British government to acknowledge the expulsion and its criminality under English and international law, to annul the expulsion order, to sponsor a formal inquiry into the circumstances of the tragedy, and to make a goodwill gesture to the Acadian people, such as erecting a monument or funding an academic chair. Perrin also required the British government to apologize for loss of human life and property. Because statutes of limitations did not apply to genocide, murder, or crimes against humanity, Perrin refrained from actually filing his petition, preferring instead to resolve the issue amicably outside of court. If the British ultimately refused to satisfy his demands, however, Perrin vowed publicly to "sue the hell out of the queen of England." He hinted about venues in which he might file his petition: a U.S. Federal District Court, the European Court of Human Rights, the United Nations International War Crimes Tribunal.

Inspired by Perrin's ardent ethnic pride and sense of empowerment, the Louisiana state legislature approved the petition, dispatching an official delegate to London in 1994 to hand deliver the document to British Prime Minister John Major. (Perrin had earlier sent the document to Prime Minister Margaret Thatcher and Queen Elizabeth II.) "We would see little value in resurrecting debate on an issue which is best seen in an historical perspective," responded a British diplomat. Despite the petition's cool reception at 10 Downing Street and Buckingham Palace, Perrin pressed forward, lecturing about his cause to sympathetic audiences in Louisiana, French Canada, Belgium, and France. He even received unsolicited support from Sinn Fein, the political arm of the Irish Republican Army, which for decades had battled the British in Northern Ireland.

Fluent in English and French, the dapper Perrin attracted media attention worldwide. The *Los Angeles Times, Montreal La presse, London Times, Paris Le monde,* and even the *Hanoi Le courrier du Vietnam* all mentioned his crusade, as did NPR, CBS, the Canadian Broadcasting Corporation, and BBC Radio. "The One-Man Acadian Liberation Front," one newspaper dubbed him. "Cajun Activist Girds for Battle," reported another, "A Cajun vs. the Brits." Perrin's cause received further media attention when he orchestrated a mock trial; unsurprisingly, the judge, longtime CODOFIL supporter Allen Babineaux, ruled that Perrin's case exhibited sufficient merit to proceed to an actual court of law. "The Queen on Trial," announced a south Louisiana newspaper, "Perrin Tells England to Stop Being a Bully."

Meanwhile, Perrin found inspiration in apologies and statements of reconciliation issued by Britain to other groups: to aboriginal Maori tribesmen of New Zealand for the confiscation of their lands in the mid–nineteenth century; to the people of Ireland for England's lack of assistance during the 1840s potato famine; to the people of India for the killing of nearly four hundred civilians by British soldiers in 1919; to the people of Dresden for its bombing during World War II. These precedents energized Perrin, even as British diplomats refused to acknowledge ongoing negotiations with the tenacious attorney.

Perrin's campaign quickly elevated him to the pantheon of leading Cajun activists, a position he further secured when he founded the Acadian Museum in Erath and its support organization, the Acadian Heritage and Culture Foundation. In 1994 he accepted Governor Edwards's invitation to succeed Bertrand as head of CODOFIL, a position that permitted Perrin not only to advance his petition but also to steer the organization in a new direction. He pushed CODOFIL to become more involved in Louisiana's economic development, marketing the state's French heritage to tourists and forging business alliances with French-speaking regions. More importantly, he sought to improve CODOFIL's image by making it more grassroots in character. Perrin envisioned a "silent army" of ordinary Cajuns, a nebulous "underground" network of cultural activists. This network, however, would include a south Louisiana ethnic group previously overlooked by CODOFIL, blacks of French-speaking heritage, otherwise known as Creoles, who had only recently founded their own preservation group, CREOLE Inc.

Although he made CODOFIL more democratic and more accessible to the general public, Perrin continued some of Domengeaux's established policies, such as promoting French Immersion and using the organization as a vocal antidefamation league. Under CODOFIL's aegis, for example, he relentlessly discouraged the use of *coonass,* ferreting out businesses and media sources that employed the word. Perpetrators inevitably received a three-page legalese "complaint" from Perrin stating that many Cajuns regarded *coonass* as derogatory, that the state had condemned the word, and that its continued use "would be a violation of applicable federal and state laws," implying a threat of civil rights litigation.

Like Domengeaux, Perrin battled organizations and individuals who made overt anti-Cajun statements. He extracted an apology from the Cambridge, Massachusetts, police department in 1999 after one of its officers asserted that Cajuns were immune to pepper spray because they, like Mexican-Americans and other ethnic groups that consumed spicy cuisine, had built up a tolerance to the sting of pepper resin. "Should you fail to apologize to our people," warned Perrin, "I will make appropriate recommendations to see to it that legal remedies . . . are utilized to insure the restoration of our good name."

Perrin also grappled with the national trend called political correctness when a Lafayette black activist group called the Un-Cajun Committee zealously protested the use of *Cajun* as a blanket term for south Louisiana culture. It even derided the term *Ragin' Cajun* because *ragin'* in reverse spelled *nigar,* implying "nigger," and the committee joined the Nation of Islam in protesting the name of Lafayette's civic arena, the Cajundome. "I'm not a Cajun," asserted one of the group's leaders. "I'm all African descent, and I'm insulted." Although the committee stated that it was not anti-Cajun, "just un-Cajun," it nonetheless proclaimed that "a cultural war has been declared on us" and accused the Cajun people of "genocide" for conspiring to deny blacks proper credit for their contributions to south Louisiana culture—a charge that prompted a swift but diplomatic reply from Perrin on behalf of all

Cajuns. "My words are unable to adequately express the disappointment which I feel," he wrote to the committee, adding, "Let us continue to strive to find ways of building our ethnic pride together and, thereby, fostering hope for all of our descendants."

In addition, Perrin reacted to the English-only movement that reasserted itself during the Reagan and Bush administrations. A reaction by WASPs against the multiculturalism of the 1960s and 1970s, this neonativist trend culminated in the 1990s when conservatives, led by activist politicians such as Newt Gingrich, gained control of Congress. "We must stop the practice of multilingual education," declared Republican presidential candidate and senator Bob Dole in 1995, "as a means of instilling ethnic pride or as a therapy for low self-esteem." Viewing such statements as grave threats to French education in Louisiana, Perrin soberly responded, "Instead of striving for English-only, Senator Dole should encourage this nation to improve our deplorably weak foreign-language skills in order to provide our children with the opportunity to compete with other countries . . . in the twenty-first century." Ironically, Perrin encountered opposition in his own backyard from some heavily Americanized south Louisianians. Congressman Billy Tauzin of Lafourche Parish not only voted for the federal English-only bill (strangely labeled the "English Language Empowerment Act") but cosponsored it. Around the same time, Louisiana state representative Robert Marionneaux Jr. of Pointe Coupée Parish proposed a bill to make English the official language of Louisiana. "Hopefully," Perrin wrote the legislator, "you will see fit to never resurrect such a terrible idea and, in the future, join with us to promote our unique heritage and culture."[33]

While Perrin helped to reinvigorate the Cajun pride movement through his petition and his CODOFIL activities, other factors also reenergized the ethnic group as it neared the end of the century. Zachary Richard founded Action Cadienne (Cajun Action), an organization more radical than CODOFIL in its efforts to save French in Louisiana. Its symbol, a fierce rooster with talons poised to attack, conveyed the group's militancy by evoking Acadiana's rural cockfighting tradition. "Nous réclamons l'immersion française et l'éducation bilingue pour chaque étudiant le désirant," it declared in its manifesto. "We demand that French immersion and bilingual education be made available to every student who desires to participate in one of these programs." Other, similar groups sprang up to support French

Immersion, including Les Amis d'Immersion (Friends of Immersion), Les Partenaires du Français (Partners of French), and the Consortium of French Immersion in Louisiana.[34]

During the same period, students at LSU founded a Cajun Student Association, which they modeled on a similar group established by high school students in Lafayette. The university itself developed a Cajun studies minor through its Department of French and Italian, offering language, linguistics, and cultural courses instructed by veteran activists Earlene Broussard and Amanda LaFleur. Not to be outdone, USL (soon renamed the University of Louisiana at Lafayette) established North America's first doctoral program in francophone studies. In the late 1990s it graduated its first students from the program, one of whom was grassroots Cajun activist and poet David Cheramie, chosen as Perrin's executive director at CODOFIL. Meanwhile, civic leaders and scholars established the Acadian Memorial in St. Martinville. This monument featured a Robert Dafford mural depicting the arrival of Acadian exiles in Louisiana, a "wall of names" identifying all known exiles who settled in the colony, and a research center designed to provide information on all aspects of Acadian/Cajun life to academics and the general public.[35]

Cajuns closed out the century with a two-week celebration that reflected their revitalized ethnic pride and empowerment: the Congrès Mondial Acadien, presided over by attorney and businessman Brian Comeaux of Lafayette. A sequel to the first Congrès, which had occurred five years earlier in Moncton, New Brunswick, the Congrès of 1999 took place across south Louisiana as part of the year-long statewide FrancoFête celebration, which marked the tricentennial of Louisiana's founding as a French colony. Just as an estimated five thousand Cajuns had made the trek to Canada for the emotional 1994 Congrès, so thousands of French-Canadians now journeyed to Louisiana to attend family reunions, festivals, dramatic presentations, genealogical symposiums, academic conferences, and town twinnings (*jumelages*). The family reunions formed the centerpiece of the Congrès, as hundreds of Broussards, Heberts, Guidrys, LeBlancs, Trahans, and other families gathered to celebrate their common heritage.[36]

Ultimately, most Cajuns did not attend the Congrès or belong to CODOFIL and other cultural preservation groups. They did not speak French, did not associate with activists at the heart of the pride and empowerment movement, or send their children to French Immersion schools. Instead, they focused on their everyday lives, working as doctors, lawyers, bankers, teachers, plumbers, electricians, welders, and any number of other modern, mainstream occupations. They shopped at Wal-Mart, K-Mart, and Winn Dixie; bought Coca-Cola, Pop Tarts, and Campbell's soup with Visas or MasterCards; and drove to suburban homes in SUVs or minivans made in Detroit, Korea, Japan, or Germany. They attended their children's soccer and baseball games; mowed their lawns on weekends; watched CNN on cable TV or satellite dishes; paid their monthly house, car, and insurance notes; and kept track of their 401(k) investments.

While acknowledging their ethnicity, Cajuns embraced their American nationality, as demonstrated during the aftermath of the September 11, 2001, terrorist attacks on the World Trade Center in New York City and the Pentagon near Washington, D.C. South Louisianians joined the nation in mourning the tragedy and showed their patriotism by exhibiting red, white, and blue bumper stickers, ribbons, T-shirts, and yard signs. And they flew thousands of American flags from their homes, businesses, and automobiles, in a display of Old Glory unrivaled since World War II. "From the Midwest to Cajun Country," reported the Associated Press nationally, "stores . . . were selling out of flags." A Lafayette merchant noted only days after the attack, "It's way beyond Desert Storm. . . . A three-month supply of flags sold out in a dozen hours." Meanwhile, artist George Rodrigue created one of his famous Blue Dog paintings to commemorate the disaster, but this canine glowed starkly white, "drained by the shock and grief," and was flanked by an American flag instead of a murky live oak. "I am proud to be from the United States of America," proclaimed the artist, who sold prints of the image to support the Red Cross. "It is our spirit, strong in the symbol of our flag, which will mend our broken hearts."[37]

As a team of scholars noted about Cajuns near the dawn of the twenty-first century, "They are in many ways just like their Anglo-American neighbors."[38]

CONCLUSION

Along with the expulsion from Nova Scotia and the Civil War, the last sixty years of the twentieth century represented one of the most crucial periods in Cajun history. During this time, the ethnic group, like other American minorities, experienced a fundamental change in character—one that actually redefined the meaning of *Cajun*. The term ceased to describe a mainly French-speaking, nonmaterialistic, impoverished people on the fringe of American society and instead referred to a largely English-speaking, consumer-oriented, middle-class community whose members closely resembled mainstream Americans. Although Americanization was compulsory during wartime and on school grounds, most Cajuns voluntarily embraced Anglo-American values and customs. Similar trends have been examined among blacks, Hispanics, American Indians, and other ethnic groups, all of which have moved toward the mainstream in recent decades.

Like these minorities, the Cajuns have entered the twenty-first century transformed yet retaining their core identity. They have not been swallowed up, for example, by the coming of the Information Age: on the contrary, in typical fashion they have adapted themselves to the digital revolution, creating

CD-ROMs as well as Internet Web sites and discussion groups dedicated to preserving their history and culture. Entering the term *Cajun* on one popular Internet search engine resulted in about 588,000 "hits" (positive responses), reflecting a growing Cajun presence on the Internet. The creation of this virtual Cajun community prompted one historian to coin the term *Cybercajun* to describe the inhabitants of this "Cyberacadiana." "They threw us out of Nova Scotia," one Cybercajun proclaimed on his Web site, "and I'll be damned if they throw us off the Internet."[1]

Cajuns have further demonstrated their ability to adapt to the modern world by pursuing high-tech careers. A few Cajuns, for example, became veritable rocket scientists, among them J. G. Thibodaux. Born in a lumber camp in the Atchafalaya swamp, he helped to develop the Nike-Cajun rocket in the 1950s, whose second stage, a sounding missile used for testing the upper atmosphere, was named in honor of his ancestry. He went on to serve as chief of the Propulsion and Power Division at Johnson Space Center, assisting NASA with the Apollo moon missions and later with the space shuttle.

While Cajuns such as Thibodaux helped to explore outer space, others explored inner space, including John P. Doucet, a molecular geneticist at Nicholls State University. Using new technologies, Doucet and other scientists studied genetic diseases that affected Cajuns more prevalently than the general population. These ailments included Friedreich's ataxia, Tay-Sachs disease, and Usher syndrome. Interest in this new scientific field led to the founding of the Center for Acadiana Genetics and Hereditary Health Care at the Louisiana State University Health Sciences Center in New Orleans as well as to DNA research at Tulane University that uncovered a common Cajun genotype, further evidence that Cajuns are indeed a bona fide ethnic group, as proclaimed by the 1980 lawsuit *Roach v. Dresser.*[2]

Cajuns now occupy positions in practically every field of human endeavor. Some have even achieved fame outside Louisiana, including chef Paul Prudhomme, painter George Rodrigue, musicians Zachary Richard and Sammy Kershaw, U.S. Senator John Breaux, human rights activist Sister Helen Prejean, baseball pitcher Ron Guidry, football quarterback Bobby Hebert, and model/actress Ali Landry. While these Cajuns have become known around the world, ordinary Cajuns have joined the international movement toward globalism. This trend is shown not only in the appeal of

Cajun food and music outside the United States but also in the efforts of Cajun entrepreneurs to seek out global markets and economic partnerships. Ideas originally put forward in the early 1970s by The International Relations Association of Acadiana have finally been realized by Le Centre International de Lafayette, a global trade development agency founded by Lafayette's city-parish government in 1990. The agency grew out of the annual Festival International de Louisiane, established in 1987 to celebrate francophone cultures worldwide. Meanwhile, the World Wide Web has further integrated the region into the new global economic and cultural community.[3]

Clearly, Cajuns have found a way to flourish in the modern world—but at what cost? Many of their folk traditions have been lost, are on the verge of disappearing, or have been transformed almost beyond recognition. The most salient example is the French language, which is moribund among younger Cajuns. Yet, as shown, Cajun ethnic pride is soaring, even as the dialect continues to move toward extinction, a trend alarming to most activists. Action Cadienne thus asserts in its manifesto that "it is impossible to conceive of a culture without being able to speak its language," implying that Cajun culture cannot exist without its traditional tongue.[4]

But census statistics, anecdotal evidence, and casual observation indicate that the primary and often sole language of most present-day Cajuns is English. French Immersion schools seem unlikely to reverse this trend, for at present they are not generating the numbers of young French speakers needed to save the dialect: only 2,058 students were enrolled in immersion programs during the 1998–99 school year, barely more than .25 percent of the entire student population. Furthermore, not all these students were Cajuns, and the French they learned was not necessarily that of their ancestors. Ultimately, only about 3 percent of Cajuns born after 1980 speak French as their first language, an astounding 95 percent decline from the World War II era. Even when youths who speak the dialect as a second language are included, the probable estimate hardly approaches the critical mass of 20 percent required for linguistic survival according to sociologists who have examined language patterns among French minorities in Anglo-dominated Canada. Unless a linguistic revolution occurs, Cajun French will cease to exist as a means of everyday communication in south Louisiana.[5]

In coming decades Cajuns will have to grapple with the difficult question, "Can an ethnic group survive without its traditional dialect?" Some seem to think so; as noted Cajun genealogist Tim Hebert has remarked, "I unfortunately was never given the chance to learn Cajun French. . . . But that doesn't mean I don't know about and value the rich heritage of the Acadian and Cajun people. I am proud of that heritage and want to help others to learn about it as well." Indeed, evidence suggests that ethnicity can persist independently of language: few black Americans, for example, have knowledge of African languages, yet they clearly maintain a distinct culture. Similarly, few Jews in America speak Hebrew or Yiddish (except on ceremonial occasions), yet they also constitute a distinct culture. Many scholars and activists, however, assert the primacy of language in cultural survival. A vocal minority in south Louisiana concurs, rejecting the notion of linguistic accommodation with mainstream America. "The future of the Cajun people of Louisiana is their children speaking the language of their ancestors," declared Action Cadienne, which regarded Cajun French as the "source of our identity." In other words, the demise of Cajun French would inevitably destroy the entire culture.[6]

It is possible, however, for Cajuns and other ethnic groups who have partly sacrificed their cultural identity to retain a shade of their heritage through symbolic ethnicity, a concept articulated by noted sociologist Herbert J. Gans. Accordingly, ethnic groups across America are replacing actual cultures with symbolic cultures, creating an "ethnicity of last resort." This symbolic ethnicity, Gans contended, permits minorities to feel ethnic by participating in traditional holidays and festivals, by consuming traditional cuisine, and by listening to traditional music, among other activities—none of which require the burden of practicing folkways on a daily basis or of belonging to preservation groups that demand active membership. Ethnicity has become a leisure-time pursuit, observed Gans, rather than a customary way of life.[7]

Symbolic ethnicity is already at work in Acadiana, as demonstrated by new French street signs that adorn many communities: although quaint, their function is primarily symbolic, for most Cajuns do not speak French, and those who do generally cannot read it. Mardi Gras is another example of symbolic ethnicity, allowing Cajuns who usually spurn folk practices to "feel" Cajun, to express their "Cajunness" when convenient, without disrupting their everyday lives. Staged events like folk and music festivals serve the same purpose, as does the consumption of ethnic cuisine, much of which is now available in the frozen food sections of supermarkets. Despite its drawbacks, symbolic ethnicity can allow Cajuns—and members of other ethnic groups—to persist indefinitely, letting them evolve and function as mainstream Americans until they choose to reassert their heritage on special occasions.

Ultimately, the future of the Cajun people remains unclear. They may succumb entirely to the process of Americanization or stagger along indefinitely on the edge of extinction, or they may rebound, flowering in a new Age of Ethnicity. Regardless, the almost instinctive ability of the Cajuns to swim in the mainstream will assure their survival for at least a few more generations. No matter their language or culture or where they find themselves, it is hoped that these new generations will devoutly heed the inscription found beside the Acadian Memorial's eternal flame. "Un peuple sans passé est un peuple sans futur"—A people without a past are a people without a future.[8]

NOTES

INTRODUCTION

1. Carl A. Brasseaux, *Acadian to Cajun: Transformation of a People, 1803–1877* (Jackson: University Press of Mississippi, 1992), 100–103; David C. Edmonds, *Yankee Autumn in Acadiana: A Narrative of the Great Texas Overland Expedition through Southwestern Louisiana, October–December 1863* (Lafayette, La.: Acadiana Press, 1979), 73; Charles Whitehorn Hilton Diary, 30 May 1865, TMs, Manuscripts Collection, Howard-Tilton Memorial Library, Tulane University, New Orleans, La. (hereafter HTML); Charles Dudley Warner, "The Acadian Land," *Harper's New Monthly Magazine*, February 1887, 340.

   The punctuation and spelling of quoted material in the text have occasionally been standardized by the author for clarity.

2. James Crawford, *Bilingual Education: History, Politics, Theory, and Practice*, 3rd ed. (Los Angeles: Bilingual Education Services, 1995), 28, 33; James Crawford, *Hold Your Tongue: Bilingualism and the Politics of "English Only"* (Reading, Mass.: Addison-Wesley, 1992), 57–58, 73, 79, 80–81, 182–83; Roger Daniels, *Coming to America: A History of Immigration and Ethnicity in American Life* (New York: HarperPerennial, 1991), 160–61, 317–18; Joe R. Feagin, *Racial and Ethnic Relations*, 2nd ed. (Englewood Cliffs, N.J.: Prentice-Hall, 1984), 199, 283; Merwyn S. Garbarino, *Native American Heritage*, 2nd ed. (Prospect Heights, Ill.: Waveland Press, 1988), 479–80; Robert Lee Maril, *Poorest of Americans: The Mexican Americans of the Lower Rio Grande Valley of Texas* (Notre Dame, Ind.: University of Notre Dame Press, 1989), 117; Jon Reyhner, "Policies toward American Indian Languages: A Historical Sketch," in *Language Loyalties: A Source Book*

on the Official English Controversy, ed. James Crawford (Chicago: University of Chicago Press, 1992), 44–46; Jon Reyhner and Deborah House, eds., "Native American Student Panel Summary," 1, transcript, National Clearinghouse for Bilingual Education Web site, www.ncbe.gwu.edu, accessed 11 January 2001.

3. Carl Lindahl, "'It's Only Folklore . . .': Folklore and the Historian," *Louisiana History* 26 (spring 1985): 141.

4. Brasseaux, *Acadian to Cajun,* 58, see image of Acadian soldier on picket duty in illustrations section between pages 88 and 89.

5. Lauren C. Post, *Cajun Sketches: From the Prairies of Southwest Louisiana* (Baton Rouge: Louisiana State University Press, 1990), 162; *1940 U.S. Census of Housing, Vol. 1, Data for Small Areas, Pt. 1, United States Summary and Alabama-Nebraska,* table 4, p. 8; table 9, p. 10; table 5, pp. 587–95; table 6, pp. 595–602; Brasseaux, *Acadian to Cajun,* 75.

6. Lewis William Newton, "The Americanization of French Louisiana: A Study of the Process of Adjustment between the French and the Anglo-American Populations of Louisiana, 1803–1860" (Ph.D. diss., University of Chicago, 1929), 9; William Faulkner Rushton, *The Cajuns: From Acadia to Louisiana* (New York: Farrar Straus Giroux, 1979), 5–6.

Despite the title of Newton's dissertation, it did not examine the Americanization of the Cajuns in the twentieth century. Instead, it focused on the Americanization of white French Creoles in antebellum Louisiana.

7. Brasseaux, *Acadian to Cajun,* 100–101.

8. Gerald N. Grob and George Athan Billias, eds., *Interpretations of American History: Patterns and Perspectives,* vol. 1, 6th ed. (New York: Free Press, 1992), 19–22; and Peter Novick, *That Noble Dream: The "Objectivity Question" and the American Historical Profession* (New York: Cambridge University Press, 1993), 469–521.

9. "Only 80,000 Cajuns? There Are that Many Thibodeauxs," editorial, *Lafayette (La.) Daily Advertiser,* 16 August 2001, 2D; Jim Bradshaw, "If You're One of 365,000 Missing Cajuns, Please Send up a Flare," *Daily Advertiser,* 12 August 2001, 3C; "Where Did All the Cajuns Go?" *New Orleans Times-Picayune,* reprinted in *Daily Advertiser,* 20 August 2001, 2C.

Regarding 1990 PUMS used in this study: Statistics were derived from a 5 percent sample of the following Louisiana census areas—00500, 00700, 00800, 00900, 01000, 01100, 01200, 01500, 01700, 01800. These areas covered the entire twenty-two-parish Acadiana region plus twelve non-Acadiana parishes. The inclusion of twelve non-Acadiana parishes probably had a negligible impact on the accuracy of the statistics because the author considered only respondents who identified themselves as Cajuns, and with one exception (Allen Parish) these parishes had only marginal Cajun populations. (The author is indebted to Professor Rogelio Saenz, head of the Department of Sociology at Texas A&M University, for his assistance in compiling, interpreting, and checking data obtained from PUMS.)

CHAPTER 1

1. Liz Hebert, "Baseball, Surfing . . . War: Before the Attack on Pearl Harbor, It Was Sunday as Usual," *Daily Advertiser,* 7 December 1991, B–1, B–3; Amanda Griffin, "Pearl Harbor to Antarctic, 'Frenchy' Was There," *Baton Rouge (La.) Advocate,* 10 May 1993, 1B; "Russell Durio, Son of Sunset Police Chief, 'Missing' from USS *Arizona,*" *Opelousas (La.)*

Daily World, 17 December 1941, 1; "Sunset Youth Missing after Jap Attacks," *Daily Advertiser,* 17 December 1941, 2; "Abbeville Boy Said Missing at Pearl Harbor," *Abbeville (La.) Meridional,* 27 December 1941, 1; "Seaman F. Ducrest Reported Missing," *St. Martinville (La.) Weekly Messenger,* 26 December 1941, 4; Gordon W. Prange, *At Dawn We Slept: The Untold Story of Pearl Harbor* (New York: McGraw-Hill, 1981), 513.

2. Russ Kintzley, "Vermilion Soldier Learns to Speak English to Stay with Outfit That Went to the Pacific Area," *Abbeville Meridional,* 8 September 1945, 3.

3. 1990 PUMS, for Persons.

4. Richard Polenberg, *One Nation Divisible: Class, Race, and Ethnicity in the United States since 1938* (New York: Viking, 1980), 46–49, 54–55; William M. Tuttle Jr., *"Daddy's Gone to War": The Second World War in the Lives of America's Children* (New York: Oxford, 1993), 51, 92; *Harvard Encyclopedia of American Ethnic Groups,* s.v. "American Identity and Americanization," 47; Philip Gleason, "Americans All: World War II and the Shaping of American Identity," *Review of Politics* 43 (October 1981): 511–12, 515–516.

5. 1990 PUMS, for Persons; "Boys Inducted into Service since Jan. 1st Are Listed," *Weekly Messenger,* 3 April 1942, 1; "Selectees Examined Friday at Lafayette Induction Center," *Weekly Messenger,* 27 November 1942, 1; "26 Vermilion Men Inducted in Army," *Abbeville Meridional,* 27 November 1943, 1; "Names Given of Selectees about to Be Inducted," *New Iberia (La.) Weekly Iberian,* 19 February 1942, 4; "Serial Numbers for Fourth Registration Released Here," *Houma (La.) Daily Courier,* 28 May 1942, 1, 2.

Statistics concerning the total number of Cajun GIs who served in World War II are estimates extrapolated primarily from 1990 census data.

6. "3 Sign up for Navy Here Today," *Daily World,* 8 December 1941, 4; "Marines to Seek Men from Iberia," *Weekly Iberian,* 8 January 1942, 3; "Marine Corps Officers to Be Here Jan. 12," *Abbeville Meridional,* 10 January 1942, 1; Booton Herndon, "Capt. Mouton Will Travel Bayous to Recruit Fighters for Marines," *Daily Advertiser,* 1 January 1942, 3; "Last Call for Bayou Battalion U.S. Marine Corps," *Abbeville Meridional,* 24 January 1942, 4.

7. 1990 PUMS, for Persons. Statistics concerning the linguistic traits of Cajun GIs who served in World War II are estimates extrapolated primarily from 1990 census data.

8. "Breaux Bridge Boys Get Nice Write-Up in Carolina Paper," *Weekly Messenger,* 30 January 1942, 3 [reprint from the *Charleston News and Courier*].

9. John Morton Blum, *United Against: American Culture and Society during World War II,* Harmon Memorial Lecture no. 25 (Colorado Springs: U.S. Air Force Academy, 1983), 1, 6–7; John Morton Blum, *V Was for Victory: Politics and American Culture during World War II* (New York: Harcourt Brace Jovanovitch, 1976), 155, 160–66, 184–85, 191, 202–3, 205–6; Daniels, *Coming to America,* 302–3, 316–17; Polenberg, *One Nation Divisible,* 76–78; William M. Simpson, "A Tale Untold? The Alexandria, Louisiana, Lee Street Riot (January 10, 1942)," *Louisiana History* 35 (spring 1994): 133–49; Harvard Sitkoff, *The Struggle for Black Equality, 1954–1992,* rev. ed. (New York: Hill and Wang, 1994), 12.

10. Robin Meche Kube, "Cajun Soldiers during World War II: Reflections on Louisiana's French Language and People," *Louisiana History* 35 (summer 1994): 345, 346, 347; "Patton—Swell; England—Nice; America—the Best Place in the World, LeBlanc Informs Rotary," *Abbeville Meridional,* 24 June 1944, 1.

11. Robert J. LeBlanc, autobiographical sketch, 1994, TMs, 111–54, original in possession of Robert J. LeBlanc, Abbeville, La.; Wallace J. Moulis and Patricia Moulis, "D-Day:

Sam Broussard's Baptism to Combat," *St. Martinville (La.) Teche News*, 23 March 1994, A–7, A–8.

12. "Eulgere Blanchard Writes from Camp," *Weekly Messenger*, 12 June 1942, 4; "LeBlanc, Former Scoutmaster, Writes to Local Troop," *Weekly Messenger*, 1 May 1942, 4; Judy Stanford, "Doing Their Part: Four Sisters from Sunset Answer the Call to Duty during WWII," *Daily Advertiser*, 15 October 1997, 1B.

13. Wallace J. Moulis, autobiographical sketch, 1994, TMs, 1, 2, 3, original in possession of Wallace J. Moulis, Falls Church, Va.; Oscar James Gonzales, "La. Flying Tiger Recalls Dogfights, Camaraderie," *The Advocate*, 4 July 1994, 3B; Michael Martin, "Lafayette 'Ranger' Endured WWII in African, Italy Battles," *The Advocate*, 6 June 1994, 3; Jonas Breaux, "Medal of Honor Winner Had to 'Grow up Fast,'" *Daily Advertiser*, 30 January 1993, 4.

14. I. Bruce Turner, "'Dear Southwesterners': World War II, Southwestern Louisiana Institute, and the Joel L. Fletcher Newsletters," 1996–97, TMs, Southwestern Archives and Manuscripts Collection (hereafter SAMC), University of Louisiana at Lafayette.

15. "Declaration of War Taken Calmly Here," *Weekly Messenger*, 12 December 1941, 1; Ralph R. Bienvenu, "The Pilot Light," column, *Abbeville Meridional*, 13 December 1941, 1.

16. E. B. (Ted) Robert, "Why They Leave the Bayou!" in E. B. (Ted) Robert, *Footnotes Not in the Book: Recollections after Fifty Years in Education and Public Service in Acadiana*, 2nd ed. (Baton Rouge, La.: Claitor's, 1969), 51.

17. "Sheriff Told to Report All Japs in This Parish," *Daily World*, 8 December 1941, 10; "Jeff Davis to Protect Plants and Utilities," *Daily Advertiser*, 12 December 1941, 3; "Police Arrest 3 Suspected Aliens Here Yesterday," *Daily World*, 10 December 1941, 1; "Local Police Busily Searching for Possible Saboteurs; Nab 3 Hoboes," *Daily World*, 14 December 1941, 3; "Sheriff, FBI Plan for Industry Protection," *Weekly Iberian*, 18 December 1941, 1, 8.

18. "Gov. Jones Speaks to Large Gathering at Defense Meeting Here Monday," *Weekly Messenger*, 13 March 1942, 1; "Gov. Jones Urges Americans to Be on the Alert," *Abbeville Meridional*, 14 March 1942, 1.

19. "5503 Iberians Volunteer for Home Defense," *Weekly Iberian*, 25 December 1941, 1; "6500 Register in St. Martin Parish for Civilian Defense," *Weekly Messenger*, 26 December 1941, 1; "Test Blackout Is Declared Success by Officials," *Weekly Messenger*, 18 September 1942, 1.

20. James H. Hughes Jr., "Strange Malady Spread Terror through the Marshlands," *Baton Rouge (La.) Morning Advocate*, 1 October 1961, 1–E.

21. Clay Blair, *Hitler's U-Boat War: The Hunters, 1939–1942* (New York: Random House, 1996), 580, 694–95; "Trawlers Bring up Wreckage in Gulf," *Houma Daily Courier*, 13 May 1942, 1; "29 Survivors of Gulf Torpedoed Vessel Brought to Houma Saturday," *Houma Daily Courier*, 25 May 1942, 1; Lenora Vaughan, "Pecan Island Paragraphs," *Abbeville Meridional*, 14 February 1942, 6; "Subs Sighted in Gulf of Mexico," *Abbeville Meridional*, 31 January 1942, 1; Harry Henderson and Sam Shaw, "Swamp Angels," *Collier's*, 21 October 1944, 22–23, 88; Alan Rider, "Angels of the Swamp," *Retired Officer Magazine*, August 1993, 34, 36.

22. E. A. McIlhenny, Avery Island, La., to Walter S. McIlhenny, San Francisco, Calif., 11 November 1942, TL, McIlhenny Company Archives (hereafter MCA), Avery Island, La.;

Jerry E. Strahan, *Andrew Jackson Higgins and the Boats that Won World War II* (Baton Rouge: Louisiana State University Press, 1994), 128, 133–34; Barry Jean Ancelet, "The Cajun Who Went to Harvard: Identity in the Oral Tradition of South Louisiana," *Journal of Popular Culture* 23 (summer 1989): 109, 110–11.

23. Louisiana Educational Survey Commission, *Louisiana Educational Survey* (Baton Rouge: Louisiana Educational Survey Commission, 1942), vol. 2, sec. 4, pp. 8, 9; Edward J. Kammer, *A Socio-Economic Survey of the Marshdwellers of Four Southeastern Louisiana Parishes*, Catholic University of America Studies in Sociology, vol. 3 (Washington, D.C.: Catholic University of America Press, 1941), 86.

24. Arnold Krammer, *Nazi Prisoners of War in America* (New York: Stein and Day, 1979), vii, xiii; Matthew J. Schott and Rosalind Foley, "Bayou Stalags: German Prisoners of War in Louisiana," 1981, TMs [photocopy], 5, 17, Matthew J. Schott Collection, SAMC; Matthew J. Schott, "Bayou Stalags of the Deep South: The POWs' 'Good War' Providence," 1994, TMs, 243–44, 248, 268, 366, 368, 369, 370, 390, original in possession of Matthew J. Schott, Lafayette, La.; "Beau Soléil Broussard: A Driving Tour," tourism brochure for the town of Broussard, La., ca. 1997; "'Great Nazi Orgy' Was Only Dinner," *Times-Picayune*, 28 December 1943, 2.

25. Raymond A. Mohl, "Cultural Assimilation versus Cultural Pluralism," *The Educational Forum* 45 (March 1981): 327, 329–30; Tuttle, *Daddy's Gone to War*, 93, 112, 115; John E. Coxe, "How Can the State Defend and Preserve Democracy through Education?" in *Education for the Defense and Preservation of the Democratic Way of Life*, ed. E. B. Robert (Baton Rouge: Louisiana State University, 1940), 10; State Department of Education of Louisiana, "Some Efforts of the State Department of Education Relating to National Defense," *Wartime Education in Louisiana Schools*, bulletin 480 (February 1942): 35–44; State Department of Education of Louisiana, "Bibliography," *Wartime Education in Louisiana Schools*, bulletin 496 (December 1942): 10–12, 13, 17.

26. 1990 PUMS, for Persons; "'Lady Who Sings in French' Gathers Louisiana Songs," *Times-Picayune*, 23 March 1941, sec. 2, p. 6.

27. John Higham, *Strangers in the Land: Patterns of American Nativism, 1860–1925*, 2nd. ed. (New Brunswick, N.J.: Rutgers University Press, 1988), 255, 259–60; Barry Jean Ancelet, *Cajun Music: Its Origins and Development* (Lafayette: Center for Louisiana Studies, University of Southwestern Louisiana, 1989), 27; Barry Jean Ancelet, Jay Edwards, and Glen Pitre, *Cajun Country* (Jackson: University Press of Mississippi, 1991), xvi, 157; James H. Dormon, *The People Called Cajuns: An Introduction to an Ethnohistory* (Lafayette: Center for Louisiana Studies, University of Southwestern Louisiana, 1983), 70.

28. "Defense Theme to Be Followed by Girl Scouts," *Daily Advertiser*, 10 December 1941, 9; "Eunice Newsboy Saves His Pennies to Help Red Cross," *Daily World*, 10 December 1941, 1; "FFA, 4-H Youths Doing Their Part," *Daily World*, 19 December 1941, 4; "Mt. Carmel Wins Wastepaper Contest," *Louisiana Education in Wartime*, April 1944, 5; "An Auto-Biography," *Weekly Messenger*, 16 October 1942, 4.

29. "The Bayou French of Louisiana," propaganda article, U.S. Office of War Information, ca. 18 August 1944, TMs, 4, National Archives and Records Administration (hereafter NARA), Washington, D.C.; "Evangeline," U.S. Treasury war bond advertisement, *Abbeville Meridional*, 11 August 1945, 8.

30. Lyle Saxon, Edward Dreyer, and Robert Tallant, comps., *Gumbo Ya-Ya: A Collection of Louisiana Folk Tales* (New York: Bonanza, 1945; reprint, New York: Bonanza, 1988), 202.

31. Ben Kaplan, Herbert Hamilton, and H. A. Wilson, *Under All . . . the Land: A Socio-Economic Study of the Rural Life in Lafayette Parish, Louisiana, 1942* (Lafayette: Southwestern Louisiana Institute, 1942), 11; Advertisement for Dudley J. LeBlanc radio program, *Daily Advertiser,* 16 November 1943, 10; John Broven, *South to Louisiana: The Music of the Cajun Bayous* (Gretna, La.: Pelican, 1983), 22–24; Ann Allen Savoy, comp. and ed., *Cajun Music: A Reflection of a People,* vol. 1 (Eunice, La.: Bluebird, 1984), 114–26. Samples of the Hackberry Ramblers' wartime fan mail are preserved in the Goldband Collection, Southern Historical Collection, University of North Carolina at Chapel Hill.

32. "A Brighter Future Looms as Opelousans Celebrate," *Daily World,* 15 August 1945, 1; "Reactions Vary as War's End Is Announced," *Houma (La.) Courier,* 16 August 1945, 1; "Church Crowded Following Victory Announcement Here," *Weekly Messenger,* 17 August 1945, 1; "Kaplan Citizens Celebrate End of War with Parade and Speaking Wednesday," *Abbeville Meridional,* 25 August 1945, 1.

33. "Receiving *Abbeville Meridional* in Berlin Is Just Like Receiving a Letter from Home, Says Soldier Who Tells of Conditions There," *Abbeville Meridional,* 27 October 1945, 5; "Iberian Saw Historic Surrender in Tokyo Bay, and Now Says He's Ready to Come Home," *Weekly Iberian,* 2 October 1945, 1.

34. 1990 PUMS, for Persons; Report of Death for Houston D. Duhon, Adjutant General's Office, U.S. War Department, Washington, D.C., 13 July 1944, TD, original in possession of U.S. Total Army Personnel Command, Department of the Army, Alexandria, Va.; *Honor Roll of Iberia Parish, Louisiana: Men and Women Serving in the Armed Forces of America, World War II* ([New Iberia, La?]: Teche Papers, 1945; reprint, New Iberia, La.: *Acadiana LifeStyle,* 1993), 2.

Statistics concerning the total number of Cajun GIs who died in World War II are estimates extrapolated primarily from 1990 census data.

CHAPTER 2

1. "Area 'Boning' on Astronomy after Flash of Meteor Bursts in Evangeline Country," *Daily Advertiser,* 17 March 1957, 1; "Area Failed Astronomy Course, Meteorite Brought Wild Rumors," *Lafayette Progress,* 23 March 1957, 1; "End of the World? Space Ship Landing? Oil Explosion? What Did You Think?" *Daily World,* 17 March 1957, 1; "Flaming Meteor Falls near Boat of 3 Baldwinites at Marone Pt.," *Franklin (La.) Banner-Tribune,* 19 March 1957, 1; "Meteor Third Seen by Vermilion Man in 75 Years; Area Excited," *Abbeville Meridional,* 21 March 1957, 1, 3; Earl Comeaux, "Les traces de mon boguet" (The Tracks of My Buggy), autobiographical sketch, 1995, TMs, n.p., original in possession of Earl Comeaux, Kaplan, La.

2. Paul Boyer, *By the Bomb's Early Light: American Thought and Culture at the Dawn of the Atomic Age* (New York: Pantheon, 1985), 352–55; James Domengeaux, "From Our Congressman James Domengeaux," *Weekly Messenger,* 17 August 1945, 3.

3. Federal Civil Defense Administration, "Probability of Fallout Debris Deposition," *Civil Defense Technical Bulletin,* June 1957, 1, and enclosed maps for south Louisiana (nos. 8

and 23), on file in Vermilion Parish Office of Emergency Preparedness, Vermilion Parish Courthouse, Abbeville, La.; "LCAFB Stands Where Rice Was Once King," *Lake Charles (La.) American Press*, 23 April 1967 [reprint of 26 September 1956 article], n.p.; "U.S. Nuclear Weapons Accidents: Danger in Our Midst," *Defense Monitor* 10 (1981), 6 (incident no. 15).

4. Louisiana Civil Defense Agency, "Shelter Listings," 11 April 1962, TD, on file in Vermilion Parish Office of Emergency Preparedness.

5. "Civilian Defense Meeting Stresses Preparedness," *Teche News*, 16 May 1957, 1; "Lafayette CD System Held up As Pattern," *Lafayette (La.) Progress*, 20 June 1953, 1; "Kill the Myths," *Daily Advertiser*, 7 January 1951, 20; "Six Survival Secrets for Atomic Attacks," *Daily Advertiser*, 7 January 1951, 20; "Opelousas Set for Raid," *Daily World*, 7 January 1951, 1.

6. Louisiana Civil Defense Agency, "Report of Operation Alert 1961," 31 July 1961, TD, 2, 3, 4, on file in Vermilion Parish Office of Emergency Preparedness; "Trained Defense Policemen Will Be the Key Fighters against Any 'Behind-the-Lines' Enemy If Lake Charles, La., Is Attacked," *Dixie* [publication of *Times-Picayune*], 23 December 1956, 7.

7. 1990 PUMS, for Persons; Harry Choates, "Korea, Here We Come," audio recording, Macy's, ca. 1950.

Statistics concerning the total number of Cajun GIs who served in Korea, the total number who died during the conflict, and their linguistic traits are estimates extrapolated primarily from 1990 census data.

8. Guilda J. Chauvin Sr., Berwick, La., to Edwin E. Willis, Washington, D.C., 10 December 1951, ALS, Edwin E. Willis Collection, SAMC; Thomas N. Richie, Louisiana Civil Defense Agency Regional Representative (Area 6), to Robert J. LeBlanc, Vermilion Parish Civil Defense Director, Abbeville, La., 26 September 1963, TLS, on file in Vermilion Parish Office of Emergency Preparedness.

9. Virginea R. Burguières, "Biographical Sketch," in Glenn R. Conrad, ed., *Creed of a Congressman: F. Edward Hébert of Louisiana*, USL History Series (Lafayette: University of Southwestern Louisiana, 1970), 22; Whittaker Chambers, *Witness* (New York: Random House, 1952), 537; *A Dictionary of Louisiana Biography*, vol. 1, s.v. "Hébert, Felix Edward"; vol. 2, "Willis, Edwin."

10. Adam Fairclough, *Race and Democracy: The Civil Rights Struggle in Louisiana, 1915–1972* (Athens: University of Georgia Press, 1995), 323; Louisiana, Joint Legislative Committee, *Subversion in Racial Unrest: An Outline of a Strategic Weapon to Destroy the Governments of Louisiana and the United States*, pt. 1, proceedings of antisubversive hearings held 6–9 March 1957, Baton Rouge, La., published March 1958, original in the Louisiana State Archives, Baton Rouge; "Subversives Not High Here," *Lafayette Progress*, 10 April 1954, 1; Joel L. Fletcher, "The Acadians of Today," *The Boardman: Official Journal of the Louisiana School Boards Association*, January 1948, 5–6.

11. Joe Choate, *The Best Answer Is America: A Biography of Dr. Alexander Sas-Jaworsky* (New York: Vantage, 1959), 19; Alexander Sas-Jaworsky v. T. W. Padfield, Minutes of Court, Suit Number 24481 (15th Judicial Court, Louisiana, 1964), 4–5, 8–9, 19, 22, 42–44, 46, 48–54, on file in Clerk of Court's Office, Vermilion Parish Courthouse, Abbeville, La.; "Dr. Sas Files $50,000 Suit for Being Called Commie," *Banner-Tribune*, 27 March 1964, 1; Alexander Sas-Jaworsky v. T. W. Padfield, Reason for Ruling (15th

Judicial Court, Louisiana, 1964), 31–32, on file in Clerk of Court's Office, Vermilion Parish Courthouse, Abbeville, La.; Alexander Sas-Jaworsky v. T. W. Padfield, Motion to Dismiss Appeal, Appeal Number 2248 (3rd Circuit Court of Appeal, Louisiana, 1968), 9, on file in Clerk of Court's Office, Vermilion Parish Courthouse, Abbeville, La.

12. "Conformity Rules the Age, Declares Optimist Speaker," *Daily Advertiser,* 2 June 1957, 25.

13. Fairclough, *Race and Democracy,* 323–24.

14. "The Study of French is Patriotic Duty of SLI Students," *Lafayette Progress,* 14 December 1950, 1.

15. T. Lynn Smith and Homer L. Hitt, *The People of Louisiana* (Baton Rouge: Louisiana State University, 1952), 107–8.

16. L. H. Boulet, "Visiting Teacher Work Explained," *Weekly Messenger,* 7 September 1945, 1; "School Attendance Law Emphasized," *Weekly Messenger,* 14 September 1945, 4; Marie D. Eastin, "Catahoula: Beloved Lake" (undergraduate term paper, Southwestern Louisiana Institute, 1960), 33, SAMC.

17. 1990 PUMS, for Persons.

18. "Conformity Rules the Age," 25.

19. Floyd Martin Clay, *Coozan Dudley LeBlanc: From Huey Long to Hadacol* (Gretna, La.: Pelican, 1973), xi, 6, 8–11, 151–58, 164, 165–72, 183–86, 218–19, 239, 240.

20. Carl A. Brasseaux, "Acadian Education: From Cultural Isolation to Mainstream America," in *The Cajuns: Essays on Their History and Culture,* USL History Series no. 11, ed. Glenn R. Conrad (Lafayette: Center for Louisiana Studies, University of Southwestern Louisiana, 1983), 138, 140; "Largest Student Body Enrolls at S.L.I.," *S.L.I. Alumni News,* September 1947, 11, SAMC.

21. Carl A. Brasseaux, *Lafayette: Where Yesterday Meets Today* (Chatsworth, Calif.: Windsor Publications, 1990), 18–19; Donald Winters, "Agriculture in the Post-World War II South," in *The Rural South since World War II,* ed. R. Douglas Hurt (Baton Rouge: Louisiana State University Press, 1998), 11, 24.

22. Eastin, "Catahoula," 16; Kammer, *Socio-Economic Survey of the Marshdwellers,* 86.

23. George Getschow and Thomas Petzinger Jr., "In Louisiana Oil Rush, One Thing Left behind Was Culture of Cajuns," *Wall Street Journal,* 25 October 1984, 1; Jerry Robertson, *Jerry Robertson's Oil Slang* (Evansville, Ind.: Petroleum Publishers, 1954), s.v. "Cajun," "Coonass."

24. *Louisiana Almanac, 1997–98 Edition,* 162; "Black Gold Spurred Amazing Growth of 'Country Town,'" *Daily Advertiser,* 29 December 1949, 1; Robert Distefano, "Oil Center—Symbol of Petroleum—Grew from Turnip Patch into Gigantic Reality," *Daily Advertiser,* 15 October 1956, 1; "Heymann Oil Center Sparks Fabulous Lafayette Growth," *Daily Advertiser,* 18 March 1966, 32–33; Jim Bradshaw, "Oil Center Is Diversifying, but Will Always Be 'the Oil Center,'" *Daily Advertiser,* 6 August 1989, 29; "Lafayette Base for Largest Independent 'Copter Operation," *Daily Advertiser,* 30 January 1959, A–31.

25. "A Tribute to Oil," *Daily Advertiser,* 15 October 1956, 1.

26. Getschow and Petzinger, "One Thing Left behind Was Culture of Cajuns," 1, 28; "Black Gold Spurred Amazing Growth," 1; "Old Master," *Time,* 20 September 1948, 94, 96.

27. Getschow and Petzinger, "One Thing Left behind Was Culture of Cajuns," 28; "Black Gold Spurred Amazing Growth," 1.

28. Statistics about Cajuns in rural and small-town Lafayette Parish in the early 1950s were derived from (chronologically): Mrs. Martin Maloney, Mrs. Jack Dennen, Charlene Walker, and Wanda Scoggins, "Scott—Where the West Begins: A Sociological Survey of Community Life" (undergraduate term paper, Southwestern Louisiana Institute, 1951), Dupré Library, University of Louisiana at Lafayette; Catherine Maloney, Mrs. Robert Longton, Anne Faye Stewart, Louise Bourne, Andre DuBois, Marion Doucet, and Velma Wise, "Broussard: A Sociological Survey of Community Life" (undergraduate term paper, Southwestern Louisiana Institute, 1951), Dupré Library, University of Louisiana at Lafayette; Louise Bourne, Frank Wallace, and Velma Wise, "Duson: A Sociological Survey of Community Life" (undergraduate term paper, Southwestern Louisiana Institute, [1952?]), Dupré Library, University of Louisiana at Lafayette; Louise Bourne, Frank Wallace, and Velma Wise, "Carencro: A Sociological Survey of Community Life" (undergraduate term paper, Southwestern Louisiana Institute, 1953), Dupré Library, University of Louisiana at Lafayette; [No authors listed] "Youngsville: A Sociological Self-Survey of Community Life," (undergraduate term paper, Southwestern Louisiana Institute, 1953), Dupré Library, University of Louisiana at Lafayette.

These surveys were prepared for course credit by undergraduate SLI students. Although probably never intended for scholarly analysis, the surveys appear to have been carefully executed under the close guidance of SLI sociology professors. The subjects questioned were never identified as Cajuns but can be reasonably assumed to be such because only white residents were queried and because surveyors repeatedly referred to their subjects as speaking French or being of French heritage.

Statistics for 1942 were derived from Kaplan et al., *Under All . . . the Land*. Unlike the early 1950s surveys, the 1942 survey queried both white and black families (396 white and 104 black). Again, it is likely that most of the white subjects were Cajuns.

Figures for all dwellings in the twenty-two-parish Acadiana region. *1950 U.S. Census of Housing, Vol. 1, General Characteristics, Pt. 3, Louisiana*, table 26, pp. 43–46; *1960 U.S. Census of Housing, Vol. 1, States and Small Areas, Pt. 4, Louisiana*, table 11, p. 14; table 12, p. 15 (Calcasieu Parish); table 16, p. 27 (Calcasieu Parish); table 28, pp. 56–60; table 30, pp. 66–70; *1960 U.S. Census of Housing, Vol. 1, States and Small Areas, Pt. 1, United States Summary*, table 7, pp. 28, 30.

29. "Age of Electricity Comes to State's 'Last Frontier,'" *Lafayette Progress*, 29 May 1954, 1; [Margret Dixon], "Pecan Island Gets a Taste of Civilization," 3 August 1952, unidentified source, Mavel Veazey Conner Scrapbook, Vermilion Parish Police Jury, Abbeville, La. (hereafter MVCS); "Southwest Louisiana Electric Co-op. Comes to 'Louisiana's Last Frontier' Pecan Island," *Rural Power Magazine*, February 1954, MVCS; Iola P. Huger, "Along the Rural Lines," entry for 26 June 1957, unidentified source, MVCS; Nick Cariello, "Pecan Island—Oasis of Quiet Far from Modern, Madding Crowd," *Daily Advertiser*, 6 December 1953, 7.

30. Eastin, "Catahoula," 13; television listings, *Daily Advertiser*, 1 July 1955, 20; 7 October 1955, 20; 11 October 1955, 24; *1950 U.S. Census of Housing, Vol. 1, General Characteristics, Pt. 3, Louisiana*, table 27, pp. 47–50; *1960 U.S. Census of Housing, Vol. 1, States and Small Areas, Pt. 4, Louisiana*, table 16, p. 27 (Calcasieu Parish); table 30, pp. 66–70; Bart Andrews, *The 'I Love Lucy' Book* (Garden City, N.Y.: Dolphin, 1985),

182–84; Keith Thibodeaux, *Life after Lucy: The True Story of Keith Thibodeaux—"I Love Lucy's" Little Ricky* (Green Forest, Ark.: New Leaf Press, 1994), 13, 30, 68. Television figures are for all dwellings in the twenty-two-parish Acadiana region.

31. John S. Fontenot, "Where Did They Go, Diggy Liggy La and Diggy Liggy Lo?" *Louisiana Renaissance,* fall 1978, 23; Richard Baudouin, "Vengéance pour la déportation des acadiens," *Louisiana Life,* spring 1995, 57.

32. Statistics about Cajun teenagers in rural and small-town Lafayette Parish in the early 1950s were derived from (chronologically): Maloney et al., "Scott—Where the West Begins" (1951); Maloney et al., "Broussard: A Sociological Survey" (1951); Bourne et al., "Duson: A Sociological Survey" (1952?); Bourne et al., "Carencro: A Sociological Survey" (1953); "Youngsville: A Sociological Self-Survey" (1953). Quotations are from "Youngsville: A Sociological Self-Survey," 26; Maloney et al., "Scott—Where the West Begins," 12; Bourne et al., "Carencro: A Sociological Survey," 11; Bourne et al., "Duson: A Sociological Survey," 14, 15; "Boy Scout Movement in Area Dates Back More Than 34 Years," *Daily Advertiser,* 30 January 1959, B–13; "Girl Scouts Aware of What's Going on in the World Today," *Daily Advertiser,* 30 January 1959, 34. Survey quotations are from Maloney et al., "Scott—Where the West Begins," 13; Bourne et al., "Duson: A Sociological Survey," 15.

33. Buzz [Kenneth] Ringle, "Iberian Teenager Presents a Reason to 'Rock-and-Roll,'" *New Iberia (La.) Daily Iberian* [ca. August 1957?], 1, 5; Johnnie Allan [John Allen Guillot], "Lonely Days, Lonely Nights," *Swamp Pop Legend: Johnnie Allan—The Essential Collection,* compact disc, Jin, 1995; Broven, *South to Louisiana,* 214; Shane K. Bernard, *Swamp Pop: Cajun and Creole Rhythm and Blues* (Jackson: University Press of Mississippi, 1996), 60–61, 63, 80–83, 84, 86–90, 134–35, 141, 148; Randy and the Rockets, "Let's Do the Cajun Twist," *Randy and the Rockets—The Essential Collection,* compact disc, Jin, 1998.

34. Ancelet, *Cajun Music,* 35–36; Ancelet et al., *Cajun Country,* 159; Bernard, *Swamp Pop,* 96; Broven, *South to Louisiana,* 34, 56–60, 61–64, 64–66, 335–37; Bill C. Malone, *Country Music U.S.A.,* rev. ed. (Austin: University of Texas Press, 1991), 230–31; Peter Lerner, "Sweet Sherry: The Early Recording Career of Jackie DeShannon," *Now Dig This* (U.K.), April 1998, 12; R. Serge Denishoff, *Waylon* (Knoxville: University of Tennessee Press, 1983), 57–58, 346.

35. "Yambilee Festival at a Glance," *Daily World,* 9 October 1956, 7; Iris Kelso, "Jackie's French Thrilled the Crowd at Crowley Festival," *Times–Picayune,* 21 May 1994, A-10; "90,000 Visitors Cheer as Kennedy Crowns Rice Queen," *Crowley (La.) Daily Signal,* 17 October 1959, 1, 2.

36. Lou Myrtis Vining, "Louisiana's Siren Land," *Travel,* January 1947, 21–23, 32; Hamilton Basso, "Bayou Country," *Holiday,* October 1949, 62; Peggy Mann, "Cajun Country," *Travel,* October 1957, 12; Bradley Smith, "Acadia Country," *American Heritage,* December 1954, 62; "Abbeville Chamber Hits Magazine Story on Area Marshes," *Daily Advertiser,* 15 December 1954, 4; "Magazine Article about Abbeville Stirs Disapproval," *Abbeville Meridional,* 16 December 1954, 1; Ben Lucien Burman, "Mysterious Marshes," *Collier's,* 24 December 1954, 86–88, 90, 92; James K. Sparkman, "The Vibrant Life in the Bayous," *Christian Science Monitor,* reprinted in *Daily World,* 13 January 1955, 22.

37. James McLean, "Acadian Bicentennial Will Bring Tourists' Dollars into Louisiana,"

Daily Advertiser, 13 April 1955, 3; Marjorie R. Esman, "Tourism as Ethnic Preservation: The Cajuns of Louisiana," *Annals of Tourism Research* 11 (1984): 455; Mann, "Cajun Country," 16.

38. John Richard "Dickie" Breaux, *How to Simply Cook Cajun* (New Orleans: Juliahouse, 1991), 15. The earliest known printed references to crawfish étouffée appeared in 1954 and are found in the cookbooks *First—You Make a Roux* ([Lafayette, La.]: Les Vingt Quatre Club, 1954); and *The Daily Iberian Cajun-Creole Cookery*, special newspaper recipe section, 18 September 1954. Advertisement for Toby's Oak Grove restaurant, *Daily Advertiser*, 22 November 1946, 12; *Cajun-Creole Cookery; First—You Make a Roux; Acadian Bi-Centennial Cook Book* (Jennings: Louisiana Acadian Handicraft Museum, 1955); Carmen Bulliard Montegut, *Recettes (recipes) du petit Paris de l'Amérique* (St. Martinville, La.: self-published, 1955), 12; *Recipes Fit for a King Using I-Ron Pot Roux* (Ville Platte, La.: self-published, ca. 1955); Rosemary Dauterive and Lydia Krause, eds., *Don's Selected Recipes for Fine Food* (Lafayette, La.: Don's Seafood and Steak House, 1956), 5; Advertisement for Don's canned crayfish bisque and crayfish étouffée, *Daily Advertiser*, 4 July 1965, 10.

39. Shane K. Bernard, "Acadian Pride, Anglo-Conformism: The Acadian Bicentennial Celebration of 1955," *Louisiana History* 41 (spring 2000): 161–74.

40. *1960 U.S. Census of Population, Vol. 1, Characteristics of the Population, Pt. 20, Louisiana*, table 28, pp. 91–95; Terry H. Anderson, *The Movement and the Sixties* (New York: Oxford University Press, 1995), 26–27, 29; C. Vann Woodward, *The Strange Career of Jim Crow*, 3rd rev. ed. (New York: Oxford University Press, 1974), 23–25, 116–18; Sitkoff, *Struggle for Black Equality*, 5–6, 35–36.

41. Joe Gray Taylor, *Louisiana: A Bicentennial History* (New York: W. W. Norton, 1976), 12, 103–4; Bennett H. Wall, ed., *Louisiana: A History* (Arlington Heights, Ill.: Forum Press, 1984), 95, 200. The "Whites Only" image appears in Basso, "Bayou Country," 54.

42. Fairclough, *Race and Democracy*, 102–3, 112, 124, 125, 129; Mark A. De Wolf III, "In the Eye of the Storm: Lafayette and the Civil Rights Movement, 1954–1971" (M.A. thesis, University of Southwestern Louisiana, 1997), 45–46, SAMC.

43. Fairclough, *Race and Democracy*, 124, 129, 130; De Wolf, "Eye of the Storm," 14; Donna Wheaton, "Sheriff D. J. 'Cat' Doucet and the Black Voters of St. Landry Parish" (M.A. thesis, University of Southwestern Louisiana, 1991), 4, 26, 42, SAMC; advertisement quoting Sheriff D. J. "Cat" Doucet as stating "I am no 'nigger lover,'" *Daily World*, 4 December 1959, 7 [Doucet's actual phrasing appears to have been "I'm not a 'nigger lover'"]; "Sheriff Doucet, No 'Nigger Lover,' Invites Rainach Group to St. Landry," *Daily World*, 27 May 1959, 1, 32.

44. Michael Tisserand, *The Kingdom of Zydeco* (New York: Arcade, 1998), 51–65; Bernard, *Swamp Pop*, 67–69.

45. Bernard, *Swamp Pop*, 69–70. The author has withheld the white female's name because she is still living; King died in 1988.

46. Fairclough, *Race and Democracy*, 9; De Wolf, "Eye of the Storm," 9, 16–18; Curney J. Dronet, *A Century of Acadian Culture: The Development of a Cajun Community, Erath (1899–1999)* ([Erath, La.]: self-published, 2000), 102–3.

47. Fairclough, *Race and Democracy*, 132; De Wolf, "Eye of the Storm," 22.

48. De Wolf, "Eye of the Storm," 18–27; Michael G. Wade, "With All Deliberate Speed: The

Integration of Southwestern Louisiana Institute," unpublished research paper, 1–31, original in possession of Michael G. Wade, Appalachian State University, Boone, N.C.; Claire Taylor and Michael Martin, "Justice for All," *La Louisiane* [University of Southwestern Louisiana alumni magazine], spring 1997, 24–27.

CHAPTER 3

1. "Rock Festival Site Set; Will Be Cypress Point," *Daily World,* 18 June 1971, 1; advertisement for "Celebration of Life" rock concert, *NOLA Express,* no. 82 (ca. June 1971), n.p., HTML; "Thousands Encamped along Atchafalaya Awaiting Fete," *Daily World,* 22 June 1971, 1; "Skinny-Dipping in the Atchafalaya River," *Daily World,* 22 June 1971, 12; Rafael Bermudez, "Rockfest Decision Still before Court," *Daily Iberian,* 22 June 1971, 1; "Health Officials Give Thumbs-up to Festival," *Daily World,* 23 June 1971, 1, 12; "Two Drown in River, Youth Shot at 'Celebration of Life,'" *Daily World,* 27 June 1971, 1, 16; "'Unreasonable Demands' Closed Rock Festival, Promoters Say," *Daily World,* 30 June 1971, 1, 2; Rafael Bermudez, "Gong to Signal Start of Bash at Sunset Today," *Daily Iberian,* 24 June 1971, 1; Ellis Byers, "Dope, Music and People Draw Youths to Festival," *Daily World,* 28 June 1971, 12; Ellis Byers, "Wind and Rain Storm Rakes Festival Site," *Daily World,* 23 June 1971, 1; "Hijinks at Rock Festival," *Daily World,* 24 June 1971, 10; Rafael Bermudez, "Basic Medical Supplies Short at Rock Festival," *Daily Iberian,* 25 June 1971, 1; "At Least Two Persons Drown at 'Celebration of Life' Festival,'" *Daily Iberian,* 27 June 1971, 1; "Fete Tabbed a 'Ripoff,'" *Daily Iberian,* 28 June 1971, 9; "Rock Festival Folded Early," *Daily World,* 28 June 1971, 1; Joseph P. Manguno, "Rock Festival Halts at Midway Mark," *Daily Iberian,* 28 June 1971, 5; "Good Ole Rock & Roll: Kapelow Speaking," *NOLA Express,* no. 85 (ca. July 1971), 14–15, HTML; Hugh Morgan and G. Michael Harmon, "Rock Festival Is Blocked by State Court Order," *Daily World,* 20 June 1971, 1; "Hearing Held Today on Fate of Rock Festival," *Daily World,* 21 June 1971, 1, 12; Joseph P. Manguno, "Judge Hearing Testimony about the Alleged Harassment of 'Celebration' Promoters," *Daily Iberian,* 21 June 1971, 1.
2. Terry H. Anderson, *The Sixties* (New York: Longman, 1999), vii, 210.
3. Advertisement for Evangeline Maid Bread, *Daily Iberian,* 20 June 1968, 17.
4. Anderson, *The Sixties,* 73–76.
5. Dormon, *People Called Cajuns,* 78; John R. Thistlethwaite, "Mugwump," column, *Daily World,* 23 September 1966, 4.
6. Anderson, *Movement and the Sixties,* 132–33, 157–58, 211, 232–33, 234; Perry H. Howard, "The Politics of the Acadian Parishes," in *The Cajuns: Essays on Their History and Culture,* ed. Glenn R. Conrad (Lafayette: Center for Louisiana Studies, University of Southwestern Louisiana, 1983), 185; Broven, *South to Louisiana,* 24–28, 38–39, 41–44, 253; Happy Fats, "Vote Wallace in '72," 45 RPM single, Reb Rebel 519, ca. 1968; Happy Fats, "Dear Mr. President," 45 RPM single, Reb Rebel 501, ca. 1965.
7. Johnny Rebel, "Who Likes a Nigger?" 45 RPM single, Reb Rebel 508, ca. 1965; Johnny Rebel, "Nigger Hatin' Me," 45 RPM single, Reb Rebel 508, ca. 1965; Johnny Rebel, "Some Niggers Never Die (They Just Smell That Way)," 45 RPM single, Reb Rebel 518, ca. 1965; Johnny Rebel, "Kajun Klu Klux Klan," 45 RPM single, Reb Rebel 504, ca. 1965; advertisements for Reb Rebel records, *The Fiery Cross,* August 1970, n.p., and February 1971, n.p., on file in Special Collections, HTML.

Clifford "Pee Wee" Trahan is identified as Johnny Rebel in Broven, *South to Louisiana,* 253, 358, 359. Late Reb Rebel owner J. D. Miller also identified Trahan as Johnny Rebel, informing Broven during an interview, "Johnny Reb, that's a young fellow by the name of Clifford Trahan." In addition, "C. Trahan" is credited as sole songwriter on several Johnny Rebel recordings, including "Who Likes A Nigger?" "Nigger Hatin' Me," "Some Niggers Never Die (They Just Smell That Way)," and "Kajun Klu Klux Klan." J. D. Miller, interview by John Broven, 1 May 1979, Crowley, La., transcript in author's possession.

8. "Louisiana Report on Klan Raps Courts, LBJ," *Beaumont Enterprise,* 27 July 1965, 1; Edwin E. Willis, address at Annual 4th Degree Banquet, Monsignor J. M. Langlois General Assembly, St. Martinville, La., 7 November 1965, TD, 5, Edwin E. Willis Papers, SAMC; Fairclough, *Race and Democracy,* 9; De Wolf, "Eye of the Storm," 9.

9. Wheaton, "Sheriff D. J. 'Cat' Doucet," 52, 59, 60–61.

10. "Parish Schools Handed Full Integration Orders," *Daily World,* 31 July 1969, 1, 3; "Ordered to Outlawry," letter to editor, *Daily World,* 5 August 1969, 13; Sidney Mixon, "Keep Children at Home Vowed," *Daily World,* 8 August 1969, 1, 16; "'School Takeover' Is Protested by Marchers," *Daily World,* 16 September 1969, 1, 10; "Registration Light at Parish Schools," *Daily World,* 3 September 1969, 1, 12; "Boycott, Pickets Halt Registration," *Daily World,* 3 September 1969, 1, 12; "Turnout of Students in Acadia Low," *Daily World,* 4 September 1969, 8; "Schools in Ascension Open; Boycott Resumes," *Daily World,* 9 September 1969, 1, 16; "Louisiana School Troubles Continue," *Daily World,* 10 September 1969, 1, 12; "Schools Open; Light Attendance by Whites," *Daily World,* 12 September 1969, 1, 16; "Evangeline First Day Smooth," *Daily World,* 12 September 1969, 1, 16; Fairclough, *Race and Democracy,* 440, 442, 443, 445, 457; Angela Simoneaux, "Judge to Hear from School Zone Critic," *Advocate,* 19 May 2000, 1B, 2B; Angela Simoneaux, "Judge, Board Discuss Desegregation," *Advocate,* 25 May 2000, 1B, 2B.

11. Anderson, *The Sixties,* 93, 153; Sitkoff, *Struggle for Black Equality,* 143; "'Take Control' Urged by Negro Attorney at NAACP Meet Here," *Daily World,* 7 August 1969, 1.

12. Michael S. Martin, "'A Peaceful Demonstration of Our Feeling toward the Death': University Students in Lafayette, Louisiana, React to Martin Luther King, Jr.'s Assassination," *Louisiana History* 41 (summer 2000): 306–7.

13. "Students Protest 'Cajun Field,'" *Daily Advertiser,* 27 May 1971, 15; Dormon, *People Called Cajuns,* 55.

14. 1990 PUMS, for Persons; George C. Herring, *America's Longest War: The United States and Vietnam, 1950–1975,* 3rd ed. (New York: McGraw-Hill, 1996), 306; Adjutant General, Department of the Army, Washington, D.C., to Alice Vice, Abbeville, La., 27 May 1969, Telegram, Acadian Museum (hereafter AM), Erath, La.; "Pod," Vietnam, to the Vice family, Vermilion Parish, La., ca. May 1969, ALS, AM.

Statistics concerning the total number of Cajun GIs who served and who died in Vietnam are estimates extrapolated primarily from 1990 census data.

15. Happy Fats, "Birthday Thank You Tommy, from Viet Nam," 45 RPM recording, Reb Rebel 513, ca. 1965; Happy Fats, "Veteran's Plea," 45 RPM recording, Reb Rebel 501, ca. 1965; Happy Fats, "What Has Happened to Old Glory?" 45 RPM recording, Reb Rebel 517, ca. 1965; Rod Bernard, "A Tear in a Lady's Eye," 45 RPM recording, SSS International 822, ca. 1970, reissued on Rod Bernard, *Cajun Blue,* compact disc, Edsel, 1999. (The "Lady" referred to in Bernard's song was the Statue of Liberty.)

16. Willis, address at Annual 4th Degree Banquet, 5; "Acadiana Neuf Purposes Are Outlined at Meeting," *Abbeville Meridional*, 22 April 1965, 8; flow chart of Acadiana Neuf and its delegate agencies, *Daily Advertiser*, 6 January 1967, 3; press release announcing establishment of Acadiana Neuf, Office of Economic Opportunity, Washington, D.C., 25 November [1964], TMs, Acadiana Neuf Collection (Cain Papers), SAMC; "Acadiana Neuf Charged with Discrimination," *Southwest Louisiana Register*, 22 April 1965, 5; letter of complaint, Charles E. Bryant, John Zippert, Rev. Edward Harris Jr., Betty Bryant, Calvin Brown, Opelousas, La., to Roland M. Hebert, executive director, Acadiana Neuf, Lafayette, La., 25 May 1966, TLS, Acadiana Neuf Collection (Cain Papers), SAMC; Geoffrey Brown, "Critics Hit Acadiana Neuf," *Southwest Louisiana Register*, 8 September 1966, n.p.; "D.A. Seizes Records of Poverty Agency," *Daily Advertiser*, 11 April 1967, 1; *A Dictionary of Louisiana Biography: Ten-Year Supplement, 1988–98*, s.v. "Angers, Robert John"; Bob Angers Jr., "Anecdotes and Antidotes," column, *Daily Advertiser*, 29 November 1967, 7; 9 February 1968, 3; 11 February 1968, 12; 12 March 1967, 5; [Bob Angers Jr.?], "South La. Facing Second Danger: Red Penetration!" *Daily Advertiser*, 23 July 1967, 4; Bob Angers Jr., "Area Poverty Worker Linked to Communist Youth Festival," *Daily Advertiser*, 8 December 1966, 1; "Hebert Says John Zippert 'Involved,'" *Daily Advertiser*, 20 December 1966, 1; "Poverty War Hearings Set," *Daily Advertiser*, 2 March 1967, 1, 6; "Reporter Says 2 'Parrot Red Line,'" *Daily Advertiser*, 8 March 1967, 1, 5; "Poverty Worker Identified as Red," *Daily Advertiser*, 9 March 1967, 1, 6; "Committee Cites Red Allegations," *Daily Advertiser*, 3 May 1967, 1; "Conclusions of Legislative Committee Printed in Full," *Daily Advertiser*, 3 May 1967, 3; "Communist Influences in S. La. True—Report," *Times-Picayune*, 4 May 1967, 9; "Local Editorial on Reds Goes into House Record," *Daily Advertiser*, 21 September 1967, 21; "Disputes Topics in Recent Letter," letter to editor, *Daily Advertiser*, 23 February 1967, 4; "Teacher Denies Any Conspiracy," letter to editor, *Daily Advertiser*, 3 March 1967, 4; "23 USL Teachers Protest Letter," letter to editor, *Daily Advertiser*, 12 March 1967, 4; William D. Reese, president, USL chapter, American Association of University Professors, to Richard D'Aquin, publisher, *Daily Advertiser*, 13 March 1967, TLS, Clyde Rougeou Collection, USL Presidential Papers (hereafter CRC), SAMC; "Public's Right to Know about University Affairs," editorial, *Daily Advertiser*, 19 March 1967, 4; Audrey Ellsworth, "Student Protest to the Vietnam War on USL Campus," [ca. 1998], TMs, 8, photocopy in author's possession; "Witch-Hunting a Real Thing," letter to editor, *Daily Advertiser*, 19 March 1967, 4; "'Witch-Hunt' at USL Foreseen," letter to editor, *Daily Advertiser*, 12 March 1967, 4; "Gives Views on Issues," letter to editor, *Daily Advertiser*, 21 February 1967, 4; "Right-Wing Nuts in Lafayette," letter to editor, *Daily Advertiser*, 12 March 1967, 5; Doug Manship Jr., "Students! Defend Your Rights!" *Vermilion* [University of Southwestern Louisiana student newspaper], 24 February 1967, 2. Angers's testimony and other material concerning allegations of subversion against Acadiana Neuf can be found in Joint Legislative Committee on Un-American Activities, *Aspects of the Poverty Program in South Louisiana*, proceedings of antisubversive hearings held 8–9 March 1967, Lafayette, La., published 14 April 1967, original in the Louisiana State Archives, Baton Rouge; see Angers testimony, 14–45.

17. "Iberian in Vietnam; 'Cajuns are Proud,'" *Vermilion*, 7 January 1966, 1; "Nixon's Cambodia Policy Supported by 908 USL Students at Referendum," *Vermilion*, 22 May 1970, 1.

18. "USL Anti-War Group Calls for Peace, Oct. 15," *Vermilion*, 10 October 1969, 1; "All-Night Vigil Held May 6," *Vermilion*, 15 May 1970, 3; "Campus Memorial Service Honors Memory of Slain Kent State Four," *Vermilion*, 15 May 1970, 3; Ellsworth, "Student Protest to the Vietnam War on USL Campus," 6–7, 8, 9–10; "Three Arrested in Connection with AFROTC Fire Bombing," *Vermilion*, 15 May 1970, 1.

19. Emile LaVoix, "Ethnic Awakening," *Undercurrents*, 1 August 1971, n.p., CODOFIL Scrapbooks (hereafter CS), SAMC.

20. Zachary Richard, "La vérité va peut-être te faire du mal," in *Faire récolte* (Moncton, N.B.: Les Éditions Perce-Neige, 1997), 116, 118 (translation by Brian Comeaux and Zachary Richard); Janis L. Pallister, "*Cadjinitude*: A New Militancy," n.d., TMs, Barry Jean Ancelet Collection, in possession of Barry Jean Ancelet, Lafayette, La. (hereafter BJAC); Ancelet, *Makers of Cajun Music*, 95, 98–99. Lyrics to "Réveille" (1973) appear in poetic form in *Cris sur le bayou: Naissance d'une poésie acadienne en Louisiane*, ed. Barry Jean Ancelet (Montreal: Éditions Intermède, 1980), 113 (translation by Barry Jean Ancelet and Zachary Richard).

21. Bernard, *Swamp Pop*, 109–11, 169–75; Rufus Jagneaux, "Opelousas Sostan," Various Artists, *Swamp Gold*, vol. 1, compact disc, Jin, 1991.

22. Bernard, *Swamp Pop*, 110–11, 173–74.

23. "Evangeline Jury Seeks to Cancel Rock Festival," *Times-Picayune*, 13 September 1972, sec. 2, p. 15; Anderson, *The Sixties*, 148.

24. C. J. "Bobby" Dugas, "Reminiscences, Observations, Predictions," 1970, TMs, 2, 4, Political Ephemera Collection, HTML.

25. Anderson, *Movement and the Sixties*, 97–101, 228–29; Anderson, *The Sixties*, 55–56, 124–25; Saxon et al., *Gumbo Ya-Ya*, 204; Eastin, "Catahoula," 25; Pat Schroeder, *24 Years of House Work . . . and the Place Is Still a Mess: My Life in Politics* (Kansas City: Andrews McMeel, 1998), 40–41; "AWS [Association of Women Students] Rallied in Favor of Women's Rights," *L'Acadien*, 1971 USL Yearbook, 137; "No Curfew System Valued," letter to editor, *Vermilion*, 4 December 1970, 6; *1940 U.S. Census of Population, Vol. 2, Characteristics of the Population, Pt. 3., Louisiana*, table 23, pp. 379–86; *1970 Census of Population, Vol. 1, Characteristics of the Population, Pt. 20, Louisiana*, table 121, p. 30; table 126, pp. 355–60; *1980 Census of the Population, Vol. 1, Characteristics of the Population, Ch. C, General Social and Economic Characteristics, Pt. 1, United States Summary*, table 86, p. 26; Ancelet et al., *Cajun Country*, 75; Nicole Denée Fontenot, "Twentieth-Century Cajun Women: Agents of Cultural Preservation" (M.A. thesis, University of Southwestern Louisiana, 1999), 111, SAMC. Fontenot's quote ("Life experiences outside the domestic realm . . .") has been reorganized slightly for clarity.

26. *The Rolling Stone Encyclopedia of Rock and Roll*, 1995 ed., s.v. "Creedence Clearwater Revival"; Creedence Clearwater Revival, "Born on the Bayou," *Chronicle, Vol. 2: 20 Great CCR Classics*, compact disc, Fantasy, 1986; Charlie Gillett, *The Sound of the City: The Rise of Rock 'n' Roll* (New York: Dell, 1972), 263. CCR bass player Stu Cook's "Cajun vibe" quote is from a 1996 interview published on an Internet fan site, "Electric Bayou: Original Homepage of Creedence Clearwater Revival and John Fogerty," located at www.jyu.fi/~petkasi/ccr-jcf/trivia.htm, accessed 13 October 2000.

27. *The Encyclopedia of Southern Culture*, s.v. "Rednecks"; *Easy Rider*, 94 min., Columbia Pictures, 1969, videocassette; Peter Fonda, *Don't Tell Dad: A Memoir* (New York:

Hyperion, 1998), 271–73; Douglas Brode, *The Films of Jack Nicholson* (Secaucus, N.J.: Citadel Press, 1987), 105.

28. Lillian Bourdier, "Theriot Raps Supreme Court, Urges Return to Patriotism," *Daily World,* 29 June 1971, 2.

29. Figures for all year-round housing units in the twenty-two-parish Acadiana region. *1970 U.S. Census of Housing, Vol. 1, Housing Characteristics for States, Cities, and Counties, Pt. 20, Louisiana,* table 36, p. 90; table 37, p. 91; table 62, pp. 163–78; table 63, pp. 179–94; *1970 U.S. Census of Housing, Vol. 1, Housing Characteristics for States, Cities, and Counties, Pt. 1, United States Summary,* table 23, p. 248; table 24, p. 254.

30. "Texaco Reaches High Achievement from Deep Horizons of Louisiana," *Daily Advertiser,* 19 October 1965, 21; "Hidden Benefits Oil Brings to Lafayette," *Daily Advertiser,* 13 February 1966, 4; Owen W. Jones and Leo W. Hough, U.S. Department of the Interior, *The Mineral Industry of Louisiana* (Washington, D.C.: U.S. Government Printing Office, 1967), 4; see also 17–18 (table 24); Dave Miller, "Floating Cities of Gulf Constantly Search for Oil," *Daily Advertiser,* 19 October 1965, 32–33.

31. "Airline Service Began in Lafayette with 1947 Flight," photo with caption, *Daily Advertiser,* 23 December 1990, 2A; "Jet Age Seen as New Impetus to Area Aviation," *Daily Advertiser,* 5 June 1957, 4; "Opening of LC Airport Marks New Era in Aviation for Area," *American Press,* 23 April 1967, B6 [reprint of article of 23 March 1962, n.p.]; "Director Outlines Progress of Louisiana Interstate Highways," *Abbeville Meridional,* 21 November 1965, 7; "Louisiana's Interstate Routes about 32 Per Cent Complete," *Morning Advocate,* 5 November 1965, 8–B; Bill Neikirk, "Plans for Bridging Atchafalaya Swamp Readied," *Times-Picayune,* 9 October 1967, sec. 3, p. 16; "That Fine New Highway over the Louisiana Swamps," editorial, *Daily Advertiser,* 25 March 1973, 14; "Interstate 10 Opens Today to Complete S. La. Link," *Daily Advertiser,* 28 March 1974, 41, 55; "I–10 Stretch from Westover to Grosse Tete Dedicated," *Morning Advocate,* 29 March 1974, 1–B; Rod Bernard, "Cajun Interstate," 45 RPM recording, SSS International 822, ca. 1970, reissued on Rod Bernard, *Cajun Blue,* compact disc, Edsel, 1999.

32. "Louisiana's Tourist Income Exceeds $500 Million Mark [in 1968]," *Morning Advocate,* 12 April 1969, 18-C; "'Acadiana' Designation May Mean International Trade, Tourism," *Daily Iberian,* 17 June 1971, 10; "Boosting Lafayette Tourism Is Local, State Business," *Daily Advertiser,* 15 February 1968, 4.

33. "Steno's Error Promoted Idea of 'Acadiana,'" *Acadiana* [KATC promotional newsletter], July 1967, 1, Vertical Files (hereafter VF), SAMC; "State Will Be Asked to Designate Area 'Acadiana,'" *Daily Advertiser,* 10 December 1970, 8; "Acadiana Relations Body Unifying Force—Angers," *Times-Picayune,* 10 December 1970, sec. 3, p. 12; "'Acadiana' Designation May Mean International Trade, Tourism," 10; House Concurrent Resolution no. 496, to establish officially the cultural region of Louisiana known as "The Heart of Acadiana," approved 6 June 1971, *1971 Legislative Calendar of the State of Louisiana,* 34th reg. sess., 221; "Acadiana as Area Name Not Approved," letter to editor, *Daily Iberian,* 24 June 1971, 4.

Max and Freda Thomas published a semiregular travel and social column in the *Crowley Daily Signal* under the title "Acadiana." Their earliest known use of the word is found in *Crowley Daily Signal,* 26 June 1956, 12.

34. "Le drapeau des acadiens louisianais," bilingual summary of origin and symbolism of Louisiana Acadian flag, ca. 22 February 1965, TD [photocopy], original in possession of Allen M. Babineaux, Lafayette, La.; House Concurrent Resolution no. 143, to establish an official flag for the cultural region of Louisiana known as "The Heart of Acadiana," approved 5 July 1974, *1974 Legislative Calendar of the State of Louisiana*, 37th reg. sess., 478; "Acadiana Flag Now Official," *Daily Advertiser*, 10 July 1974, 3; "Acadian Flag," *Daily Advertiser*, 17 September 1967, 10; "Acadian Flag to Fly Here," *Daily Advertiser*, 30 January 1968, 1; "Acadian Flag Raised," *Daily Advertiser*, 14 February 1968, 1; "Acadian Flag Is to Fly at City Hall," *Daily Advertiser*, 30 July 1968, 1; "Flag Bearers," *Vermilion*, 26 September 1968, 8; "One Moment in Time," *Daily Advertiser*, 22 January 1994, 2A [reprint of 1965 photograph documenting public introduction of Acadian flag]; "Flag Display Criticized," *Daily Advertiser*, 10 July 1974, 6.

The flag's symbolism is explained in Thomas J. Arceneaux, "The Louisiana Acadian Flag," *Acadiana Profile* (January-February 1969), inside front cover, 1; and Rushton, *The Cajuns*, 264. For comparison with SLI seal, see *S.L.I. Alumni News*, January 1957, 5, VF, SAMC.

35. Paul C. Tate, Mamou, La., to Wasserman Productions, New York, 16 August 1967, TL [photocopy], Raymond Spencer Rodgers Collection (hereafter RSRC), SAMC; [Paul C. Tate], "Memorandum in Support of Demand that Louisiana Portion of NBC Bell Telephone Hour Special (Bill Dana) Be Deleted," ca. 16 August 1967, TD [photocopy], RSRC.

36. Bern Keating, Charles Harbutt, Franke Keating, "Cajunland: Louisiana's French-Speaking Coast," *National Geographic*, March 1966, 352–53, 361; "Let's Tell It Like It Is about the Acadians," editorial, *Daily Advertiser*, 2 July 1969, n.p., CS.

37. Larry L. King, "If a Bayou Baby Sticks His Finger down a Crayfish Hole before He's Six Months Old, He's a Cajun," *Holiday*, May 1970, 80–81.

38. 1990 PUMS, for Persons; "Young in Cajun Country Don't Dig French Language," *Daily Advertiser*, 16 April 1968, 14.

39. Douglas E. Kneeland, "Cajuns Seek French Culture out of Mixed Past," *New York Times*, 9 May 1968, 49, 56; "Young in Cajun Country Don't Dig French Language," 14.

CHAPTER 4

1. Clyde C. Vidrine, *Just Takin' Orders: A Southern Governor's Watergate* (Baton Rouge, La.: self-published, 1977), 237–40; Candice Lee, "Inauguration Day Is Festive, Warm," *Morning Advocate*, 10 May 1972, 15–A; John McMillan, "'There He Is!' Says One; 'Who? . . . There's Who?'" *Times-Picayune*, 10 May 1972, sec. 1, p. 6; Ed Cullen, "Monsieur Edwards Had a Pretty Fine Parade, *n'est-ce pas?* Top Cajun Takes Walk to Capitol," *Morning Advocate*, 10 May 1972, 14–A; C. M. Hargroder, "Racial Bars to Fall, Vow," *Times-Picayune*, 10 May 1972, sec. 1, p. 1; Gerald Moses, "Bilingual Oath Starts New Era," *Morning Advocate*, 10 May 1972, 1–A, 6–A; "Text of Edwards Speech Given," *Times-Picayune*, 10 May 1972, sec. 2, p. 2; Sidney J. Romero, ed., *"My Fellow Citizens . . .": The Inaugural Addresses of Louisiana's Governors* (Lafayette: Center for Louisiana Studies, University of Southwestern Louisiana, 1980), 359–63; Gerald Moses, "Cajun Power Leads to Election Sweep," *Morning Advocate*, 2 February 1972, 1–A, 12–A; "Claims Cajun Power," *Morning Advocate*, 2 February 1972,

14–A; Roy Reed, "Louisiana's Cajuns, a Minority with Power," *New York Times,* 9 May 1972, 43. Although two politicians of Acadian descent, Alexandre Mouton [1843–46] and Paul O. Hébert [1853–56], served as Louisiana governors, the author does not consider them Cajuns because the ethnic group did not coalesce until after the Civil War.

2. Carolyn Ramsey, *Cajuns on the Bayou* (New York: Hastings House, 1957), xv; Dormon, *People Called Cajuns,* 74–75.

3. Anderson, *The Sixties,* 92–93, 163–67, 207; Anderson, *Movement and the Sixties,* 176–77, 293–310, 407–8, 414; Dormon, *People Called Cajuns,* 80–81; Polenberg, *One Nation Divisible,* 243–49.

4. Ruth Mouton Hamilton (Mrs. C. E. Hamilton), president, France-Amérique de la Louisiane-Acadienne, Lafayette, La., 13 November 1951, form letter explaining the group's origin and purpose, TL, France-Amérique de la Louisiane-Acadienne Collection (hereafter FALAC), SAMC; "'France-Amérique de la Louisiane-Acadienne' Organized at Lafayette," France-Amérique de la Louisiane Cultural Relations Committee bulletin, December 1951, 1, FALAC; Hosea Phillips, "Report on France-Amérique de la Lne-Acadienne [*sic*], Prepared by H. Phillips for Delivery by Mrs. C. E. Hamilton in Paris, June 1959," TD, FALAC.

5. Raymond Spencer Rodgers, Professional Personnel Record, Louisiana Department of Education, 15 September 1966, D [photocopy], RSRC; Raymond Spencer Rodgers, Academic Personnel Data Sheet, University of Southwestern Louisiana, 1966, D [photocopy], RSRC; Robert M. Crisler, head, Department of Social Studies, University of Southwestern Louisiana, Lafayette, to Raymond Spencer Rodgers, Department of Political Science, University of South Alabama, Mobile, 26 March 1966, TLS [photocopy], RSRC [letter confirming Rodgers's appointment as USL associate professor beginning the 1966–67 academic year]; Raymond Spencer Rodgers, "Is French Dying in State?" *Daily Advertiser,* 19 October 1966, 1, 8; Raymond Spencer Rodgers, "Community Action Needed to Preserve French in Area," *Daily Advertiser,* 23 October 1966, 21; Raymond Spencer Rodgers, "How to Boost Employment for Southwest Louisiana," *Daily Advertiser,* 18 December 1966, 7; Raymond Spencer Rodgers, "Answering DeGaulle in French," *Daily Advertiser,* 5 December 1967, 2; Raymond Spencer Rodgers, "The Capacity of Louisiana to Conclude International Agreements, and Current Developments," *Proceedings of the Louisiana Academy of Sciences* 30 (1967): 102–18; "Dr. Rodgers Appointed Liaison Head," *Daily Advertiser,* 2 April 1967, 2; John J. McKeithen, governor of Louisiana, Baton Rouge, to Daniel Johnson, premier of Quebec, Canada, 15 August 1967, TLS [photocopy], RSRC [letter confirming Rodgers's appointment as McKeithen's aide-de-camp in negotiating the Quebec-Louisiana Cultural Agreement]; Raymond Spencer Rodgers, "The Survival of French in Louisiana," October 1966, TD [photo-copy], 2, RSRC; Ellis Pregeant, "Rodgers: 'Academic Freedom,'" interview, *Vermilion,* 14 December 1967, 16.

6. "French Group Organized," *Daily Advertiser,* 3 March 1967, 1, 6; "Furthering French Culture Aired at Meet Yesterday," *Daily Advertiser,* 19 May 1967, 6; Vincent Marino, "C of C [Chamber of Commerce] Protests Naming of Rodgers," *Daily Advertiser,* ca. September 1968, 2, RSRC; "French Renaissance in Louisiana," *Acadiana Profile,* January-February 1969, 8.

7. "Bi-Lingual Project Meet Tomorrow," *Daily Advertiser,* 19 January 1968, 2; "Bilingual Meet Airs 'Natural Resource,'" *Daily Advertiser,* 21 January 1968, 10.

8. "French Education Push Supported," *Daily Advertiser,* 4 February 1968, 1; O. C. (Dan) Guilliot, Edgar G. Mouton Jr., Fredric G. Hayes, and J. Luke LeBlanc, Lafayette, La., form letter to other south Louisiana legislators, 9 February 1968, TL [photocopy], RSRC; "French Teaching Meeting Planned," *Daily Advertiser,* 13 February 1968, 1; "Push Begins for Bi-Lingual State," *Daily World,* 18 February 1968, n.p., CS; "Solons Pushing French Culture," *Times-Picayune,* 24 May 1968, sec. 1, p. 10; "Pelican, French Tongue Dying in State, Report," *Times-Picayune,* 8 April 1968, sec. 3, p. 4; Anne L. Simon, "CODOFIL: A Case Study of an Ethnic Interest Group" (M.A. thesis, University of Southwestern Louisiana, 1977), 13, SAMC. Contemporary newspaper articles referred to the petition as a "resolution." Its absence from state publications, such as the *Legislative Calendar* and the *Official Journal* of the House and Senate, suggests it was actually a round robin–type letter rather than a formal legislative document. Sections of the petition were quoted by state newspapers, but no copy of the entire document is known to exist.

9. Act 409, to authorize the establishment of the Council for the Development of Louisiana-French, approved 20 July 1968, *Acts Passed by the Legislature of the State of Louisiana at the Regular Session of 1968,* 2:921–22; Act 22, to change the name of the Council for the Development of Louisiana-French to the Council for the Development of French in Louisiana, approved 27 December 1968, *Acts Passed by the Legislature of the State of Louisiana at the Extraordinary Session of 1968,* 94–95; Raymond Spencer Rodgers, n.p., to James Domengeaux, [Lafayette, La.?], 1 December 1968, TL [photocopy], RSRC.

10. "Lafayette Lawyer to Head Group," *Daily Advertiser,* 11 September 1968, 1, 3; *Dictionary of Louisiana Biography,* vol. 1, s.v., "Domengeaux, James 'Jimmy'"; Vernon A. Guidry Jr., "Efforts to Preserve State's Acadian Heritage Pushed," *Morning Advocate,* 1 December 1968, 4–E; "Pelican, French Tongue Dying in State," 4; "Push Begins for Bi-Lingual State," n.p. Domengeaux is referred to as a newcomer to the French-preservation movement in Bob Angers Jr., "Anecdotes and Antidotes," column, *Daily Advertiser,* 7 February 1968, 11; see also complaint about Domengeaux's lack of experience as a French preservationist in "French Council Hassle Develops," *Daily Advertiser,* 17 September 1968, 6.

11. Anderson, *Movement and the Sixties,* 183–238; Anderson, *The Sixties,* 102–28.

12. Act 256, to further the preservation and utilization of the French language by removing discrimination against French[,] . . . to provide that all legal notices may be published in the French language . . . and to reconfirm the traditional authority of state officials and institutions to publish in the French language . . . any public document, approved 19 July 1968, *Acts Passed by the Legislature of the State of Louisiana at the Regular Session of 1968,* 1:599–600; Act 257, to direct institutions . . . presently offering teacher certification in high school French to similarly offer teacher certification programs in elementary school French, approved 19 July 1968, *Acts Passed by the Legislature of the State of Louisiana at the Regular Session of 1968,* 1:600–601; Act 408, to further the preservation and utilization of the French language and culture of Louisiana by strengthening its position in the public schools of the state, approved 20 July 1968, *Acts Passed by the Legislature of the State of Louisiana at the Regular Session of 1968,* 2:919–21; Act 458, to further the preservation and utilization of French . . . by authorizing the

establishment of a non-profit French language television broadcasting corporation, approved 20 July 1968, *Acts Passed by the Legislature of the State of Louisiana at the Regular Session of 1968,* 2:1097–98. See also Act 21, to amend and reenact . . . Act 408 of the 1968 Regular Session . . . with respect to teaching French and the culture of Louisiana in the public elementary and high schools in the state, approved 27 December 1968, *Acts Passed by the Legislature of the State of Louisiana at the Extraordinary Session of 1968,* 93–94.

13. "French Renaissance in Louisiana," 7–11.

14. "Lafayette Lawyer to Head Group," 1, 3; Bob Angers Jr., "Acadians Map Plans for French," *Daily Advertiser,* 28 October 1968, 1, 2; Minutes of CODOFIL organizational meeting, Baton Rouge, La., 27 October 1968, TD, passim, CRC, SAMC; "CODOFIL Calls School Programs 'Criminal Waste,'" *Morning Advocate,* 3 August 1972, n.p., CS; "Pelican, French Tongue Dying in State," 4.

15. "Elementary and Secondary Education Amendments of 1967," Public Law 90–247; 81 Stat. 783, Title VII, sec. 702, approved 2 January 1968, *Laws of the 90th Congress—1st Session,* 918; "Education Amendments of 1974," Public Law 93–380; 88 Stat. 484, Title VII, sec. 703(a)(4)(B), approved 21 August 1974, *Laws of the 93rd Congress—2nd Session,* 567; Simon, "CODOFIL: A Case Study," 15, 24, 62–63, 65–66, see also table 6, "Federal French Language Programs in Louisiana, 1970–1977," 105; Arnold H. Leibowitz, *The Bilingual Education Act: A Legislative Analysis* (Rosslyn, Va.: InterAmerica Research Association/National Clearinghouse for Bilingual Education, 1980), 15, 17, 20, 30.

16. "Domengeaux Tells of French Plans," *Daily Advertiser,* 16 November 1969, 1, 6; Barbara Vorenkamp, "French Teachers Arrive in City," *Daily Advertiser,* 9 September 1970, sec. 1, pp. 1, 2; "French Tutors Arrive in State," *Times-Picayune,* 10 September 1970, sec. 3, p. 7; Simon, "CODOFIL: A Case Study," 1–2, 15, 45, 62.

17. Simon, "CODOFIL: A Case Study," 45–47, 55, 67; "French Renaissance in Louisiana," 7–11; Trent Angers, "French-Speaking Ability Stressed by Merchants," *Times-Picayune,* 3 April 1972, 3; Roy Reed, "Cajun Country in Louisiana Waging Underdog Fight to Keep French Alive," *New York Times,* 7 May 1972, 71; David Snell, "A Waning Echo in Cajun Country," *Life,* 14 March 1969, 18B; Transcript of CBS Evening News segment on Cajun culture, broadcast 12 October 1968, TD [photocopy], RSRC; "Survey Shows: French Runs Deep in Louisiana Parishes," *Acadiana Profile,* January-February 1970, 11; "Acadiana Still 'French Country,'" *Daily Advertiser,* 20 March 1970, sec. 1, p. 3.

18. "Convention Passes French Language Provision," *Daily Advertiser,* 7 January 1974, 1, 5; Simon, "CODOFIL: A Case Study," 70; "New Theater Has French Flavor," *Daily Advertiser,* 27 April 1972, 25; "Scholarships Are Awarded by CODOFIL," *(Baton Rouge) State Times,* 17 May 1974, 14B; "CODOFIL Asks POW 'Humanity,'" *Times-Picayune,* 1 November 1970, sec. 1, p. 12; F. Edward Hébert, "The New Louisiana Story," *Congressional Record,* vol. 120, pt. 4 (5 March 1974), 5419; Chris Segura, "Morrison Co-Authors CODOSIL Bill," *Times-Picayune,* 22 June 1975, sec. 1, p. 22; Rhonda Smith, "Co De Span," *Tech-Talk* [Louisiana Tech University student newspaper], 3 October 1985, n.p., CS; Rushton, *The Cajuns,* 291; "CODOFINE and CODOFIL," *Daily Advertiser,* 11 May 1973, 51.

19. "French Movement Gets Attention," *Daily Advertiser*, 22 July 1970, 3 [reprint of article from *Philadelphia Enquirer*, 29 June 1970, n.p.]; "Theriot Appeals for Acadian Awareness," n.p., n.d., CS.

20. Walter Coquille, *Mayor of Bayou Pom Pom* (New Orleans: American Printing, 1929), passim; "The Lord of Pom Pom," Walter Coquille obituary, *Newsweek*, 9 December 1957, 38; F. R. Duplantier, "Cajun Humor: Is It Funny Only in French?" *La gazette des acadiens* (Jennings, La.), December 1976, 6–7; Broven, *South to Louisiana*, 278; Howard Jacobs, "Attacks on Cajun Humor Draw Variety of Responses," *Times-Picayune*, 7 July 1974, sec. 2, p. 4; "CODOFIL Responds to Cajun Humor Issue," *Times-Picayune*, 21 July 1974, sec. 3, p. 12; Ancelet, "Cajun Who Went to Harvard," 112.

21. James Domengeaux, "Cajun Not Same Thing as C–A [*sic*]," letter to editor, *Daily Advertiser*, 19 January 1975, n.p., CS; "Scot-Irish 'Frenchy' Explains Derivation," letter to editor, *Morning Advocate*, 5 August 1981, n.p., BJAC; "French Still Use Coonass Tag," editorial, *Mamou (La.) Prairie*, 15 December 1977, n.p., CS; Chris Segura, "Afro-Cajuns: Cultural Survival at Stake," *Daily World*, 12 November 1998, 9–A; "A 'Disgusting' Prostitute or a Davy Crockett Hat?" *Times-Picayune*, 25 October 1972, 9; "The Coonass Dilemma," letter to editor, *Lafayette (La.) Times of Acadiana*, 13 January 1999, 4; Barry Jean Ancelet, "On Coonass" [unpublished essay], n.d., n.p., TD, BJAC; "Cajun Coonass" photograph, National Archives and Records Administration, Special Media Archives Services Division (Still Picture Reference Team), College Park, Md., photograph identification number 342-FH-3A-32507-79171a.c., April 1943; Joe N. Silverberg, "From Our Point of View," column, *Daily Comet*, 12 January 1971, 2; Allan Katz, "Edwards under Fire for 'Coonass' Jibe," *New Orleans States-Item*, 24 October 1972, 14; James Domengeaux, Lafayette, La., to Ray Authement, president, University of Southwestern Louisiana, Lafayette, 21 February 1976, TL [photocopy], CS; James Domengeaux, Lafayette, La., to Ray Authement, president, University of Southwestern Louisiana, Lafayette, 24 February 1976, TL [photocopy], CS.

Domengeaux himself apparently originated the *conasse* etymology. In Katz, "Edwards under Fire," 14, the journalist states that Domengeaux "said he has researched the matter." For more about Domengeaux's etymology of *coonass*, see James Harvey Domengeaux, "Native-Born Acadians and the Equality Ideal," *Louisiana Law Review* 46 (July 1986): 1151 (asterisked footnote), 1168–69. (James Harvey Domengeaux is the nephew of CODOFIL chairman James Domengeaux.)

22. "French Council Hassle Develops," 1, 6; Bob Angers Jr., "Harmonious Relations Said Needed at French Meeting," *Daily Advertiser*, 11 October 1968, 2; Marino, "C of C Protests Naming of Rodgers," 1, 2; "Governor Asked to Reconsider Appointment," *Morning Advocate*, 13 September 1968, 15–A; Jim LaCaffinie, "Another Quebec Delegation Visits—This Time without Protocol Problem," *Morning Advocate*, 22 December 1968, n.p., CS.

23. Raymond Spencer Rodgers, Lafayette, La., to William Dodd, secretary, State Board of Education, Baton Rouge, La., 28 November 1967, TLS [photocopy], RSRC; Raymond Spencer Rodgers, [Lafayette, La.?], to Graduate Dean Olivier, [University of Southwestern Louisiana, Lafayette], 22 June 1967, TLS [photocopy], RSRC; Raymond Spencer Rodgers, Winnipeg, Canada, letter to editor, *Daily Advertiser*, Lafayette, La., 1 October 1968, TLS [photocopy], RSRC; Raymond Spencer Rodgers, Winnipeg, Canada,

to the Givens Agency, Lafayette, La., 18 December 1968, TLS [photocopy], RSRC; John J. McKeithen, governor of Louisiana, Baton Rouge, to Wilfred C. Lockhart, president, University of Winnipeg, Canada, 15 August 1968, TL [photocopy], RSRC; "Louisiana Seeks Local Prof," *Winnipeg (Canada) Free Press,* 24 August 1968, n.p., RSRC; "Governor Wants Ro[d]gers to Head Acadian Heritage," *Daily World,* 30 August 1968, 11; minutes of CODOFIL organizational meeting, 9; Marino, "C of C Protests Naming Rodgers," 2; James Domengeaux, Lafayette, La., to Ray Authement, academic vice president, University of Southwestern Louisiana, Lafayette, 26 January 1968, TLS, SAMC.

24. "CODOFIL Head: Auditor Wrong," *Times-Picayune,* 30 May 1973, sec. 1, p. 17; "CODOFIL Spending Cited," *Daily Advertiser,* 28 May 1973, 16; "Domengeaux Disputes Report," *Daily Advertiser,* 30 May 1973, 17; Earl McRae, "Louisiana libre!" *Toronto (Canada) Star,* 13 May 1973, n.p., CS; "French Teacher Proposal Attacked," *Daily Advertiser,* 21 November 1972, 1, 2; George Arceneaux, *Youth in Acadia: Reflections on Acadian Life and Culture in Southwest Louisiana* (Baton Rouge: Claitor's, 1974), 91; Pierre V. Daigle, *Tears, Love and Laughter: The Story of the Acadians* (Church Point, La.: Acadian Publishing Enterprise, 1972), 11–12, 71, 128; Howard Jacobs, "School Role in Study of French Clarified," *Times-Picayune,* 27 September 1972, sec. 1, p. 15; "Cajun Debaters 'Hilarious Hamlets,'" *States-Item,* n.d. [late 1972–early 1973?], n.p., CS; Simon, "CODOFIL: A Case Study," 37; Jerry Estill, "French Group Disgruntled—Say They Have Been Duped," *State-Times,* 24 May 1973, 1-B, 13-C; "Strike Set by Teachers from France," *Morning Advocate,* 29 April 1973, n.p., CS; "CODOFIL Fires 5 Teachers," *Times-Picayune,* 9 June 1973, n.p., CS.

25. Ross H. Munro, "French Is Dying in Louisiana," *Toronto Globe and Mail,* 29 March 1973, n.p., CS; S. J. Young, "Polar Views on CODOFIL," *Bayou Bengal,* 18 December 1970, 11; "PREFAM Meets in Rayne Monday," *Daily Advertiser,* 21 November 1971, n.p., CS; "CODOFIL Will Be Replaced Says PREFAM Organizer," *Abbeville Meridional,* 2 December 1971, n.p., CS; Daigle, *Tears, Love and Laughter,* 128–29.

26. "145 from France Are Teaching Louisiana's Children a Tongue That Was Nearly Stilled," *New York Times,* 3 October 1972, 14; "French Language Instruction Falters in South Louisiana," editorial, *Daily Advertiser,* 19 March 1972, 46.

27. Munro, "French Is Dying in Louisiana," n.p.; 1990 PUMS, for Persons; "French Teachers May Be [a] Little Bit Discouraged," *Daily Advertiser,* 28 November 1975, n.p., CS; Sam Hodges, "French Language Program in Trouble?" n.p., n.d. [*Shreveport (La.) Times,* February 1981?], CS.

28. "'Let Foes Beware the Bayou Blitz' Lewis Tells Departing Selectees," *Daily World,* 9 July 1941, 1.

29. "Entire Range of Folk Music Slated," *Newport Daily News,* 20 July 1964, 14; Jane Nippert, "Basic Musical Cultures Launch Folk Festival," *Newport Daily News,* 24 July 1964, 1, 4; Jane Nippert, "Festival Program Runs Wide Gamut," *Newport Daily News,* 25 July 1964, 1; Robert Shelton, "Newport Begins Its Folk Festival," *New York Times,* 24 July 1964, 16; Robert Shelton, "Folk Music Gains in Newport Event," *New York Times,* 26 July 1964, 56; Ancelet, *Cajun Music,* 37–40; Ancelet, *Makers of Cajun Music,* 29, 30, 121, 123; Ancelet et al., *Cajun Country,* xx, 161; Broven, *South to Louisiana,* 243–45; Dewey Balfa, "Valse de Newport," in *Yé yaille, chère! Traditional Cajun Dance Music,* comp. and ed. Raymond E. François (Lafayette, La.: Thunderstone, 1990), 428–29.

30. Bona Arsenault, *Histoire et généalogie des Acadiens,* 2 vols. (Quebec: Le Conseil de la Vie Française en Amérique, 1965) [later expanded to six volumes]; Bona Arsenault, *History of the Acadians* (Quebec: Le Conseil de la Vie Française en Amérique, 1966); Dudley LeBlanc, *The Acadian Miracle* (Lafayette, La.: Evangeline Publishing, 1966); Father Donald J. Hébert, *Southwest Louisiana Records,* 48 vols. (1750–1916) (Rayne, La.: Hébert Publishing, 1974–98). Hébert also published *South Louisiana Records,* 12 vols. (1794–1920) (Rayne, La.: Hébert Publishing, 1978–85), documenting church and civic records from southeast Acadiana. Robert L. Olivier, *Tidoon: A Story of the Cajun Teche* (Gretna, La.: Pelican, 1972), 66; Robert L. Olivier, *Tinonc: Son of the Cajun Teche* (Gretna, La.: Pelican, 1974).

31. Daigle, *Tears, Love and Laughter,* 57, 65; Revon Reed, *Lâche pas la patate: Portrait des acadiens de la Louisiane* (Montreal: Éditions Parti Pris, 1976); Rushton, *The Cajuns,* 282–83.

32. "Rodrigue's Art Shown at Center," *Daily Advertiser,* 12 July 1970, 18; "Louisiana Artist Preserves Image of Gourmet Society," *Daily Advertiser,* 28 January 1971, 31; George Rodrigue, *The Cajuns of George Rodrigue* (Birmingham, Ala.: Oxmoor House, 1976); "'Thrust into Courage of Past' Citation by Author to Artist," *Eunice (La.) News,* 6 January 1976, n.p., CS; Eleanor Yount, "Floyd Sonnier Portrays Acadian Heritage," n.p., 10 April 1977, 26, CS; "Meet Bec Doux, Cajun Friends," *Daily Advertiser,* 10 April 1970, n.p., CS; Judy Broussard, "How 'Bec Doux' Happened," *Daily Advertiser,* 23 May 1971, 30; Deb David, "Kaplan Pair Tries to Save Cajun, Fulfil Dream with Comic Strip," *Daily Advertiser,* 10 June 1979, 49; Patti Taylor, "Camera Angles," column, *Acadiana* [KATC promotional newsletter], July 1967, 3, VF, SAMC; Patti Taylor, "Camera Angles," column, *Acadiana,* November 1967, 3, VF, SAMC; "Polycarp 'Mr. Acadiana,'" *Acadiana,* November 1967, 1, VF, SAMC; "'Dogs Mostly Native,'" *Vermilion,* 12 July 1963, 4; "Football Returns to USL, Season Opens on Sept. 20," *Vermilion,* 9 September 1963, 4; "Ragin' Cajuns Meet Lions," *Vermilion,* 20 September 1963, 8; "Augie's Doggies Turn Cajun," *L'Acadien,* 1975 USL Yearbook [in reference to 1974 football season], 276.

33. *Dictionary of Louisiana Biography,* vol. 1, s.v. "LeBlanc, Dudley J. ('Couzin Dud')"; Wall, *Louisiana,* 358–59, 360–61, 362; "More French Use Asked by Edwards," *Daily Advertiser,* 6 April 1972, 1; John Maginnis, *The Last Hayride* (Baton Rouge: Gris Gris Press, 1984), 24; John Hill, "Edwards Gets 10 Years," *Daily Advertiser,* 9 January 2001, 1A, 7A.

34. Les Blank with Skip Gerson, *Spend It All,* 41 min., Flower Films, 1971, film documentary; Paul Goldsmith, *The Good Times Are Killing Me,* 1975, film documentary; Broven, *South to Louisiana,* 63–64, 238; Doug Kershaw, *Lou'siana Man* (New York: MacMillan, 1971), 23, 31, 41; Licensing contract between Floyd Soileau [Flat Town Music Company], Ville Platte, La., and Apple Corps Limited, London, England, signed by George Harrison, Floyd Soileau, and members of Lesa Cormier and the Sundown Playboys, dated 2 October 1972, TDS, original in possession of Floyd Soileau, Flat Town Music Company, Ville Platte, La.; Full-page advertisement for Lesa Cormier and the Sundown Playboys, "Saturday Night Special," 45 RPM single 1852, Apple, 1972, *Billboard,* 7 October 1972, back page.

35. Barry Jean Ancelet, introduction, *Cajun Music and Zydeco* [photographic collection], by Philip Gould (Baton Rouge: Louisiana State University Press, 1992), xi–xv;

Ancelet, *Makers of Cajun Music,* 31–32, 124; Dormon, *People Called Cajuns,* 86–87; Simon, "CODOFIL: A Case Study," 75; Angie Delcambre, "Eating Gumbo with a Silver Spoon: The Attempted Revival of Cajun Culture in South Louisiana" (honors program thesis, Stanford University, 1994), 24, photocopy in author's possession; "Tribute Paid to Cajun Music," *Daily Advertiser,* 25 March 1974, 10; Martha Aycock, "Coliseum Is Full of Cajun Spirit," *Daily Advertiser,* 27 March 1974, 1, 4; "'Academic Exercise' Turns into Mass Rally for Cajuns," *Daily Advertiser,* 28 March 1974, 12; Jim Bourgeois, "Tribute Concert Staged in Blackham," *Vermilion,* 5 April 1974, 14; Carol Raymond, "Lafayette Man Collects Louisiana Folklore [Barry Jean Ancelet]," *Daily Advertiser,* 25 July 1976, n.p., CS; Sarah Spell-Johnson, "Ancestral Voices," *La Louisiane,* fall 1995, 29, passim.

36. James H. Dormon, "Louisiana's Cajuns: A Case Study in Ethnic Group Revitalization," *Social Science Quarterly* 65 (December 1984): 1052–53; Ancelet, *Cajun Music and Zydeco,* xv.

37. The author has granted anonymity to the radical Cajun activist quoted in this paragraph.

38. Jacques Henry, "From *Acadien* to *Cajun* to *Cadien:* Ethnic Labelization and Construction of Identity," *Journal of American Ethnic History* 17 (summer 1998): 44–45, 47; House Concurrent Resolution no. 68, to express the intent of the Legislature with respect to the proper designation to be accorded those citizens . . . who are of French-Acadian descent, approved 27 May 1974, *1974 Legislative Calendar,* 37th reg. sess., 463; Howard Jacobs, "'Cajun' Is Endorsed by CODOFIL Head," *Times-Picayune,* 29 August 1974, 11; Dormon, "Louisiana's Cajuns," 1054; Stan Tiner, "Column One," column, *Shreveport (La.) Journal,* 12 June 1981, n.p., CS; Royal Brightbill, "South Louisiana French Still Using 'Coonass,'" *Thibodaux (La.) Comet,* 7 December 1977, n.p., CS; "Reagan Uses 'Coonass' Term in Talk Here," *State Times,* 7 May 1976, n.p., CS; "Reagan 'Blooper' Draws Cheer," *Daily World,* 7 May 1976, n.p., CS; Carl A. Brasseaux, *In Search of Evangeline: Birth and Evolution of the Evangeline Myth* (Thibodaux, La.: Blue Heron Press, 1988), 52.

39. Barry Jean Ancelet, letter to editor, *Gris Gris,* n.d., TLS [photocopy], BJAC.

40. Anderson, *Movement and the Sixties,* 408–9; Anderson, *The Sixties,* 206–9; Peter N. Carroll, *It Seemed Like Nothing Happened: America in the 1970s* (New Brunswick, N.J.: Rutgers University Press, 1990), 250; Joshua A. Fishman, Michael H. Gertner, Esther G. Lowy, and William G. Milán, *The Rise and Fall of the Ethnic Revival: Perspectives on Language and Ethnicity,* Contributions to the Sociology of Language no. 37 (New York: Mouton Publishers, 1985), 490.

41. Mrs. Leroy Faul et al. v. Superintendent of Education, Louis F. Gaudet, and the School Board of Jefferson Davis Parish, Appeal Number 6828 (3rd Circuit Court of Appeal, Louisiana, 1979), *Southern Reporter,* 2nd Series (1979), 1267–74; Act 714, to provide a procedure for petitioning a parish or city school board for the inclusion of the teaching of a second language in the general curriculum, approved 17 July 1975, *Acts Passed by the Legislature of the State of Louisiana at the Regular Session of 1975,* 2:1529–31; Barbara Ryder, "*En défense de la langue française:* An Interview with CODOFIL Chairman James Domengeaux," *Louisiana Renaissance,* winter 1978–79, 24. *Acadiana Profile* dropped its subtitle "A Magazine for Bilingual Louisiana" in 1976.

CHAPTER 5

1. Most of these Cajun-related items were found for sale on the Internet auction house eBay, www.eBay.com, accessed 1999–2000. Elizabeth Mullener, "Counterfeit Cajun Can't Come Close," *Times-Picayune,* 16 August 1988, A8.

2. Carroll, *Seemed Like Nothing Happened,* 220; Howard, "Politics of the Acadian Parishes," 188; Tom Squitieri, "Cajuns Can KO Carter," *Daily Advertiser,* 26 October 1980, 1, 4.

3. Michael Schaller, *Reckoning with Reagan: America and Its President in the 1980s* (New York: Oxford University Press, 1992), 60, 74–76.

4. Katrinna Chéri Huggs, "The Gospel According to Paul," *Times of Acadiana,* 24 August 1994, 19, 20; Bob Marshall and Gene Bourg, "Banned: La. Redfish Declared Off-Limits to All," *Times-Picayune,* 8 January 1988, A-1, A-4; Mimi Sheraton, "Eat American! Summer's Bounty Inspires Young Chefs," *Time,* 26 August 1985, 58; Christopher Cox and Chet Kaufman, "Cajun Cooking Coast to Coast," *Baton Rouge (La.) Sunday Magazine,* 22 June 1986, 22; "Opelousas Hails Native Son Prudhomme Today," *Daily Advertiser,* 7 March 1988, 6.

5. Tim Talley, "La. Cooking Becomes Big Business," *Morning Advocate,* 1 November 1987, 12A; Rhonda McKendall, "Cajun Will Add Spice to Soviet Way of Life," *Times-Picayune,* 17 May 1988, A-1, A-4; Joe Gyan Jr., "Chef John Folse Returns from U.S.S.R.," *Morning Advocate,* 5 June 1988, 1B, 5B.

6. Talley, "La. Cooking," 1A; Cox and Kaufman, "Cajun Cooking," 20–21; James Edmunds, "First, You Don't Make a Roux," *Times of Acadiana,* 29 August 1985, 16; James Edmunds, "New York Eats Boudin," *Times of Acadiana,* 5 May 1983, 15; Mullener, "Counterfeit Cajun," A-8; Gene Bourg, "Cajun Rage May Die before Real Food's Tasted," *Times-Picayune,* 17 December 1985, D-12; Jack Wardlaw, "State: Fake Cajun Food Blackening La. Image," *Times-Picayune,* 7 March 1989, B-1; "Cajun Food Fight Brewing," *Daily Advertiser,* 2 April 1989, 11; Marcelle Tessier, "Imitation Cajun," n.p., [1989?], CS; Bennigan's online menu, www.bennigans.com, accessed 18 December 1999; Chili's online menu, www.chilis.com, accessed 18 December 1999; TGI Friday's online menu, www.tgifridays.com, accessed 18 December 1999; Shoney's online menu, www.shoneysrestaurants.com, accessed 17 March 2000; Angers, *Truth about the Cajuns,* 72; McDonald's and Burger King television menus and commercials, observed by author, New Iberia, La., 1999–2000; George Ritzer, *The McDonaldization of Society: An Investigation into the Changing Character of Contemporary Social Life* (Thousand Oaks, Calif.: Pine Forge Press, 1993), 2, 7–8, 40–41; "Popeye's Famous Fried Chicken," in John R. Kemp, *New Orleans: An Illustrated History* (Woodland Hills, Calif.: Windsor Publications/Preservation Resource Center of New Orleans, 1981), 292; Popeye's Web site, www.popeyes.com, accessed 18 December 1999, 9 January 2000, 7 December 2000, 7 October 2001; Popeye's and Copeland's menus, observed by author, Lafayette, La., 1997, 2000; Data about "Certified Logo Program," Louisiana Department of Agriculture and Forestry Web site, www.ldaf.state.la.us, accessed 19 December 1999; Public posting on USENET newsgroup alt.culture.cajun, 9 September 1999.

7. Esman, "Tourism as Ethnic Preservation," 455, 463, 464; Angers, *Truth about the Cajuns,* 7–8, 94, 111; Mason Florence and David Appell, "The Cheapest Places on Earth," *Arthur*

Frommer's Budget Travel, spring 1999, front cover, 7, 112–22; Ancelet et al., *Cajun Country,* 94; public postings on USENET newsgroup alt.culture.cajun, 26 February 1997, 17 March 1998; Barry Jean Ancelet, "Cajun Land," *Southern Exposure,* fall 1989, 52; advertisement for antitourist T-shirt, Floyd's Record Shop 2000 Catalog, Ville Platte, La., 15; Mike Tidwell, "Hitchhiking on Shrimp Boats through Louisiana's Cajun Country, the Author Discovers an Evocative—and Imperiled—Way of Life," *Washington Post,* 22 August 1999, E01; Margaret Moser, Ed Ward, Louis Black, Nick Barbaro, and Lee Nichols, "The *Austin Chronicle* Guide to Southwestern Louisiana," *Austin (Tex.) Chronicle,* 26 April 1996, n.p.; *1990 U.S. Census of Population, Social and Economic Characteristics, Louisiana,* sec. 1, table 137, pp. 196, 197, 198; *1990 U.S. Census of Population, Social and Economic Characteristics, Texas,* sec. 1, table 137, p. 190; Priit Vesilind, "Upbeat, Downbeat, Offbeat New Orleans," *National Geographic,* January 1995, 118.

Figures for Houston and New Orleans are based on a comparison of Harris County, Texas (metro Houston) and Orleans Parish, Louisiana (metro New Orleans).

8. Sleeve advertisement for *Thunder Bay,* MCA Home Video, 1990, videocassette; advertisement for *Bayou, Daily Advertiser,* 2 June 1957, 26, 3 June 1957, 8; "'Southern Comfort' Uneasy Film," *Times-Picayune/States-Item,* 20 October 1981, sec. 1, p. 12; Mathé Allain, "They Don't Even Talk Like Us: Cajun Violence in Film and Fiction," *Journal of Popular Culture* 23 (summer 1989): 72; Kendall Hamilton and Yahlin Chang, "Oh, You Silly Boy," *Newsweek,* 9 November 1998, 68; Lisa Schwarzbaum, "We'll Pass," *Entertainment Weekly,* 13 November 1998, 52; Roger Ebert, "The Big Easy," movie review, *Chicago Sun-Times,* 21 August 1987, n.p.; Barry Jean Ancelet, "Drinking, Dancing, Brawling Gamblers Who Spend Most of Their Time in the Swamp: That's a Composite Description of Cajuns in Film," *Times of Acadiana,* 20 June 1990, 14; Angers, *Truth about the Cajuns,* 20–21; author's notes concerning Cajun characters on television programs; "Larry Hagman Plays a Gambling Judge in 'Orleans,'" *Daily Advertiser,* 12 January 1997, 6E.

Information about these and other Cajun-related films were found on the Internet Movie Database, www.imdb.com, accessed 1999–2000.

9. Mike Hasten, "State's Economy Dependent on Oil and Gas Industry," *Daily Advertiser,* 20 October 1983, 29; *Louisiana Almanac,* 645 (historic average crude oil prices); Carl Redman, "Oil Glut Taking Its Toll on Louisiana Employment," *Morning Advocate,* 28 March 1983, 1-A, 8-A; Chuck Springton, "The Outlook for 1984," *Times of Acadiana,* 26 January 1984, 16–20; David Snyder, "Oil Boom Bust Casts a Shadow over Cajun Camelot," *Times-Picayune,* 20 March 1983, sec. 1, pp. 1, 12; "The Oil Depression," *Daily Advertiser,* 15 February 1987, 33; Thomas Petzinger Jr., and George Getschow, "In Louisiana, Big Oil Is Cozy with Officials and Benefit Is Mutual," *Wall Street Journal,* 22 October 1984, 1, 23; Thomas Petzinger Jr., and George Getschow, "In Louisiana, Pollution and Cancer Are Rife in the Petroleum Area," *Wall Street Journal,* 23 October 1984, 1, 24; George Getschow and Thomas Petzinger Jr., "Louisiana Marshlands, Laced with Oil Canals, Are Rapidly Vanishing," *Wall Street Journal,* 24 October 1984, 1, 26; Getschow and Petzinger, "One Thing Left behind Was Culture of Cajuns," 1, 28.

10. Elizabeth Mullener, "True Cajun Spice Fades with Years," *Times–Picayune,* 14 August 1988, A-10; *1990 U.S. Census of Population, Social and Economic Characteristics, Metropolitan Areas,* sec. 1, table 26, pp. 545, 546, 563, 576, 609, 620, 622, 629, 635, 650,

653, 660, 665; Bruce Dobie, "Cajuns in Exile," pt. 1, *Times of Acadiana,* 16 September 1987, 16–21; Bruce Dobie, "Cajuns in Exile," pt. 2, *Times of Acadiana,* 23 September 1987, 11–17; Jane Nicholes, "Coming Home," *Times of Acadiana,* 11 November 1990, 18–19.

11. Clifford J. Clarke, "Religion and Regional Culture: The Changing Pattern of Religious Affiliation in the Cajun Region of Southwest Louisiana," *Journal for the Scientific Study of Religion* 24 (December 1985): 384–95; Tony Alamo, *Fugitive Pope* [anti-Catholic pamphlet] (Van Buren, Ark.: Music Square Church, [ca. 1990]); "Protestant Churches Grow in Membership," *Daily Advertiser,* 28 March 1974, 37; Jesse Duplantis Ministries Web site, www.jdm.org, accessed 30 October 2000; 1965 Southern Bell telephone directory, greater Lafayette, yellow pages, 42–43; 1998–99 BellSouth telephone directory, greater Lafayette, yellow pages, 203–7.

12. Kathy LeJeune, "French Students Find Louisiana Too American," n.p., 2 August 1978, CS; CODOFIL flyer concerning organization's possible termination, 1 February 1993, VF, SAMC; David Marcantel, "Coonass Controversy Continues," letter to editor, *Gris Gris,* 18 June 1979, n.p., BJAC.

13. Francis Debyser, Jan Lobelle, Andre Paquette, Robert Paris, and Lawrence Richard, "1978 Evaluation of Louisiana State-Wide CODOFIL French Program," 10 March 1978, D, ii, 1, 4, 5, 6, BJAC; "State French Program Examined by Experts," *Daily Advertiser,* 13 March 1978, n.p., BJAC; "Language Specialist Recommends Change in CODOFIL Thrust," *Morning Advocate,* 14 March 1978, 17-C; "Acadia Kills CODOFIL," *Jennings (La.) Daily News,* 20 June 1978, n.p., CS; Vicki Ferstel, "CODOFIL Stirs Emotions at Meeting," *Daily News,* 21 June 1978, n.p., CS; John Gravois, "Parish Drops CODOFIL Program," *Courier and Terrebonne Press,* n.d. [June 1978?], CS; Bonnie Landry, "St. Mary Might Drop CODOFIL," *Daily Iberian,* 26 June 1978, n.p., CS; Sandra Lantz, "Bilingual Program Disappears from Budget: CODOFIL Cut in Evangeline," *Daily World,* 8 September 1978, n.p., CS; Susan Harrison, "Iberia Drops CODOFIL for Next School Year," *Daily Iberian,* 16 November 1978, n.p., CS.

14. James Donald Faulk, *Cajun French I* (Abbeville, La.: Cajun Press, 1977); "Teacher Attempts to Put Cajun French in Writing," *Daily Advertiser,* 11 July 1977, 5; Cory Toevs, "Vermilion Man Launches Crusade to Save Language," *Abbeville Meridional,* 24 November 1977, n.p., BJAC; James Domengeaux, "Statement of Position of the Council for the Development of French in Louisiana (CODOFIL), James Domengeaux, Chairman, in Support of the Recommendation of the Textbook and Media Advisory Council of the Department of Education Concerning Its Action in Refusing to Authorize the Supplemental Use of the Textbook, *Cajun French One* [sic], Authored by James Donald Faulk[,] in French Language Curriculum Instructions in Louisiana's High Schools," [1979?], TDS, 5, BJAC; Laurie Smith, "Author Hopes to Help Preserve Language of Cajun French," *State Times,* 19 August 1977, n.p., BJAC; "Cajun French Language Gains Academic Status," *Crowley (La.) Post-Signal,* 23 September 1977, n.p., BJAC; "'French' Battle Lines Beginning to Develop," *Morning Advocate,* 6 April 1979, n.p., BJAC; "Cajun French Text Battle Lines Drawn," *Morgan City (La.) Daily Review,* 16 April 1979, n.p., BJAC; "Advisory Board Drops Cajun Text's Approval," *Morning Advocate,* 19 April 1979, n.p., BJAC; Woody Baird, "CODOFIL Chief Trying to Block Cajun French Book," *Times-Picayune,* 19 April 1979, n.p., BJAC; "CODOFIL Frowns on Cajun French Textbook," *American Press,* 6 April 1979, n.p., BJAC; "CODOFIL versus

Local Man," *Abbeville Meridional,* 9 April 1979, n.p., BJAC; Rushton, *The Cajuns,* 289–90; Barry Jean Ancelet, "A Perspective on Teaching the 'Problem Language' in Louisiana," *French Review* 61 (1988): 349–50; Miles Hawthorne, "Folklorist Seeks 'Cultural Equity,'" *Daily Advertiser,* 20 April 1980, n.p., BJAC; Woody Baird, "Lomax at Odds with CODOFIL," *Daily Advertiser,* 19 June 1980, n.p., BJAC; Woody Baird, "Attempt to Save Cajun Culture May Be Killing It, Expert Says," *Shreveport Times,* 19 June 1980, n.p., BJAC.

15. Christopher Rose, "La. Bidding French Adieu Despite Agency's Efforts," *Times-Picayune,* 24 December 1990, A–8; Richard Mackie, "PM Says Special Status Needed to Protect French," *Toronto Globe and Mail,* 20 October 1992, 1; "Cajunization," editorial cartoon, *Toronto Globe and Mail,* 21 October 1992, n.p., BJAC.

16. Ancelet et al., *Cajun Country,* xviii; Ancelet and Morgan, *Makers of Cajun Music,* 137.

17. "*La renaissance de la langue française:* French Language Revival," *Times of Acadiana,* 10 May 1995, 28.

18. Jean Arceneaux, "Enfants du silence, I," in *Cris sur le bayou: Naissance d'une poésie acadienne en Louisiane,* ed. Barry Jean Ancelet (Montreal: Éditions Intermède, 1980), 65; Ancelet, "Teaching the 'Problem Language,'" 347. Domengeaux expressed his negative views concerning Cajun French in "Cajun French Language Gains Academic Status," n.p., and "CODOFIL Frowns on Cajun French Textbook," n.p.

19. Ancelet, "Teaching the 'Problem Language,'" 348, 350, 352–53; Mike Maher, "Written down at Last? USL Profs Begin Course with Cajun French Text," *Gris Gris,* 4 June 1979, n.p., CS.

20. Ancelet, "Teaching the 'Problem Language,'" 351–52.

21. Hodges, "French Language Program in Trouble?" n.p.; Ann Wakefield, "La cause française, comment ça va?" *Times of Acadiana,* 19 December 1985, 31; Katrinna Chéri Huggs, "Commes des petites éponges (Like Little Sponges)," *Times of Acadiana,* 10 May 1995, 23, 25, 29–30; former immersion teacher, public posting on USENET newsgroup alt.culture.cajun, 21 October 1999.

22. Ancelet, "Teaching the 'Problem Language,'" 350–51; David Barry, "A French Literary Renaissance in Louisiana: Cultural Reflections," *Journal of Popular Culture* 23 (summer 1989): 47–63; Pallister, "Cadjinitude," 11–12; Darrell Bourque, "Plainsongs of the *Marais Bouleur:* A Selection," *Journal of Popular Culture* 23 (summer 1989): 37–45; Biographical sketch of Tim Gautreaux, *Zoetrope: All-Story,* vol. 3, no. 2 (1999), online literary journal, www.zoetrope-stories.com, accessed 13 October 2000; Charlie Bier, "The Work of Burke," *Times of Acadiana,* 19 January 2000, 11–12; Steven Del Sesto and John L. Gibson, eds., *The Culture of Acadiana: Tradition and Change in South Louisiana* (Lafayette: University of Southwestern Louisiana, 1975); Greg Guirard, *Cajun Families of the Atchafalaya: Their Ways and Words* (St. Martinville, La.: self-published, 1989); Philip Gould, *Les cadiens d'asteur: Today's Cajuns* (Lafayette, La.: Acadiana Press, 1980); Todd Mouton, "Master of Allusion: Robert Dafford's Downtown Mural Renders Culture and Conflict on a Cajun Planet," *Times of Acadiana,* 8 December 1999, 20–23, 25–26; Biographical sketch of Francis X. Pavy, www.pavy.com, accessed 13 October 2000; Katrinna Chéri Huggs, "How Much for That Blue Doggie in the Window?" *Times of Acadiana,* 23 February 1994, 13–17; Rick Bragg, "An Artist and a Dog That Became a Cultural Icon," *New York Times,* 16 September 1998, E2; Mary Tutwiler, "Blue Dog

Unleashed," *LifeStyle Lafayette (Lafayette, La.)*, 12 November–2 December 1999, 13–15; "Capitol Questions," www.c-span.org, accessed 4 February 2000.

Information about these and other Cajun-related films were found on the Internet Movie Database, www.imdb.com, accessed 1999–2000.

Billy Tauzin, a Louisiana congressman and former Blue Dog leader prior to becoming a Republican, has asserted that the term was actually a play on the phrase *Yellow Dog Democrat*, used to describe fiercely loyal party members.

23. Ancelet, *Cajun Music*, 44–50; Ancelet and Morgan, *Makers of Cajun Music*, 143, 146; Ancelet et al., *Cajun Country*, 161–62; Arsenio Orteza, "A Little Bit of Zack's World," *Times of Acadiana*, 24 June 1998, 18–19, 21–24; Todd Mouton, "A Tale of Two Cultures," *Times of Acadiana*, 11 August 1999, 16–21.

24. John St. Ores, "Eunice Celebrates Prairie Acadian Culture," *Daily Advertiser*, 10 July 1997, 1B; Ancelet, *Cajun Music*, 41; Katrinna [Chéri] Huggs, "Make Mine French," *Times of Acadiana*, 24 June 1987, 14–15; Nissa Darbonne, "Lifting Economic Spirits," *Daily Advertiser*, 20 April 1997, 1D; Lisa Sylvester, "KRVS Graduates from College to Success," *Daily Advertiser*, 18 January 1981, 48; Robert S. Wolf, "Two-Stepping on the Air: Zydeco and Cajun Radio," *Daily Advertiser*, 9 January 1997, 1B; Kermit Bouillion, "Lafayette Station Revives French Music on Tube," *Eunice News*, 25 September 1980, n.p., CS.

25. Johnnie Allen [John Allen Guillot], *Memories: A Pictorial History of South Louisiana Music, 1920s-1980s, Vol. 1, South Louisiana and East Texas Musicians* (Lafayette, La.: Johnnie Allan/JADFEL, 1988); Bernard, *Swamp Pop*, 108.

26. Linda Keenan with Karen Collins and Ben Pagac, "History of Cajun and Zydeco Music in the Washington/Baltimore Area," 1995–96, revised 1997, TD, original in possession of Linda Keenan, Washington, D.C.; Mary Chapin Carpenter, "Down at the Twist and Shout," *Shooting Straight in the Dark*, compact disc, Columbia, 1980; Bruce Murray, "Honor Lifts Cajun Music to New Heights," *Daily Advertiser*, 22 March 1998, 1A, 4A.

27. "These Are Cajun Times," *Cajun Times* (U.K.), April 1995, 1–2; "A Thick Cajun Stew: Filé Gumbo," *Cajun Times*, April 1995, 5; Ron Knowles, "Cajun and Zydeco Music and Dance in the UK," *Cajun Times*, July–September 1998, 20, 22, 24; Glyn Roberts, "A Cajun History of the North," *Cajun Times*, April–June 1999, 18, 20; Tim Rutherford, "10 Years of Filé Gumbo: A Brief Personal Memoir," *Cajun Times*, July–September 1999, 27.

28. "Cajun Claims Discrimination in Job Firing," *Times-Picayune*, 20 April 1980, sec. 1, p. 10; Calvin J. Roach v. Dresser Industrial Valve and Instrument Division, a Division of Dresser Industries, Inc., Deposition of Calvin Joseph Roach, Civil Action no. 78–0157 (U.S. District Court, Western District of Louisiana, Alexandria Division, 1979), 11–24, 101–3, 110–11, 116, 169, on file at U.S. District Court, Western District of Louisiana, U.S. Courthouse, Shreveport, La.; Calvin J. Roach v. Dresser Industrial Valve and Instrument Division, a Division of Dresser Industries, Inc., Testimony of Calvin Joseph Roach, Civil Action no. 78–0157 (U.S. District Court, Western District of Louisiana, Alexandria Division, [1980]), 4–14, on file at U.S. District Court, Western District of Louisiana, U.S. Courthouse, Shreveport, La.; Mike Hasten, "Cajuns Can Claim Status under Equal Job Act," *Daily Advertiser*, 10 August 1980, 17; "Cajun Origins Recognized by Federal Court," *Mamou Prairie*, 14 August 1980, n.p., VF, SAMC; Calvin J. Roach v. Dresser Industrial Valve and Instrument Division, a Division of Dresser Industries, Inc., Ruling of Judge Edwin F. Hunter Jr., Civil Action no. 78–0157 (U.S. District Court,

Western District of Louisiana, Alexandria Division, 1980), on file at U.S. District Court, Western District of Louisiana, U.S. Courthouse, Shreveport, La.

29. "Cajuns Ask Minority Status," *New York Times*, 23 May 1988, n.p., CS; "Blacks Opposing Cajun Bill," *Daily Advertiser*, 23 May 1988, 20; Ed Anderson, "Cajuns a Minority? House Says Yes," *Times-Picayune*, 19 May 1988, A-24; Ed Anderson, "Lawmakers Drop Cajun Minority Bill," *Times-Picayune*, 9 July 1988, A-1, A-4.

30. "Cajuns Get New Respect from [Census] Bureau," *Daily Advertiser*, 1 August 1993, A-12; "Legal Status Sought by Solons for 'Acadian, Cajun' Stickers," *Times-Picayune*, 18 May 1974, sec. 1, p. 7; "La. Senate Agrees with House, Acadians Are 'Cajuns[,]' Not. . . ," *Times-Picayune*, 22 May 1974, n.p., BJAC; "What's Good Word? Solons Agree It Sure Ain't C—A—," *Daily Advertiser*, 26 May 1974, 18; House Concurrent Resolution no. 68, 463; "'Coonass' Will Become Extinct If Lawmakers Have Their Way," *Times-Picayune/States-Item*, 3 June 1981, sec. 1, p. 26; "Senate Goes on Record against 'Nasty' Word," *Daily Advertiser*, 16 June 1981, n.p., CS; Matt Scallan, "'Coonass' Bill Passes; Haik Says It's Stupid," *Daily Iberian*, 12 July 1981, n.p., CS; "'Coonass' OK with Iberians," *Daily Iberian*, 8 June 1981, n.p., CS; Senate Concurrent Resolution no. 170, to condemn the use of the term *coonass* and to condemn the sale or promotion of any items containing that term, approved 13 July 1981, *1981 Legislative Calendar of the Legislature of the State of Louisiana*, vol. 2, 7th reg. sess., 1085.

31. Kathleen Thames, "Chairman of CODOFIL Insulted by Crawgator," *Daily Advertiser*, 12 August 1983, n.p., CS; Bruce Schultz, "Attorney Angry over Firm's Crawgator Cup," *Morning Advocate*, 13 August 1983, n.p., CS; "Gulf's 'Crawgator' Cup Draws Attorney's Wrath," *State-Times*, 13 August 1983, n.p., CS; "Crawgator Opposed," letter to editor, *Daily Advertiser*, 28 August 1983, n.p., CS; "Crawgator Promotion Insults Millions of Acadians," editorial, *Daily Advertiser*, 28 August 1983, n.p., CS; James Edmunds, "The Crawgator—Round Two," *Times of Acadiana*, n.d. [August–September 1983?], n.p., CS.

32. "CODOFIL Founder Domengeaux Dies," *Daily Advertiser*, 12 April 1988, 1, 2; *Dictionary of Louisiana Biography*, s.v. "Domengeaux, James 'Jimmy.'"

33. Baudouin, "Vengéance pour la déportation," 55–58; Louise McKinney, "Perrin's Petition," *World and I*, September 1995, 209, 210, 213; Jim Yardley, "Rematch: A Cajun vs. the Brits," *Atlanta Journal-Constitution*, 4 July 1995, B-4; "Those Weighty Issues: Lafayette Attorney Warren Perrin Wields Considerable Clout When It Comes to His Acadian French Heritage," *Times of Acadiana*, 5 May 1999, 32–33; Warren A. Perrin, "The Petition to Obtain an Apology for the Acadian Deportation: 'Warren A. Perrin, et al. Versus Great Britain, et al.,'" *Southern University Law Review* 27 (fall 1999): 3–4, 30, 31, 33–37, 44–45; Christopher Rose, "Cajun Holds Ancient Grudge against British," *Times-Picayune*, 4 June 1990, A–8; Senate Concurrent Resolution no. 159, to urge and request the government of Great Britain to end the exile of the Acadian People, approved 1 June 1993, *1993 Legislative Calendar of the Legislature of the State of Louisiana*, vol. 2, 19th reg. sess., 1222–23; résumé of Warren A. Perrin, 2000, TD, 1 p., original in possession of Warren A. Perrin, Lafayette, La.; Eric Lawlor, "The One-Man Acadian Liberation Front," *L.A. Times Magazine*, 4 September 1994, 26–28, 41; "Cajun Activist Girds for Battle Royal over Queen's Treatment of Forebears," *Dallas Morning Star*, 5 April 1995, n.p., original in possession of AM; Ron Delhomme, "The Queen on Trial: Perrin Tells England to Stop Being a Bully," *Daily Advertiser*, 13 August 1999, 9A; Ron Delhomme, "Mock Trial of Acadians vs. Crown Draws

Crowd," *Daily Advertiser,* 14 August 1999, 1A, 9A; Dave Francis, "Mock Trial Highlights Attempt at British Apology to Acadians," *Advocate,* 14 August 1999, 3B; "Queen Gets Mixed Response," *Daily Advertiser,* 23 October 1992, E-6; Warren A. Perrin, form complaint letter concerning use of *coonass,* n.d., TD, 3 pp., original in possession of Warren A. Perrin, Lafayette, La.; Robert Estrin, "Police Regret Pepper Spray Comment," Associated Press article, 13 August 1999, www.ap.org, accessed 15 August 1999; Warren A. Perrin, Lafayette, La., to Ronnie Watson, police commissioner, Cambridge, Mass., 25 August 1999, TLS, original in possession of Warren A. Perrin, Lafayette, La.; Ronnie Watson, Cambridge, Mass., to Warren A. Perrin, Lafayette, La., 31 August 1999, TLS, original in possession of Warren A. Perrin, Lafayette, La.; B. Drummond Ayres Jr., "On Bayou, Non-Cajuns Fight for Recognition," *New York Times,* 23 November 1997, 10; James H. Dormon, "Ethnicity and Identity: Creoles of Color in Twentieth-Century South Louisiana," in *Creoles of Color of the Gulf South,* ed. James H. Dormon (Knoxville: University of Tennessee Press, 1996), 173, 178 n. 4; Ruth Foote, "Farrakhan Plan Stirs Label Debate," *Advocate,* 24 July 1997, 1B, 2B; Carissa D. Mire, "Nation of Islam Protests Cajundome Naming," *Vermilion,* 7 November 1997, 1; manifesto of Un-Cajun Committee, n.d., TD, 2, photocopy in possession of Warren A. Perrin, Lafayette, La.; Warren A. Perrin, Lafayette, La., to Adofo Harmon, Un-Cajun Committee, Lafayette, La., 1 August 1997, TLS, photocopy in possession of Warren A. Perrin, Lafayette, La.; Daniels, *Coming to America,* 318, 397–99; Margot Hornblower, "Putting Tongues in Check," *Time,* 9 October 1995, 42; Warren A. Perrin, Lafayette, La., to Congressman Randy "Duke" Cunningham, [Washington, D.C.], 26 October 1995, TLS, photocopy in possession of Warren A. Perrin, Lafayette, La.; Congress, House, English Language Empowerment Act, 104th Cong., 2nd sess., H.R. 123, approved 1 August 1996, Library of Congress Web site, www.loc.gov, accessed 28 November 1999, 15 January 2000; House Bill no. 701, to designate English as the official state language, *1999 Legislative Calendar of the Legislature of the State of Louisiana,* vol. 1, 25th reg. sess., 238; Warren A. Perrin, Lafayette, La., to Representative Robert Marionneaux Jr., Livonia, La., 20 May 1999, TDS, photocopy in possession of Warren A. Perrin, Lafayette, La.

34. "Action Cadienne," *Times of Acadiana,* 14 June 1995, 3; Angela Simoneaux, "Group Promoting French Immersion Program," *Advocate,* 19 July 1995, 4B; manifesto of Action Cadienne, ca. 1995, published pamphlet in author's possession; Huggs, "Comme des petites éponges," 23, 25; "*La renaissance de la langue française,*" 28; Report on French Immersion conference sponsored by Action Cadienne, 12 August 1999, Action Cadienne Web site, www.actioncadienne.org, accessed 7 March 2000.

35. "*La renaissance de la langue française,*" 28; Cajun studies program synopsis, Louisiana State University Web site, www.lsu.edu, accessed 7 March 2000; *The 30th Anniversary of CODOFIL,* 23 min., CODOFIL Foundation/Louisiana Public Broadcasting/Louisiana Educational Television Authority, 1998, videocassette, AM; Kenneth Hickson, "3,000 Exiles Honored in Wall of Names at Acadian Memorial," *Daily Iberian,* 1 June 1998, 1; Acadian Memorial Web site, www.acadianmemorial.org, accessed 13 October 2000.

36. Congrès mondial acadien-Louisiane 1999, press release, original in author's possession; Shala Carlson, "Two Fêtes Are Better Than One," *Times of Acadiana,* 27 May 1998, 13–17, 19; Patrick Courreges, "The Grand Finale: Concert in the Cajundome Ends Congrès mondial acadien," *Daily Advertiser,* 16 August 1999, 1A.

37. Pauline Arrillaga, "Amid Tragedy and Terror, Americans Raise Old Glory in an Enduring Sign of Solidarity," Associated Press article, 13 September 2001, www.ap.org, accessed 28 October 2001; Bruce Schultz, "U.S. Flag Sales Very Brisk in Lafayette," *Advocate*, 14 September 2001, 15A; George Rodrigue, "Finding Comfort through Art—and the Blue Dog," letter to editor, *Times of Acadiana*, 31 October 2001, 5.

38. Ancelet et al., *Cajun Country*, xxiii.

CONCLUSION

1. Stephen Webre, "Among the Cybercajuns: Constructing Identity in the Virtual Diaspora," *Louisiana History* 39 (fall 1998): 443–56; Nancy Regent, "Cajuns on the Web," *Advocate*, 23 December 1996, 1B, 2B; C. Richard Cotton, "Web Site Offers Potpourri on Cajun Culture," *Advocate*, 30 November 1998, 1B, 2B; www.google.com, accessed 7 October 2001.

2. "Genetics of the Acadian People," booklet distributed at symposium held in conjunction with Congrès Mondial Acadien, 9 August 1999, McNeese State University, Lake Charles, La.; Angela Simoneaux, "Acadian Genealogy Offers History, Genetic Research," *Advocate*, 6 August 1999, 1B, 2B; Angela Simoneaux, "Acadians' Genetic Secrets Studied," *Advocate*, 10 August 1999, 1B, 2B; "Researchers, Studying DNA from Cajuns, Identify Characteristics Unique to Group," *Morning Advocate*, 2 June 1991, 1B, 2B.

3. Darbonne, "Lifting Economic Spirits," 1D; "Philippe Gustin: A Teacher of International Business Solutions," *Acadiana @ Work*, March 2000, 10, 12.

4. Manifesto of Action Cadienne.

5. Data on number of French Immersion students found in CODOFIL, "Réunion annuelle du CODOFIL," 16 October 1999, D, photocopy in author's possession; Louisiana Department of Education, "1998–1999 Louisiana State Education Progress Report" (Baton Rouge: Louisiana Department of Education, 2000), T-1; Brasseaux, *Acadian to Cajun*, 90.

6. Manifesto of Action Cadienne.

7. Herbert J. Gans, "Symbolic Ethnicity: The Future of Ethnic Groups and Cultures in America," *Ethnic and Racial Studies* (January 1979): 1–20.

8. The eternal flame inscription is from Cajun poet Antoine Bourque, pseudonym of historian Carl A. Brasseaux. Brasseaux, *Acadian to Cajun*, vii (epigraph).

INDEX